Pass CLAiT Plus

USING OFFICE 2003

P. Evans

PAYNE-GALLWAY

www.payne-gallway.co.uk

Acknowledgements

Published by Payne-Gallway Publishers
Payne-Gallway is an imprint of Harcourt
Education Ltd., Halley Court, Jordan Hill,
Oxford, OX2 8EJ

Copyright © P. Evans 2006

First published 2006

10 09 08 07 06

British Library Cataloguing in Publication Data
is available from the British Library on request

10-digit ISBN 1 904467 98 9

13-digit ISBN 978 1 904467 98 4

Copyright notice

Cover picture © Katherine Palmers-Needham

Typeset by TechType, Abingdon

Printed by Scotprint Ltd.

Ordering Information

You can order from:

Payne-Gallway,
FREEPOST (OF1771),
PO Box 381, Oxford OX2 8BR

Tel: 01865 888070
Fax: 01865 314029
E-mail: orders@payne-gallway.co.uk
Web: www.payne-gallway.co.uk

**We are grateful to the following organisations for
permission to use copyright material:**

Microsoft, Excel, Powerpoint, FrontPage, Outlook and
Windows are either registered trademarks or trademarks
of Microsoft Corporation in the United States and/or
other countries.

Every effort has been made to contact copyright owners
of material published in this book. We would be glad
to hear from unacknowledged sources at the earliest
opportunity.

Contents

Chapter 1   Integrated E-Document Production   4

Chapter 2   Manipulating Spreadsheets and Graphs   49

Chapter 3   Creating and Using a Database   93

Chapter 4   E-Publication Design   136

Chapter 5   Designing an E-Presentation   177

Chapter 6   E-Image Manipulation   217

Chapter 7   Website Creation   250

Chapter 8   Electronic Communication   299

Index   325

To pass this unit you must be able to:

- ✓ access, open, save, protect and print files

- ✓ create and print mail merge documents and use mail merge features

- ✓ integrate files to create an integrated business document

- ✓ format tabular data

- ✓ enter data accurately and amend existing data

- ✓ format page layout and manipulate text according to a house style.

Before you start this chapter, you or your tutor should download a zipped file called **Resources for Chapter 1** from **www.payne-gallway.co.uk/claitplus**. It will automatically unzip. Specify that the contents are to be saved in your **My Documents** folder.

The practice tasks that follow cover all the techniques you need to learn in order to pass a New CLAiT Plus Unit 1 INTEGRATED E-DOCUMENT PRODUCTION assignment.

Practice tasks

Scenario

You are working as an administrative assistant for Crossways High School. You have been asked to prepare some documents for the Headteacher.

Task 1   Creating a mail merge document

Mail merge is a special feature included in most word processing packages. It allows the user to create a **master document** and then merge it with data from a spreadsheet, database or other text file. This file is called the **source data file**. During the mail merge process data from **fields** in individual records in the source data file is inserted into specially marked places in the master document. This produces a set of documents which each contain virtually the same information. This task takes you through the steps you need to follow to create a mail merge master document.

Creating a subfolder

Before you get started it is a good idea to create a subfolder in your **My Documents** folder or network home directory folder where you can store files created as you work through the practice tasks.

- Double-click the icon on your desktop to see the contents of your **My Documents** folder. The **My Documents** window will be displayed.

- Right-click in any blank part of the **My Documents** window. Then click **New** and **Folder**.

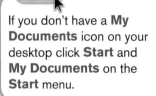

TIP

If you don't have a **My Documents** icon on your desktop click **Start** and **My Documents** on the **Start** menu.

My Documents

- Type the name **Unit 1 PT** for the new subfolder, then click anywhere in the window.

TIP

If your computer doesn't let you right-click in the **My Documents** window click the **Make a new folder** icon in the **File and Folder Tasks** section on the left of the **My Documents** window.

Creating a mail merge master document

The Headteacher has asked you to create a mail merge master document to produce a set of notices. These will be used to inform staff about room changes made necessary by special events taking place around the school over the next few weeks.

To get started you need to load **Microsoft Word**. This can be done in one of two ways:

Word 2003

- *either* double-click the **Microsoft Word** icon on the main screen in **Windows**,

- *or* click the **Start** button at the bottom left of the screen, then click **All Programs**, **Microsoft Office**.

The main **Word** document window will be displayed. It should look something like the one on the next page, with a blank document ready to start work on.

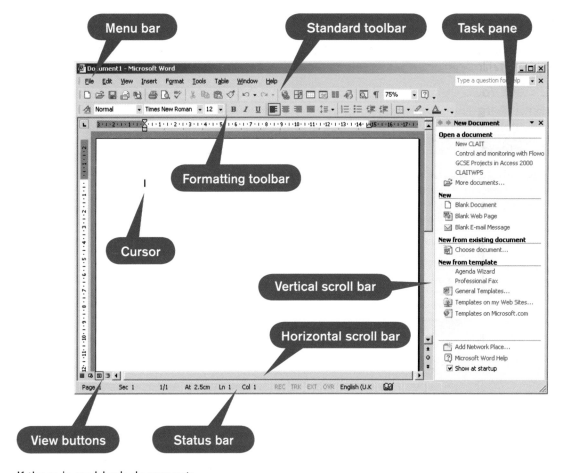

If there is no blank document:

New button

- *either* click the **New** button on the **Standard** toolbar,

- *or* click **Blank Document** in the **Task pane**.

The first thing you need to do is make sure the **page orientation** for the document is set to **portrait** and the selected paper type is **A4**.

- Click **File** on the menu bar and then click **Page Setup**.

- The **Page Setup** dialogue box will be displayed. The **Margins** tab should already be selected – if it isn't just click on it.

- Click **Portrait** in the **Orientation** section if it isn't already selected.

- Click the **Paper** tab.

- **A4** should already be selected in the **Paper size** section – if it isn't click on the down arrow on the right of the first box, and then click **A4** in the list of paper sizes.

- Click **OK** to close the **Page Setup** dialogue box.

> **TIP**
>
> If you can't see the **Task pane** or prefer not to work with it on the screen, click **View** in the menu bar and **Task pane**.

Attaching a datafile

A datafile has been prepared for you containing the information about room changes. You need to attach this datafile to the mail merge master document.

▶ Click **View**, **Toolbars** on the menu bar, and then click **Mail Merge** in the list of toolbars. The **Mail Merge Toolbar** will appear at the top of the screen.

▶ Click the **Open Data Source** button on the **Mail Merge** toolbar.

The **Select Data Source** dialogue window will appear.

Open Data
Source button

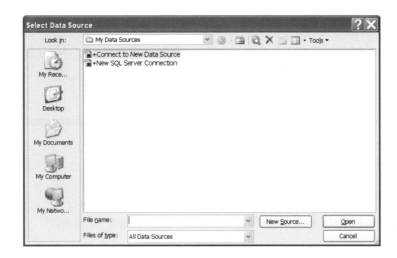

The datafile you need to use is a Microsoft Excel workbook called **rooms**. Your tutor will tell you where to find this file. In the example below it is in the user's **My Documents** folder.

▶ Click the **My Documents** icon on the left of the window.

The contents of your **My Documents** folder will be listed.

▶ Click on the file called **rooms**, and then click **Open**.

The **Select Table** dialogue box will appear.

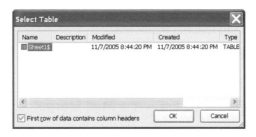

▶ Click **Sheet1$** in the list if it is not already selected.

▶ Click **OK**.

Inserting merge fields

Next you need to write the document text and insert **merge fields** to indicate where information from the attached datafile needs to be added when the mail merge process is performed. The process of inserting merge fields can be speeded up by adding the **Insert Merge Fields** button to the **Mail Merge** toolbar. Follow the steps below to add this button.

▶ Click the **Toolbar Options** arrow on the right of the **Mail Merge** toolbar.

▶ Position the mouse pointer over **Add or Remove Buttons**, and then **Mail Merge.**

Insert Merge Field button

▶ Click **Insert Merge Fields** in the drop-down list of options, and then click anywhere in the document. The **Insert Merge Fields** button will be added to the **Mail Merge** toolbar.

▶ The cursor should already be flashing at the top of your new document – if it isn't, just point at the top of the page and click the left mouse button.

▶ Type: **Room Changes**

▶ Press the **Enter** key twice to leave a blank line.

▶ Type: **Please note that:**

▶ Press the **Enter** key twice to leave a blank line.

Insert Merge Field button

▶ Click the **Insert Merge Fields** button on the **Mail Merge** toolbar.

A drop-down list of available merge fields will appear.

▶ Click **Room** in the list. **<<Room>>** will appear to show that this is a place in the document where information from the datafile will be inserted when the mail merge process is carried out.

▶ Press the **Enter** key twice to leave a blank line.

▶ Type: **Will be out of use on**

▶ Press the **Spacebar** once.

Insert Merge Field button

▶ Click the **Insert Merge Fields** button on the **Mail Merge** toolbar.

▶ Click **Date** in the list of fields; **<<Date>>** will appear.

▶ Press the **Enter** key twice to leave a blank line.

▶ Type: **Due to**

▶ Press the **Spacebar** once.

▶ Click the **Insert Merge Fields** button on the **Mail Merge** toolbar.

Insert Merge Field ▾

▶ Click **Reason** in the list of fields; **<<Reason>>** will appear.

Insert Merge Field button

▶ Press the **Enter** key twice to leave a blank line.

▶ Type: **An alternative room will be allocated on the daily cover list**

▶ Check through your work and compare it carefully with the finished example below before you carry on.

Room Changes

Please note that:

«Room»

Will be out of use on «Date»

Due to «Reason»

An alternative room will be allocated on the daily cover list

TIP

Checking your work carefully during an assignment is very important. Missing words, sentences or punctuation all count as **critical errors** that will cause you to fail a final assessment. Any mistakes you find in a document must be corrected. This can be done by pointing and clicking to the right of the text you want to change, before deleting it by pressing the **Backspace** key.

Formatting the document text

Now you need to format the document text by changing the **font size** and **font type**.

▶ Hold down the **Ctrl** key, and then press the **A** key to select all the document text.

▶ Click the down arrow in the **Font name** box at the top of the screen.

▶ Scroll up through the list of available fonts and click on the font called **Arial**.

Click the down arrow in the **Font size** box at the top of the screen.

Scroll up through the list of available font sizes and click on size **20**.

> **TIP**
>
> You can choose a **font type** or **font size** if none are specified at this stage during an assignment.

Bold button

Next you need to change the emphasis of the document text by formatting all the text as **bold**.

Leave the document text selected.

Click the **bold** button on the **Formatting** toolbar.

Center button

Next you need to set the text alignment in this document to be **centred**.

Click the **center** button on the **Formatting** toolbar.

Your document should now look like the example below.

Room Changes

Please note that:

«Room»

Will be out of use on «Date»

Due to «Reason»

An alternative room will be allocated on the daily cover list

Saving and printing

Now you need to save this document.

Save button

Either click **File** on the menu bar, and then click **Save**.

Or click the **Save** button on the **Standard** toolbar.

The **Save As** dialogue box will appear.

Double-click the **Unit 1 PT** folder.

Type the name **roomchanges** in the **File name** box and click the **Save** button.

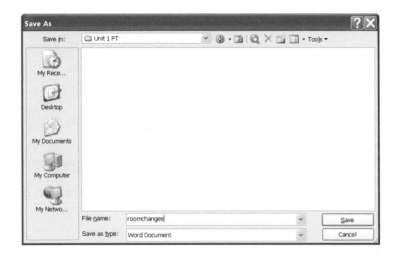

The **Save As** dialogue window will disappear. The filename **roomchanges** will be displayed at the top of the screen. This document will now be saved with this name whenever you click the **Save** button on the **Standard** toolbar.

Next you need to print the document showing the merge fields. The standard print facility will do this.

 Click the **Print** button on the **Standard** toolbar.

Print button

Password protecting a document

Next you need to password protect the document. This will prevent unauthorised access to the document by asking for a password whenever it is opened. If the password is entered incorrectly the document will not open.

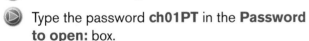 Click **Tools** on the menu bar and then click **Options...**

The **Options** dialogue box will be displayed.

 Click the **Security** tab.

 Type the password **ch01PT** in the **Password to open:** box.

Click **OK**. The **Confirm Password** dialogue box will be displayed.

 Type the password **ch01PT** in the **Reenter password to open:** box.

 Click **OK**. The password is now set. You will need to use this password next time this document is opened.

TIP

Don't forget the password that you use for a document – there's no other way to open it without the correct password. You should also note that passwords are **case sensitive**. This means that if a combination of upper and lower case letters is used when setting up the password exactly the same combination must be used when opening the document again.

Closing the document and exiting Word

Now you need to close this document and shut **Word** down. You can perform both these instructions in a single operation.

 Click **File** on the menu bar, and then click **Exit**, or click **(X)** in the top right-hand corner of the screen.

TIP

If you want to close a document without closing down **Word**, select **File** and then **Close** on the menu bar.

Task 2   Using mail merge queries

The Headteacher has asked you to print a set of notices for the room changes affecting the Main Hall only. This task takes you through the steps you'll need to follow to do this using a **mail merge query**.

Opening a password protected file

 Load **Word**.

To get started you need to save the current blank document. This will be used to store some screen prints that will provide evidence some tasks have been carried out.

 Click **File**, **Save As** on the menu bar.

 Double-click the **Unit 1** folder.

 Type the name **screenprints** in the **File name** box and click the **Save** button.

Next you need to load the password protected mail merge master document called **roomchanges** that you created and saved in Task 1.

▶ Click **File** on the menu bar, and then click **Open**.

▶ Or click the **Open button** on the **Standard** toolbar.

Open button

The **Open** dialogue box will appear.

▶ Double-click the **Unit 1 PT** subfolder if its contents are not already displayed.

▶ Click on **roomchanges** and **Open**. The **Password** dialogue box will appear.

▶ Type the password **ch01PT** in the box but don't click OK – you need to take a screen print of this dialogue box as evidence that password protection was set for the document.

Taking a screen print

▶ Take a screen print of the **Password** dialogue box by holding down the **Alt** key and then pressing the **Print Scr** key.

▶ Click **OK**. The **roomchanges** mail merge master document will be opened.

▶ Click the icon at the bottom of the screen to view the **screenprints** document.

📕 screenprints - Mi...

▶ Click **Edit** on the menu bar, and then click **Paste**. The screen print will appear.

You will need to put the next screen print you take on a new page in this document. To go to a new page, you need to insert a **page break**.

▶ Click **Insert** on the menu bar, and then click **Break**. The **Break** dialogue window will appear.

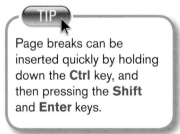

TIP

Page breaks can be inserted quickly by holding down the **Ctrl** key, and then pressing the **Shift** and **Enter** keys.

▶ Click **Page break** in the list of break types if it isn't already selected.

▶ Click **OK** and a new blank page will appear. The **screenprints** document is now ready for the next screen print. You can save it and return to work on the mail merge master.

▶ Click the **Save** button on the **Standard** toolbar.

▶ Click **File** and then **Close** on the menu bar.

Save button

One   Integrated E-Document Production

Chapter 1

Creating a mail merge query

Now you need to create a mail merge query to find all the room changes affecting just the Main Hall.

Mail Merge
Recipients button

▶ Click the **Mail Merge Recipients** button on the **Mail Merge** toolbar.

The **Mail Merge Recipients** dialogue box will appear.

▶ Click the down arrow at the top of the second column where the rooms are listed.

▶ Click **Main Hall** in the drop-down list of options.

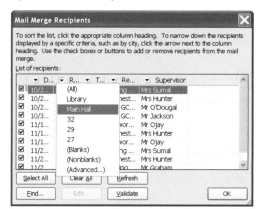

The datafile records matching the criteria **Main Hall** will be listed.

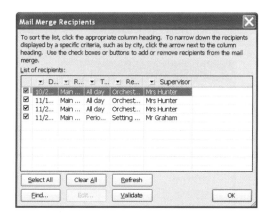

▶ Click **OK**.

Next you need to generate a set of mail merged documents matching the merge query.

Merge to New
Document button

▶ Click the **Merge to New Document** button on the **Mail Merge** toolbar.

The **Merge to New Document** dialogue box will appear.

▶ Click the radio button next to **All** if it is not already selected.

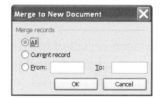

 Click **OK**. A new document will appear containing the results of the mail merge.

Room Changes

Please note that:

Main Hall

Will be out of use on 28/10/2006

Due to Orchestra Rehearsal

An alternative room will be allocated on the daily cover list

Now you need to print this document.

 Click the **Print** button on the **Standard** toolbar.

Finally you need to save the new mail merged document.

 Click **File** on the menu bar, and then click **Save**.

 Or click the **Save** button on the **Standard** toolbar.

The **Save** dialogue box will appear.

 Double-click the **Unit 1 PT** folder if it is not already selected.

 Type the name **mainhall** in the **File name** box and click the **Save** button.

Print button

Save button

> **TIP**
>
> The merged documents created by a mail merge are not normally saved because they can be produced again at any time simply by opening the master document and running the mail merge again. You will be asked to save the merged documents in a CLAiT Plus Unit 1 assignment simply to provide evidence that the mail merge was performed correctly.

 Close any open documents and shut **Word** down.

Task 3   Combining files to create a new document

The Headteacher has asked you to prepare a letter of invitation to the school Open Evening. The text and images for the invitation have already been prepared and saved in two separate files. This task takes you through the steps you need to follow to combine these files to create the new document.

Draft document

The draft document shown below has been provided to give some additional information about the way the information sheet must be laid out and formatted.

Insert the image file **slogo** centred between each margin

Open Evening

We sincerely hope that you will be able to come to our open evening on the 10th of July. Come and see what our school has to offer. The evening will give parents of current and prospective pupils a chance to tour our facilities, speak to students and teachers, and share in the life of the school.

The Headteacher, Mrs Barbara Wheat, will open the evening at 7.00 pm with a short presentation about the school. This presentation will include an overview of the excellent improvements in GCSE examination results over the last five years. The graph below illustrates the remarkable progress we have made.

Insert the graph **results** here

Start page 2 here

Page break

Activities

A wide range of activities will be available for you to try throughout the evening. A leaflet giving more information will be provided when you arrive. Full details will also be posted on the school website **www.crossways-high.org.uk** next week.

Some of the activities will include:

Music and dance in the Performing Arts Studio
Video editing in the ICT Suite
Weird science in the Physics Laboratory
Quick Cook challenge in the Cafe des Arts Bistro

Add a bullet character to each of these 4 lines

Set the bulleted text to 1.5 line spacing

Uniform

Seabridge School Supplies Ltd. will be present showing their range of approved school uniform clothing. The most popular items along with their costs (specially discounted for the evening) are shown in the table below.

Insert the datafile **uniform** and format as specified in Task 4

We look forwarded to welcoming you. Please bring the whole family along and join in all the fun!

If you have any questions about the evening please telephone the school on 0169 273784.

Saving a text file in Microsoft Word document format

To get started you need to open the text file containing the text for the invitation and save it in Microsoft Word document format.

▶ Load **Word**.

The text file you need to use is called **openeve**. Your tutor will tell you where to find this file. In the example below it is in the user's **My Documents** folder. Your tutor will tell you where to find this file if it is in a different location.

Open button

▶ Click **File** on the menu bar, and then click **Open**.

▶ Or click the **Open button** on the **Standard** toolbar.

The **Open** dialogue box will appear.

▶ Click the **My Documents** icon on the left of the window if the contents of your **My Documents** folder aren't already visible.

▶ Click the down arrow next to the **Files of type:** box.

▶ Scroll down through the drop-down list of options and click **Text Files**.

▶ Click on the file called **openeve**, and then click **Open**. The file will be opened.

▶ Click **File** on the menu bar, and then click **Save As...**

▶ Double-click the **Unit 1 PT** folder.

▶ Click the down arrow next to the **Save as type:** box.

▶ Scroll up through the drop-down list of options and click **Word Document**.

▶ Click **Save**.

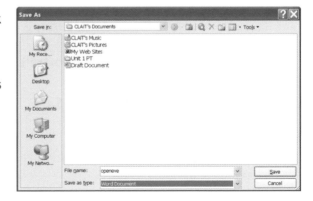

Setting up the document

Now you need to set the **pager margins**, **page orientation**, **paper size**, **font size**, **font type**, **text alignment** and **line spacing** for the new document.

▶ Click **File** on the menu bar and then click **Page Setup**.

The **Page Setup** dialogue box will be displayed.

▶ Click the **Margins** tab if it isn't already selected.

The top and bottom margins for this document need setting to **2.0 cm**.

The left and right margins for this document need setting to **3.0 cm**.

▶ Click inside the boxes for the **top** and **bottom** margins. Replace each value with **2.0 cm**.

▶ Click inside the boxes for the **left** and **right** margins. Replace each value with **3.0 cm**.

The margin settings for a document determine how much blank space will be left between the text and the page edges. Changing the margin settings is one method that can be used to fit more text on each page of a document. You could be asked to set any combination of the top, bottom, left or right margins during a New CLAiT word processing assignment.

▶ The page orientation needs to be **Portrait**. Click **Portrait** in the **Orientation** section if it isn't already selected.

Next you need to set the **paper size** to **A4**.

▶ Click the **Paper** tab.

▶ Click the down arrow on the right of the first box in the **Paper size:** section, and then click **A4** in the list of paper sizes.

▶ Click **OK**.

Now you need to format the document text by changing the font type and size.

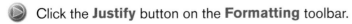 Hold down the **Ctrl** key, and then press the **A** key to select all the document text.

Change the font type to **Arial**.

Change the font size to **12**.

Leave the text selected.

Now you need to set the **text alignment** for this document. The alignment buttons on the **Formatting** toolbar provide the quickest way to change the alignment of text in a document. Text can be **left aligned**, **right aligned**, **centred** or **fully justified**.

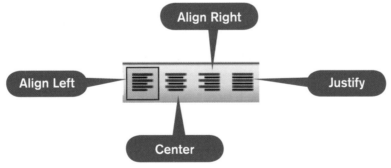

The text in this document must be **fully justified**.

Click the **Justify** button on the **Formatting** toolbar.

Justify button

Left Align button

 TIP

The default text alignment for documents is **left**. If left alignment is specified for a document you won't need to do anything if the left align button is already selected. The alignment of text can be changed at any time by clicking on a line or inside a paragraph then choosing an alignment option on the **Formatting** toolbar.

Finally you need to set the **line spacing** for this document. **Line spacing** is used to change the amount of space between lines of text. Normal text is single spaced. Common line spacing options include 'single', '1.5 times', and 'double'. You need to set the line spacing for this document to **Single**.

 Click **Format** on the menu bar, and then click **Paragraph**.

The **Paragraph** dialogue box will be displayed.

 Click the arrow next to the **Line spacing** box.

 Click **Single**, if it is not already selected, in the drop-down list of options that appears. Click **OK**.

Single line spacing is the default setting for **Word** documents. If you're asked to use single line spacing it is still a good idea to check the setting. You might be asked to use a different type of line spacing when setting up a document.

 Click anywhere in the document to remove the text highlighting.

  Click the **Save** button on the **Standard** toolbar to save these changes to the document keeping the file name **openeve**.

Save button

Formatting the document text

Text must be **highlighted** before it can be formatted. Highlighting makes a selected portion of text turn black with the individual characters white. There are a number of different techniques for selecting text in Microsoft Word. You have already used Ctrl A to select all the document text. Some of the more commonly used techniques for selecting individual portions of text are described below.

First you need to format the document heading.

- Click anywhere in the document heading **Open Evening**.
- Click the mouse button <u>three</u> times to highlight the heading.
- Change the font type to **Times New Roman**.
- Change the font size to **26**.
- Click the **bold** button on the **Formatting** toolbar to set the emphasis for this text to bold.

Bold button

Next you need to format the document subheadings. We will use a different technique to select the text this time.

- Position the pointer in the left margin just to the left of the first subheading **Activities**.

  The pointer will change shape into a white arrow.

- Click <u>once</u> on the left mouse button to highlight just this line of text.

- Change the font type to **Times New Roman**.
- Change the font size to **16**.
- Click the **italic** button on the **Formatting** toolbar to set the emphasis for this text to italic.
- Format the other subheading **Uniform** in exactly the same way.

Italic button

The top section of your document should now look like the example below.

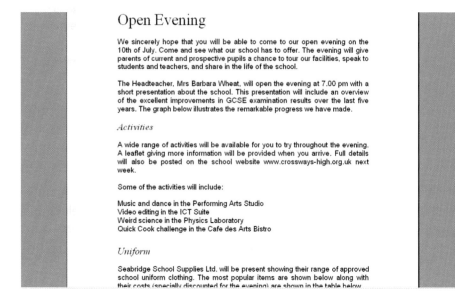

Next you need to add bullets and change the line spacing for the activities listed at the bottom of the document.

▶ Click at the start of the line beginning **Music and dance…**

▶ Click and hold down the left mouse button.

▶ Drag down and across to the end of the line ending **…Arts Bistro**. If you go too far, keep your finger on the left mouse button and drag the mouse in the opposite direction. Four lines of text should be highlighted like the example below.

> Some of the activities will include:
>
> Music and dance in the Performing Arts Studio
> Video editing in the ICT Suite
> Weird science in the Physics Laboratory
> Quick Cook challenge in the Cafe des Arts Bistro

Bullets button

▶ Click the **Bullets** button on the **Formatting** toolbar to bullet these lines of text. The bullets will appear and the text will stay highlighted – leave it like this.

You need to set the line spacing for the highlighted text to **1.5 lines**.

▶ Click **Format** on the menu bar, and then click **Paragraph**.

The **Paragraph** dialogue box will be displayed.

▶ Click the arrow next to the **Line spacing** box.

▶ Click **1.5 lines** in the drop-down list of options that appears.

▶ Click **OK**.

▶ Click anywhere in the document to remove the text highlighting.

Your bulleted list should look like the example below.

> Some of the activities will include:
>
> • Music and dance in the Performing Arts Studio
> • Video editing in the ICT Suite
> • Weird science in the Physics Laboratory
> • Quick Cook challenge in the Cafe des Arts Bistro

Importing an image

Now you need to insert the image **slogo** in the position shown on the Draft Document.

▶ Hold down the **Ctrl** key, and then press the **Home** key to position the cursor at the start of the document.

▶ Press **Enter** to create a blank line space at the start of the document.

▶ Click above the heading **Open Evening** to position the cursor back at the start of the document.

Insert Picture button

▶ Click **Insert** on the menu bar, and then click **Picture, From File…**

▶ *Or* click the **Insert Picture** button on the **Drawing** toolbar at the bottom of the screen.

The **Insert Picture** dialogue box will appear. The image file you need to use is called **slogo.gif**. Your tutor will tell you where to find this file. In the example below it is in the user's **My Documents** folder. Your tutor will tell you where to find this file if it is stored in a different location.

▶ Click on the file called **slogo**, and then click **Insert**.

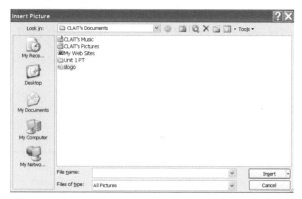

The image will be inserted in the document.

Resizing and positioning an image

Now you need to resize the image to approximately half of its current size.

▶ Click <u>once</u> on the image to select it. Small square **sizing handles** will appear around the image.

▶ Move the mouse pointer over the bottom right sizing handle until it changes shape into a diagonal two-headed arrow.

▶ Click and hold the left mouse button.

▶ Drag up and across towards the top left corner of the image. As you drag a dotted line will show you how big the image will be when you let go of the mouse button. When the outlined area is roughly the same size as the one shown below, let go of the mouse button.

TIP

Never use the side sizing handles to resize an image – this will distort it. For Unit 1 assignments you should resize images so that they stay in proportion. This means always use the corner sizing handles to resize images.

Now you need to position the image in the centre of the page with the text below it.

Text Wrapping button

▶ Click <u>once</u> on the image if it isn't already selected with the sizing handles visible.

▶ Click the **Text Wrapping** button on the **Picture** toolbar.

▶ Click **Top and Bottom** in the list of text wrapping options. This will place any text near the image above and below it.

TIP

Click **View**, **Toolbars** and **Picture** if you can't see the **Picture** toolbar.

TIP

You'll normally need to use either **square** text wrapping to flow text around an image or **top and bottom** text wrapping to place text above and below an image.

Format Picture button

▶ Click the **Format Picture** button on the **Picture** toolbar.

The **Format Picture** dialogue box will be displayed.

▶ Click the **Layout** tab.

▶ Click the **Center** radio button in the **Horizontal alignment** section, and then click **OK**.

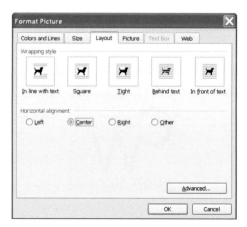

TIP

Clicking twice on an image will also display the **Format Picture** dialogue box.

This section of your document should now look like the example below.

Open Evening

Importing a graph

You need to insert a graph image contained in a **Microsoft Excel** workbook called **results** in the position shown on the Draft Document. To get started you need to load **Excel**. You can do this in one of two ways:

▶ *either* double-click the **Microsoft Excel** icon on the main screen in Windows,

Microsoft Office Excel 2003

or click the **Start** button at the bottom left of the screen, then click **Programs**, then click 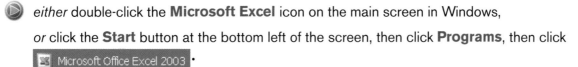 •

The main Excel window will be displayed with a blank **workbook**.

▶ Click **File** on the menu bar, and then click **Open**.

▶ *Or* click the **Open** button on the **Standard** toolbar.

Open button

The **Open** dialogue box will appear.

▶ Click the **My Documents** icon on the left of the window to view the contents of your **My Documents** folder.

▶ Click on the file called **results**, and then click **Open**.

The file will be opened – it should look like the one below.

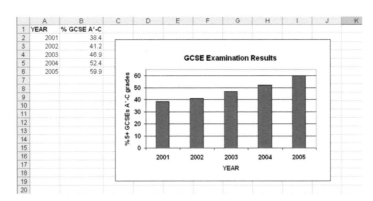

▶ Click <u>once</u> on a blank section anywhere around the edge of the graph to select it.

▶ Click **Edit** on the menu bar, and then click **Copy** – a flashing dashed line will appear around the graph.

▶ *Or* click the **Copy** button on the **Standard** toolbar.

Copy button

25

▶ Click the **Word** icon at the bottom of the screen to view the **openeve** document.

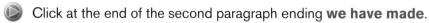

▶ Click at the end of the second paragraph ending **we have made**.

▶ Press **Enter** <u>twice</u> to leave a blank line between the end of the paragraph and the point where the graph will be inserted.

> **TIP**
>
> When a New CLAiT Plus assignment tells you to *'insert a clear line space'* it means leave a single blank line above or below a paragraph or image. To do this position the cursor above the point where you need the blank line, click the mouse button, and then press **Enter** *twice*.

Paste button

▶ Click **Edit** on the menu bar, and then click **Paste**.

▶ *Or* click the **Paste** button on the **Standard** toolbar.

The graph will appear in the document.

▶ Click <u>once</u> on the graph to select it.

> **TIP**
>
> You might need to use the corner sizing handles to resize a graph at this stage during an assignment to make it fit on the page.

Text Wrapping button

▶ Click the **Text Wrapping** button on the **Picture** toolbar, and select **Top and Bottom** text wrapping.

Format Picture button

▶ Click the **Format Picture** button on the **Picture** toolbar.

▶ Click the **Layout** tab in the **Format Picture** dialogue box, and select **Horizontal alignment** section.

▶ Click the radio button next to **Center**, and then click **OK**.

This section of your document should now look like the example below.

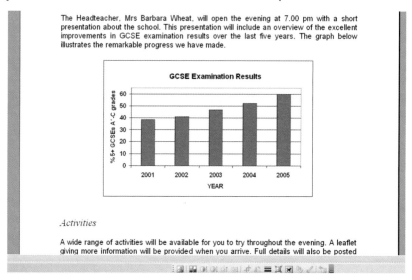

Save button

▶ Click the **Save** button to save these changes to the document keeping the filename **openeve**.

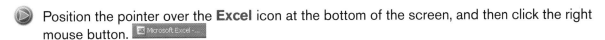 Position the pointer over the **Excel** icon at the bottom of the screen, and then click the right mouse button.

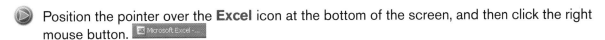 Click **Close** on the pop up menu to shut **Excel** down and close the **results** workbook.

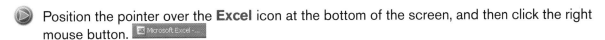 Click **No** if you're prompted to save changes to the file.

Inserting a page break

When the first page in a document is full Word automatically inserts a **page break** to start a new page. This has already been done in your **openeve** document. Page breaks are often needed at specific location in a document, for example, after a title page or at the start of a new section or chapter. When this situation arises a **manual page break** must be inserted by the user. You need to insert a manual page break after the graph as shown in the Draft Document. The technique to do this has already been covered in Task 2 on page 13.

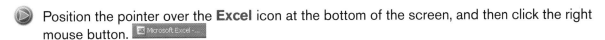 Click at the start of the subheading **Activities**.

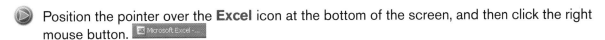 Insert a page break.

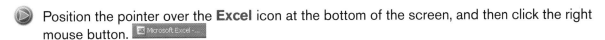 Save these changes to the document.

Adding a header and footer

Next you need to insert a **header** that contains your name and centre number, and a **footer** that contains the document filename.

 Click **View** on the menu bar, and then click **Header and Footer**.

 Type **your name (first name and last name)** and **centre number** in the header section. You will need to ask your tutor for the correct centre number.

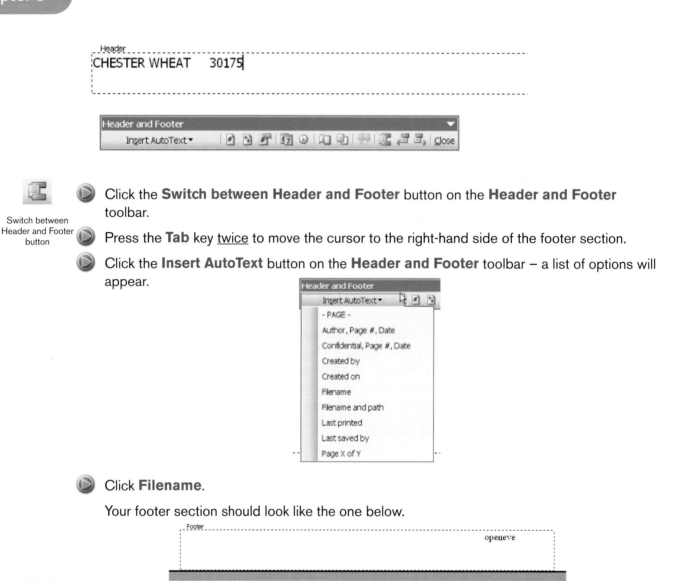

Header

CHESTER WHEAT   30175

Click the **Switch between Header and Footer** button on the **Header and Footer** toolbar.

Press the **Tab** key <u>twice</u> to move the cursor to the right-hand side of the footer section.

Click the **Insert AutoText** button on the **Header and Footer** toolbar – a list of options will appear.

Click **Filename**.

Your footer section should look like the one below.

Footer
openeve

Click the **Close** button on the **Header and Footer** toolbar.

Click the **Save** button on the **Standard** toolbar to save the document keeping the name **openeve**.

Close the document and shut **Word** down.

Task 4   Datafiles and tables

Seabridge School Supplies has provided a datafile that you will need to insert into the invitation for the Open Evening. This task takes you through the steps needed to import a datafile into a Word document, display the data as a table, and then format the table.

Importing a datafile

▶ Load **Word** and open your copy of the **openeve** document.

▶ Click at the end of the paragraph ending **in the table below** on the second page of the document.

▶ Press **Enter** <u>twice</u> to leave a blank line between the end of the paragraph and the point where the datafile will be inserted.

The datafile you need to import is called **uniform**. In the example below this datafile is in the user's **My Documents** folder.

▶ Click **Insert** on the menu bar, and then click **File...**

The **Insert File** dialogue box will appear.

▶ Click the **My Documents** icon on the left of the window to view the contents of your **My Documents** folder.

▶ Click the down arrow next to the **Files of type:** box, and then click **All files** in the drop-down list of options.

▶ Click on the file called **uniform**, and then click **Open**.

The data will be imported and should look like the example below.

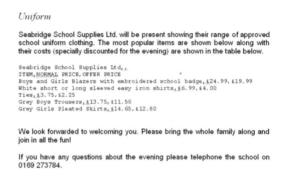

Converting data into table format

Next you need to convert the imported data so that it is displayed in a table.

▶ Highlight the imported data taking care not to highlight any of the other text in the document.

▶ Click **Table** on the menu bar, and then click **Convert, Text to Table...**

The **Convert Text to Table** dialogue box will appear.

▶ Click **OK**. The data will be displayed in a table with the contents highlighted.

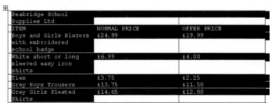

Next you need to apply some formatting to the table contents. Start by changing the font type and size of the text.

⊙ Use the **Font** box on the **Formatting** toolbar to change the font type to **Arial**.

⊙ Use the **Font Size** box on the **Formatting** toolbar to change the font size to **12**.

Next centre align the text in the second and third columns of the table.

⊙ Click away from the table to remove the highlighting.

⊙ Highlight the text in the second and third columns of the table.

Seabridge School Supplies Ltd		
ITEM	NORMAL PRICE	OFFER PRICE
Boys and Girls Blazers with embroidered school badge	£24.99	£19.99
White short or long sleeved easy iron shirts	£6.99	£4.00
Ties	£3.75	£2.25
Grey Boys Trousers	£13.75	£11.50
Grey Girls Pleated Skirts	£14.65	£12.80

⊙ Click the **Center** button on the **Formatting** toolbar to set the alignment for this text to center.

Center button

⊙ Click away from the table to remove the highlighting.

Merging and formatting cells

Next you need to format some specific parts of the table. This will be easier if you use the **Tables and Borders** toolbar.

⊙ Click **View**, **Toolbars** on the menu bar, and then click **Tables and Borders** in the drop-down list of toolbars. The **Tables and Borders** toolbar will appear.

Now you need to merge the three cells in the first row of the table to form one single cell.

⊙ Position the pointer on the left of the first row of the table and click the left mouse button to highlight the entire row.

Seabridge School Supplies Ltd		
ITEM	NORMAL PRICE	OFFER PRICE
Boys and Girls Blazers with	£24.99	£19.99

⊙ Click the **Merge Cells** button on the **Tables and Borders** toolbar.

The cells will be merged forming a single cell across the top of the table.

Merge Cells button

Seabridge School Supplies Ltd		
ITEM	NORMAL PRICE	OFFER PRICE

Now you need to format this cell and its contents. First you need to centre align the text and shade the cell background with a grey fill colour.

⊙ Centre align the text in this cell.

Shading Color
button

Click the small down arrow next to the **Shading Color** button on the **Tables and Borders** toolbar. A choice of cell shading colour options will appear.

Click the **Grey-65%** square on the palette.

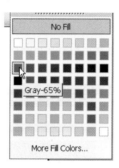

Next you need to format the text in this cell.

Font Color button

Click the small down arrow next to the **Font Color** button on the **Drawing** toolbar. A choice of font colour options will appear.

Click the white coloured square on the palette.

Use the **Font Size** box to change the font size to **14**.

Bold button

Click the **Bold** button to make the text bold.

Click away from the table to remove the highlighting. The first row of your table should look like the example below.

Seabridge School Supplies Ltd		
ITEM	NORMAL PRICE	OFFER PRICE

Next you need to format the text in the second row of the table.

Highlight the second row of the table.

Bold button

Click the **Bold** button on the **Formatting** toolbar to make all the text bold.

Formatting table gridlines

Next you need to increase the thickness of the gridlines for the entire table using the **Tables and Borders** toolbar.

Click **View**, **Toolbars**, and then click **Tables and Borders** on the menu bar.

Click anywhere inside the table.

Click **Table**, **Select**, and then click **Table** on the menu bar to highlight the table.

Tables can also be selected by resting the pointer on the upper-left corner of the table until the table move handle appears, and then clicking on the table move handle.

▶ Click the down arrow next to the **Line Weight** box on the **Tables and Borders** toolbar.

▶ Click **1 pt** in the drop-down list of options.

▶ Click the down arrow next to the **Borders** button on the **Tables and Borders** toolbar.

▶ Click **All Borders** in the drop-down list of options to apply this change to the entire table.

▶ Click away from the table to remove the highlighting. Your table should now look like the example below.

Line Weight button

Borders button

All Borders

Seabridge School Supplies Ltd		
ITEM	NORMAL PRICE	OFFER PRICE
Boys and Girls Blazers with embroidered school badge	£24.99	£19.99
White short or long sleeved easy iron shirts	£6.99	£4.00
Ties	£3.75	£2.25
Grey Boys Trousers	£13.75	£11.50
Grey Girls Pleated Skirts	£14.65	£12.80

Adjusting column widths

Now you need to adjust the width of the columns so that none of the table contents appears on more than two lines.

▶ Position the pointer over the line separating the first and second columns. The pointer will change into a double-headed arrow.

	NORM/
Blazers	£2
ed school	
long	£

▶ Click and hold the left mouse button and drag to the right.

▶ Let go of the mouse button. The width of the first column will increase.

ITEM	N
Boys and Girls Blazers with embroidered school badge	
White short or long sleeved	

▶ If the text in the first column of your table is still displayed on three lines adjust the column width again until it takes up two lines.

▶ Position the pointer over the line separating the second and third column.

▶ Click the left mouse button <u>twice</u> when the pointer changes into the double-headed arrow. The width of the column will be adjusted automatically to fit the widest item in it.

▶ Position the pointer over the line on the right of the third column.

▶ Click the left mouse button <u>twice</u> when the pointer changes into the double-headed arrow. Your table should now look like the example below.

Seabridge School Supplies Ltd		
ITEM	NORMAL PRICE	OFFER PRICE
Boys and Girls Blazers with embroidered school badge	£24.99	£19.99
White short or long sleeved easy iron shirts	£6.99	£4.00
Ties	£3.75	£2.25
Grey Boys Trousers	£13.75	£11.50
Grey Girls Pleated Skirts	£14.65	£12.80

Now you can save and print the document.

- Save the document keeping the name **openeve**.
- Click the **Print** button to print one copy of the document.
- Close the document and shut **Word** down.

Task 5   Making changes to an existing document

An information leaflet about the school curriculum needs to be prepared for the Open Evening. The text for this leaflet has already been prepared but some changes need to be made to it. This task describes how to edit and reformat the text in an existing document.

Opening a pre-prepared text file

To get started you need to open a pre-prepared text file **curriculum**. Your tutor will tell you where to find this file. In the example below it is in the user's **My Documents** folder. Your tutor will tell you where to find this file if it is in a different location.

- Load **Word**.

- Click **File** on the menu bar, and then click **Open**.

Open button

- *Or* click the **Open button** on the **Standard** toolbar.

  The **Open** dialogue box will appear.

- Click the **My Documents** icon on the left of the window to view the contents of your **My Documents** folder.
- Click the down arrow next to the **Files of type:** box.
- Scroll down through the drop-down list of options and click **Text Files**.
- Click on the file called **curriculum**, and then click **Open**.

Amending the text

First you need to add some text.

- Point and click at the end of the paragraph headed **Geography** after the text **...of the curriculum.**
- Press the **Spacebar** once and type the following sentence:

    The GCSE option is a popular choice with an outstanding pass rate in Key Stage 4.

Now you need to delete some text.

- In the paragraph headed **Information and Communication Technology** highlight the text:

    unrestricted access to broadband Internet and

- Press the **Backspace** or the **Delete** key on the keyboard to delete the text.

Next you need to move some text.

- In the paragraph headed **English** highlight the second sentence:

   Pupils normally sit GCSE English and GCSE English Literature examinations at the end of Key Stage 4.

Once text is highlighted there are a number of ways to move it – the technique you're going to use is **cut and paste**.

- Click the **Cut** button on the **Standard** toolbar. The sentence will disappear.

Cut button

- Point and click after the last sentence of the paragraph ending **...during English lessons** making sure there is one space before the cursor.

- Click the **Paste** button on the **Standard** toolbar and the sentence will reappear. This paragraph should look now like the example below.

Paste button

English

Pupils follow the the National Curriculum programmes of study in Key Stages 3 and 4. Pupils are given opportunities to read, write, listen and talk for a range of purposes and audiences during English lessons. Pupils normally sit GCSE English and GCSE English Literature examinations at the end of Key Stage 4.

Find and replace

The **find and replace** facility in **Word** allows you to look for one word and replace it with another. This can be done selectively for just part of a document or globally. Selective find and replace will check each time it finds the search word whether or not you want it replacing. Global find and replace finds every occurrence of the search word and replaces it without asking first. You are going to replace the word **exam** with the word **examination** wherever it appears in this document.

- Click **Edit** on the menu bar, and then click **Replace**...

   The **Find and Replace** dialogue box will appear.

- Click the **More** button if the **Search Options** section of the window is not already displayed.

- Click in the **Find what** box and type **exam**

- Click in the **Replace with** box and type **examination**

- Click the check box next to **Find whole words only**. This will avoid parts of words being replaced, for example, <u>exam</u>ination ending up as <u>examination</u>ination.

 Click **Replace All** to carry out a global find and replace.

A message will appear telling you that **3** replacements have been made.

 Click **OK** and **Close**.

Inserting special symbols

Next you need to insert a special symbol to replace the letter **e** in the word **Cafe** so that it becomes **Café**.

 In the last sentence of the last paragraph highlight the letter **e** at the end of the word **Cafe**.

> Textiles Technology. The s
> and Cafe des Arts bistro for
> Catering and Hospitality.

 Click **Insert** on the menu bar, and then click **Symbol**…

The **Symbol** dialogue box will appear.

 Use the scroll bar on the right to move down through the list of available symbols.

 Click on the **é** symbol.

- Click **Insert**, and then click **Close**.

- The symbol will be inserted. The word **Cafe** will now read **Café**.

Using superscript formatting

Next you need to use superscript formatting in the paragraph headed **History** so that the text **19th** is displayed as **19th**.

- In the second sentence of this paragraph highlight the letters **th** at the end of the text **19th**.

- Click **Format** on the menu bar, and then click **Font**…

    The **Font** dialogue box will appear.

- Click the check box next to **Superscript** in the **Effects** section.

- Click **OK**. The text will now be displayed as th.

Checking spellings and grammar

Next you need to use the Spellcheck facility to correct any errors in the text.

- Hold down the **Ctrl** key, and then press the **Home** key to position the cursor at the start of the document and start the spellcheck from this point.

- Click the **Spelling and Grammar** button. The **Spelling and Grammar** dialogue box will appear.

Spell button

The first error highlighted in red is a repeated word where the same word appears twice.

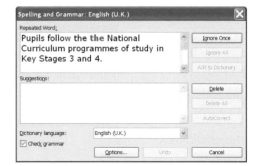

- Click the **Delete** button to remove one of the repeated words.

The next error highlighted in red is a spelling error and the suggested spelling is correct.

▶ Click the **Change** button to accept and make the correction.

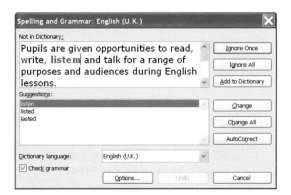

The next error highlighted in green is a grammatical error. The grammar of this document does not need to be changed so this error can be ignored.

▶ Click the **Ignore Once** button to ignore this error and carry on.

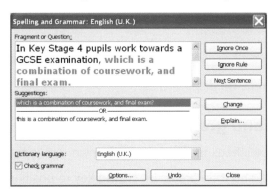

▶ Click **Yes** when the message below appears.

The next error highlighted in red is a name that is spelt correctly but does not appear in the Dictionary. This error can be ignored.

▶ Click the **Ignore Once** button to ignore this error.

▶ Work through the rest of the spellcheck and click **OK** when it is complete.

Adding a footer

The next thing you need to do is add some information to the footer of this document.

- Click **View** on the menu bar, and then click **Header and Footer**.
- Click the **Switch between Header and Footer** button on the **Header and Footer** toolbar to move to the footer section.

Switch between Header and Footer button

- Type **your name (first name and last name)** and **centre number**.

Your footer section should now look something like the one below.

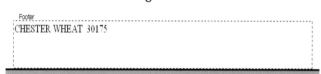

Footer
CHESTER WHEAT 30175

- Click the **Close** button on the **Header and Footer** toolbar.

Close button

Saving and printing

Now you need to save this text file as a **Word** document and print it.

- Save this file as a **Word** document with the filename **opencur**
- Click the **Print** button to print one copy of the document.
- Close the document and shut **Word** down.

TIP

The technique for saving a text file in **Word** document format is described in **Task 3** on page 17.

Print button

Task 6   Archiving files

The Headteacher has asked you to archive all the files that were used in the preparation of the Open Evening documents. Archiving involves making a copy of a set of files before moving them to a storage device such as a CD-ROM or Backup Tape. Archived files are often copied into a compressed or 'zipped' file to save storage space. This task describes how to create a zipped archive file.

Creating a zipped archive file

- Double-click the icon on your desktop to view the contents of your **My Documents** folder.

Now you need to select all the files that need to be archived.

My Documents

▶ Hold down the **Ctrl** key, and then press each file in turn until the files **curriculum**, **openeve**, **results**, **rooms**, **slogo** and **uniform** are highlighted.

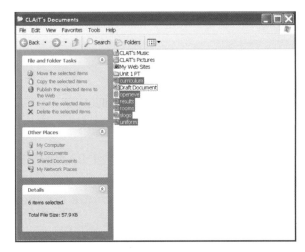

▶ Click **File** on the menu bar, and then click **Send To, Compressed (zipped) Folder**.

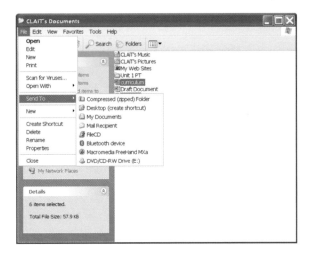

A zipped folder icon will appear with the same name as the first highlighted file.

Next you need to give the zipped folder a new name that gives a better idea about its contents.

▶ Click anywhere in the **My Documents** window to deselect the highlighted files.

▶ Click once on the zipped folder.

▶ Click the **Rename this file** icon in the **File and Folder Tasks** section on the left of the **My Documents** window.

▶ Type **OpEvArchive** and click anywhere in the subfolder window.

Taking a screen print of the archived file

Next you need to take a screen print of the **Unit 1** subfolder showing the zipped file to provide evidence of archiving.

- Load **Word**.
- Click **File** on the menu bar, and then click **Open**.
- *Or* click the **Open button** on the **Standard** toolbar.
- Double-click the **Unit 1 PT** folder if it is not already selected.
- Click on **screenprints** and **Open**.
- Click your **My Documents** icon at the bottom of the screen .
- Hold down the **Alt** key, and then press the **Print Scr** key to take a screen print of the **My Documents** window.
- Click the **screenprints** icon at the bottom of the screen.
- Hold down the **Ctrl** key, and then press the **End** key to move to the end of the document.
- Click **Edit** on the menu bar, and then click **Paste**. The screen print will appear.
- Save and print this document.
- Close the document and shut **Word** down.

That's the end of the practice tasks. Now try the full New CLAiT Plus assignment that follows.

TIP

You should have created and saved the **screenprints** document in **Task 2** on page 12.

Open button

Practice assignment

Scenario

You are working as an Administrative Officer for Boomerang Boarding Kennels. You are helping to organise promotional materials for the launch of a new site.

You will be required to produce a mail merge notice, an invitation and an information leaflet.

To produce the documentation you will need the following files:

FILENAME	FILE TYPE
activities	datafile
launch	text file
klogo	image file
feedback	spreadsheet containing a graph
supplies	datafile
facilities	rich text file

You will also need to refer to the Draft Document.

You will need to use system software and application software that will allow you to:

- create a range of business documents
- create mail merge documentation
- combine text, graphics and datafiles
- control page layout, columns and use of tables.

Assessment Objectives	TASK 1
	Before you begin this task ensure you have the datafile **activities**.
	You have been asked to create a master mail merge document about launch day activities. This will be used to produce notices informing staff which activities they will be supervising on the day. The datafile **activities** has already been prepared for you.
2a	1 a) Using suitable software, create a new mail merge master document.
2b	b) Use A4 paper in portrait orientation.
5a	c) Key in the following text, inserting merge fields from the **activities** datafile. Follow
6a	the line endings and ensure there is a clear line or paragraph space where shown.
6c	

LAUNCH DAY ACTIVITIES

[insert **Event** merge field]

will be led by

[insert **Employee** merge field]

in [insert **Location** merge field]

at [insert **Time** merge field]

d) Insert your name and centre number as a header or footer in the master document.

2c | 2 Format the document as follows:

Alignment: **centre**

Emphasis: **bold**

You may use any legible font type, font sizes and margins to suit your document.

1b | 3 Save the master document using the filename **events**.

1d | 4 Print a copy of the document **events** on one page, showing the merge fields.

1b | 5 a) Using the password **LdayEvts1** protect the file **events** from unauthorised access.

1c | b) Save the file keeping the same filename.

| c) Close the document.

Assessment Objectives | **TASK 2**

You have been asked to print just the notices for activities in Kennel Block 2. To save disk space, normal company policy states that merged documents should not be saved. On this occasion you will be required to save the merged file.

You will need to produce a screen print to evidence file protection.

1a | 1 a) Prepare to open the document **events** that you saved in Task 1.

1e | b) Take a screen print to show evidence that password protection has been set.

| c) Save this screen print for printing later.

| d) Open the document **events**.

2d | 2 Create a mail merge query to find the activities where the **Location** is **Kennel Block 2**.

1d | 3 a) Merge the query in a new document.

1e | b) Print the results.

More copies of the mail merge may need to be printed at a later date.

1b | 4 As an exception to normal policy, save this document as **kblock2**

Assessment Objectives	TASK 3
	Before you begin this task ensure you have the following files:
	launch
	klogo
	feedback
	You have been asked to prepare a letter of invitation for the Launch Day. The text and images have been prepared. You will need to combine the files into one document and format as specified in the instructions.
1b 3a	1 Using suitable software open the text file **launch** and save this as **openday** in your software's file type.
6a	2 Format the entire document as follows:
6b	Paper size: **A4 portrait**
6f	Top Margin: **2 cm** (other margins may be set to suit your document)
	Alignment: **left**
	Font: **Arial**
	Emphasis: **none**
	Font size: **12**
	Line spacing: **single** (except where specified)
	3 Format the heading **Seaford Grange Site Grand Opening** as follows:
	Alignment: **centre**
	Font: **Times New Roman**
	Emphasis: **bold**
	Font size: **24**
6f	4 Format the subheadings as follows:
	Alignment: **left**
	Font: **Times New Roman**
	Emphasis: **bold, italic**
	Font size: **16**
	The two subheadings are:
	Family Activities
	Seaford Pet Supplies
3c	5 Referring to the Draft Document on page 48 make the following amendments:
5b	a) Import the image **klogo**.
6b 6e	b) Centre this graphic between the margins of the page. The image may be resized, but the original proportions must be maintained.

c) Import the graph contained in the file **feedback**. Ensure that all data in the graph is legible. The graph must fit on the first page of your document. You may resize the graph to achieve this.

d) Ensure there is at least one clear line space above the graph.

e) Insert a page break below the graph, as specified.

f) Insert bullets and double line spacing where indicated in the draft document.

g) Ensure that the original alignment, font size and font style are retained.

6c	6	Create the following headers and footers:
6d		Header: **your name and centre number**
		Footer: **automatic filename**
1b	7	Save the file retaining the filename **openday**.

Assessment Objectives | **TASK 4**

Before you begin this task ensure you have the following files:

supplies
openday (that you created in Task 3).

Seaford Pet Supplies has provided a datafile that you will need to insert into the letter of invitation for the Launch Day. You will then need to check the layout of the document before printing.

3b	1	Using the file **openday** that you created in Task 3, refer to the Draft Document on page
4a		48 and import the datafile **supplies**. Ensure this is displayed as a table.
6f	2	Format all the data in the table as follows:
4c		Font: **Arial**
		Font size: **12**
		Alignment: **centre**

Text may be wrapped, but words must not be split.

4b	3	To make the table easier to read some additional formatting is required.
4d		

a) Merge the 4 cells in the first row of the table.

b) Apply dark shading to the first row of the table only.

c) Format the text **Seaford Pet Supplies** to be red.

d) Embolden the data in the first and second rows of the table only.

e) Display gridlines and borders for the entire table.

f) Adjust the column widths so that no entry is displayed on more than two lines.

g) Ensure that the text of the table is entirely within the page margins.

h) Ensure that there is at least one clear line space above and below the table.

6b	4	Check the document to ensure:

a) all instructions have been carried out

b) all items are positioned within the margins of the page

c) the imported datafile is not split across pages

d) page breaks have been inserted where specified

e) there are no additional line spaces at the top of pages

f) subheadings are not split from related text

g) spacing between subheadings and related text is consistent

h) there are no widows or orphans

i) spacing between paragraphs is consistent

j) text, images and lines are not superimposed

k) there is at least one clear line space above the graph and above and below the table containing the imported datafile.

1b	5	Save the file retaining the filename **openday**.
1d	6	Print one copy of the document **openday**.

Assessment Objectives | **TASK 5**

Before you begin this task ensure you have the file **facilities**.

An information leaflet about the new site facilities needs to be included in the welcome packs that will be given to guests on the launch day. The text has already been prepared, but some changes need to be made.

1a	1	Open the text file **facilities**.
5b	2	In the first paragraph delete the words:
		All kennels are built to the highest standard.
5c	3	Replace all instances of the word **vet** with the word **veterinary** wherever it occurs.
		Ensure that you maintain case and that you replace whole words only.
5a	4	In the paragraph headed **Health** replace the second **a** in the name **Manfred Hartel**
5d		with a special character so that it becomes **Manfred Härtel**.
5e	5	Spellcheck the document and correct any errors. Delete any duplicate words, but do not change the grammar of the document.
		Specialist words have already been checked and no changes should be made to them. Spellings must be in English (UK).
6c	6	Insert your name and centre number as a header or footer in this document.
1b	7 a)	Save your document with the filename **seaford**
1d	b)	Print one copy of the document **seaford**.
	c)	Close all open files and exit the software securely.

Assessment Objectives

TASK 6

Your Manager has asked you to archive the source files used in the preparation of the documents for the Woodwind Festival. You may use any method of archiving.

1f

1 Archive the files **launch**, **facilities**, **feedback**, **activities**, **supplies** and **klogo**.

1e

2 a) Take a screen print as evidence of the archiving.

b) Print both this screen print and the screen print saved at Task 2. Ensure that your name is printed on the printout(s).

c) Close any programs and exit the system securely.

Insert the image file **klogo** centred between each margin

Seaford Grange Site Grand Opening

We sincerely hope that you will be able to come to the grand opening of our new site at Seaford Grange. This event will give current and prospective clients a chance to tour our fantastic new site and speak to the staff.

Boomerang Boarding Kennels have an excellent reputation for quality service and care. The graph below summarizes the feedback we have had from clients.

Insert the graph **feedback** here

The event will open at 12.30 pm with a buffet lunch followed by a short presentation about the company from the Site Manager, Mrs Susan Marshall. Tours and fun activities for all the family will continue until the closing firework display at 7.00 pm.

Page break

Start page 2 here

Family Activities

A great choice of fun family activities will be available for you to try throughout the afternoon. Some of the activities will include:

Bouncy Castle
Canine Karaoke
Dog Grooming
Dog Show
Marketplace Stalls
Mountain Bike Adventure Trail
Magic with Silly Billy the clown

Add a bullet character to each of these 7 lines

Set the bulleted text to 1.5 line spacing

Seaford Pet Supplies

Local company Seaford Pet Supplies will be hosting a marketplace stall selling their range of organic pet food and treats. Special discounts will be available on all products. Some of the most popular products and prices are shown in the table below.

Insert the datafile **seaford** and format as specified in Task 4

We do hope that you will be able to join us for this exciting event. Please bring the whole family along and join in all the fun!

Please telephone Patsy Black at the Stanley Green site on 01621 761981 if you have any further questions about this event.

Two   Manipulating Spreadsheets and Graphs

To pass this unit you must be able to:

✓ identify, input and amend data in spreadsheet software accurately

✓ use formulae and functions in spreadsheets

✓ produce exploded pie, bar/line graphs and XY scatter graphs

✓ use formatting and alignment techniques in spreadsheets and graphs/ charts

✓ save and print spreadsheets and graphs/charts.

Before you start this chapter, you or your tutor should download a zipped file called **Resources for Chapter 2** from **www.payne-gallway.co.uk/claitplus**. It will automatically unzip. Specify that the contents are to be saved in your **My Documents** folder.

The practice tasks that follow cover all the techniques you need to learn in order to pass a New CLAiT Plus Unit 2 MANIPULATING SPREADSHEETS AND GRAPHS assignment.

Practice tasks

Task 1   Creating a new spreadsheet

Scenario

You are working in the office of a holiday car rental company. Your manager has created some outline spreadsheets. You have been asked to complete the spreadsheets and produce reports and graphs for your manager.

Saving a datafile in Excel workbook format

You have been asked to use a pre-prepared datafile to produce a report on income from rentals in August.

To get started you need to open the pre-prepared datafile and save it in Microsoft Excel workbook format.

 Create a subfolder called **Unit 2 PT** in your **My Documents** folder or network home directory folder where files created as you work through these practice tasks can be stored.

The steps you need to follow to create a subfolder are described in **Chapter 1** on **page 5**.

Microsoft Office
Excel 2003

Next you need to load Excel. This can be done in one of two ways:

▶ *either* double-click the **Microsoft Excel** icon on the main screen in Windows,

▶ *or* click the **Start** button at the bottom left of the screen, then click **Programs**, then click .

The datafile you need to use is called **august**. Your tutor will tell you where to find this file. In the example below it is in the user's **My Documents** folder.

Open button

▶ Click **File** on the menu bar, and then click **Open**.

▶ Or click the **Open button** on the **Standard** toolbar.

The **Open** dialogue box will appear.

▶ Click the **My Documents** icon on the left of the window.

The contents of your **My Documents** folder will be listed.

▶ Click the down arrow next to the **Files of type:** box.

▶ Scroll down through the drop-down list of options and click **Text Files**.

▶ Click on the file called **august**, and then click **Open**.

The datafile will be opened – it should look like the example below.

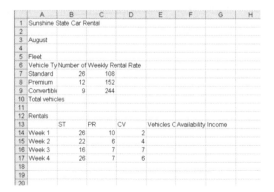

▶ Click **File** on the menu bar, and then click **Save As...**

▶ Type the new name, **reservations**

50

▶ Double-click the **Unit 2 PT** subfolder in your **My Documents** folder.

▶ Click the down arrow next to the **Save as type:** box.

▶ Scroll up through the drop-down list of options and click **Microsoft Office Excel Workbook**.

▶ Click **Save**.

Merging cells

Now you can carry on setting up and formatting this spreadsheet. Text labels and numbers on a worksheet can be formatted by selecting the appropriate cells and using the buttons on the **Formatting toolbar**. The formatting options available on the formatting toolbar are shown below.

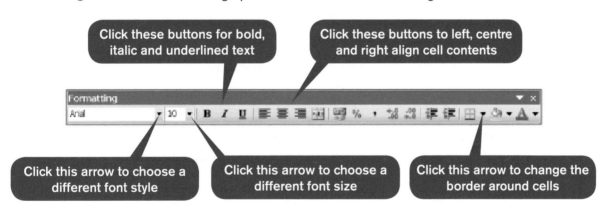

TIP

More formatting options are available by clicking **Format**, and then **cells** on the menu bar. You will learn about some of these as you work through the rest of this task.

The text label **Sunshine State Car Rental** in cell **A1** needs formatting so that it is centred across columns **A** to **G** with a border around it. You need to start by merging cells **A1** to **G1** to form a single cell at the top of the spreadsheet.

◉ Click in cell **A1** and hold the left mouse button.

◉ Drag the mouse to the right as far as cell **G1**.

◉ Let go of the mouse button – the cells you need to format will be highlighted.

◉ Click **Format**, and then click **Cells...** on the menu bar.

The **Format Cells** dialogue box will appear.

◉ Click the **Alignment** tab.

◉ Click the **Merge cells** check box in the **Text control** section.

◉ Click **OK**.

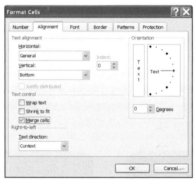

TIP

If you don't highlight the right group of cells just click back where you started and try again. Cells can also be highlighted by clicking where you want to start, holding the **SHIFT** key down and using the arrow keys.

◉ Click the down-arrow in the **Font size** box on the formatting toolbar.

◉ Scroll up through the list of available font sizes and click on size **16**.

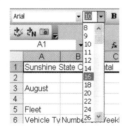

TIP

Excel applies standard or 'default' alignment options when you first enter data in cells. When text is entered in a cell it is automatically left aligned. Similarly when numbers are entered in cells they are automatically right aligned. If you're asked to left align text or right align numbers in an assignment you won't need to do anything.

Bold button

Center button

◉ Click the **bold** button on the **Formatting** toolbar.

◉ Click the **center** button on the **Formatting** toolbar.

TIP

You will be asked to format the size of text labels as **small**, **medium** or **large**. As a general rule use a font size of 12 points for small, 18 points for medium, and 24 points for large.

The final formatting that this part of the spreadsheet needs is a border around the merged cells.

- ▶ Click the down arrow next to the **Outside Border** button on the **Formatting** toolbar.

Outside Border
button

- ▶ Click the **Outside Borders** button in the list of border options.

- ▶ Click away from the highlighted cells on any blank part of the spreadsheet.

    This part of your spreadsheet should look like the example below.

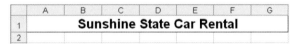

	A	B	C	D	E	F	G
1				Sunshine State Car Rental			
2							

Wrapping text and adjusting column widths

Next you need to use text wrapping and change the width of columns **B** and **C** so that the text labels in cells **B6** and **C6** are displayed on two lines.

- ▶ Highlight cells **B6** and **C6**.

	A	B	C	D
1			Sunshine State	
2				
3	August			
4				
5	Fleet			
6	Vehicle Ty	Number of	Weekly Re	ntal Rate
7	Standard	26	108	
8	Premium	12	152	

- ▶ Click **Format**, and then click **Cells...** on the menu bar.
- ▶ Click the **Alignment** tab in the **Format Cells** dialogue box if it is not already selected.
- ▶ Click the **Wrap text** check box in the **Text control** section.
- ▶ Click **OK**. The text in these cells will be wrapped but will take up three lines.

	A	B	C	[
1			Sunshine Sta	
2				
3	August			
4				
5	Fleet			
6	Vehicle Ty	Number of vehicles	Weekly Rental Rate	
7	Standard	26	108	
8	Premium	12	152	

Now you need to adjust the width of these columns so that the text labels are displayed on two lines.

Position the mouse pointer on the line between the column headers **B** and **C**. The pointer will change to a double-headed arrow.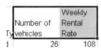

Press and hold down the left mouse button.

Drag the mouse to the right – the column will start to widen. Let go of the mouse button when the text label **Number of vehicles** is displayed on two lines.

Use the same technique to widen column **C** so that the text label **Weekly Rental Rate** is also displayed on two lines.

Next you need to change the widths of columns **A**, **E** and **F** so that the remaining text labels in the cells can be seen in full. This can be done using a different technique.

Position the mouse pointer on the line between the column headers **A** and **B**. The pointer will change to a double-headed arrow.

Double-click the left mouse button. Column **A** will automatically widen to fit the text label.

Use the same technique to change the widths of columns **E** and **F**.

Your spreadsheet should look like the example below.

	A	B	C	D	E	F	G
1	Sunshine State Car Rental						
2							
3	August						
4							
5	Fleet						
6	Vehicle Type	Number of vehicles	Weekly Rental Rate				
7	Standard	26	108				
8	Premium	12	152				
9	Convertible	9	244				
10	Total vehicles						
11							
12	Rentals						
13		ST	PR	CV	Vehicles Out	Availability	Income
14	Week 1	26	10	2			
15	Week 2	22	6	4			
16	Week 3	16	7	7			
17	Week 4	26	7	6			

TIP

For New CLAiT Plus all of the data in each column must be visible. You will lose marks if the contents of any cell cannot be seen in full. If you see ##### displayed in a cell, this means the contents of the cell cannot be displayed because it is too narrow. If this happens just make the column wider.

Using standard functions and naming cells

First you need to enter a formula in cell **B10** to calculate a figure for **Total vehicles**. The standard function **AutoSum** provides the quickest way to do this.

EXCEL provides a large number of built-in standard **mathematical** functions. Two of the most commonly used functions are **SUM** and **AVERAGE**. You can click the **Insert Function** button on the left of the Formula bar to see a list of functions and receive help using them. This is explained in more detail later.

Insert Function button

▶ Click in cell **B10**.

▶ Click the **AutoSum** button on the **Standard** toolbar.

Autosum button

Excel will automatically outline cells **B7** to **B9** and the formula **=SUM(B7:B9)** will be displayed in cell **B10**.

		Number of	Weekly
6	Vehicle Type	vehicles	Rental Rate
7	Standard	26	108
8	Premium	12	152
9	Convertible	9	244
10	Total vehicles	=SUM(B7:B9)	
11		SUM(**number1**, [number2], ...)	
12	Rentals		

▶ Press **Enter**. The result of the calculation will be displayed in cell **B10**.

Next you need to name this cell. Once a cell has been named the name can be used in formulae rather than the cell reference.

▶ Click in cell **B10** if it is not already selected.

▶ Click in the **Name Box** containing the text **B10** just above columns **A** and **B**.

▶ Type **vehicles**, and then press **Enter**.

You'd get the same answer by entering the formula: =B7+B8+B9. The AutoSum function just provides a quicker way to calculate totals if a set of numbers are together in a row or column.

vehicles	▼
A	

The name **vehicles** will be displayed in the cell name box.

Now you need to enter a formula in cell **E14** to calculate a figure for **Vehicles Out** in **Week 1**.

▶ Click in cell **E14**.

▶ Click the **AutoSum** button.

Autosum button

Excel will automatically outline cells **B14** to **D14**. The formula **=SUM(B14:D14)** will be displayed in cell **E14**.

12	Rentals						
13		ST	PR	CV	Vehicles Out	Availability	Income
14	Week 1	26	10	2	=SUM(B14:D14)		
15	Week 2	22	6	4	SUM(**number1**, [number2], ...)		
16	Week 3	16	7	7			

▶ Press **Enter**. The result of the calculation will be displayed in cell **E14**.

Replicating formulae

Now you need to copy or 'replicate' the formula in cell **E14** down **Column E** so a figure for **Vehicles Out** is shown for each week.

Click back in cell **E14**. You'll see a small black square – called the **fill handle** – in the bottom right-hand corner of the cell.

Hold the pointer over the fill handle. Click and hold the left mouse button when it changes into a thin black cross.

Drag down the column as far as cell **E17**.

Let go of the mouse button. The formula will be replicated in cells **E15** to **E17**.

Auto Fill Options button

The **Auto Fill Options** button might appear after you've used the fill handle – you don't need to use this – just ignore it.

Click on any blank part of the spreadsheet to remove the highlighting in the selected cells. Your spreadsheet should now look like the example below.

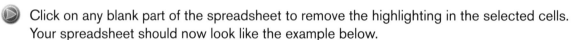

	A	B	C	D	E	F	G
1			**Sunshine State Car Rental**				
2							
3	August						
4							
5	Fleet						
6	Vehicle Type	Number of vehicles	Weekly Rental Rate				
7	Standard	26	108				
8	Premium	12	152				
9	Convertible	9	244				
10	Total vehicles	47					
11							
12	Rentals						
13		ST	PR	CV	Vehicles Out	Availability	Income
14	Week 1	26	10	2	38		
15	Week 2	22	6	4	32		
16	Week 3	16	7	7	30		
17	Week 4	26	7	6	39		

TIP

Undo button

If you make a mistake when you're using the fill handle just click the **Undo** button on the **Standard toolbar** and try again.

Conditional functions

Insert Function button

Next you need to enter a formula in cell **F14** that will calculate the **Availability** of vehicles in **Week 1**. If the number of **Vehicles Out** is greater than the result of multiplying the value in the named cell **Vehicles** by **80%** then **Low** should be displayed in the cell, otherwise **OK** should be displayed in the cell. You need to use a **conditional function** called **IF** to do this.

▶ Click in cell **F14**.

▶ Click the **Insert Function** button on the left of the Formula bar.

The **Insert Function** dialogue box will appear.

▶ Click the down arrow next to the **Or select a category:** box, and then click **Logical** in the drop-down list of options.

▶ Click **IF** in the list of functions.

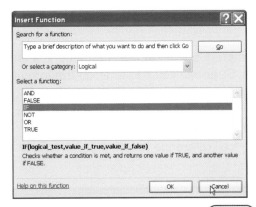

▶ Click **OK**. The **Function Arguments** dialogue box will appear.

▶ Click in the Logical_test box and type **E14>vehicle*80%**

▶ Click in the **Value_if_true** box and type **Low**

▶ Click in the **Value_if_false** box and type **OK**

TIP

If you're asked to leave a cell blank if the result of a conditional function is either true or false just enter two double quotation marks "" in either the **Value_if_true** box or the **Value_if_false** box.

Your **Function Arguments** dialogue box should now look like the example below.

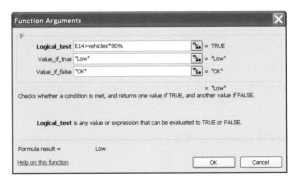

▶ Click **OK**. The result of the calculation will be displayed in cell **F14**.

▶ Use the **fill handle** to copy the formula in cell **F14** down as far as cell **F17**.

This section of your spreadsheet should look like the example below.

13		ST	PR	CV	Vehicles Out	Availability	Income
14	Week 1	26	10	2	38	Low	
15	Week 2	22	6	4	32	OK	
16	Week 3	16	7	7	30	OK	
17	Week 4	26	7	6	39	Low	

Absolute cell references

Normally, when you enter a formula in a cell, you use a cell reference such as **A1**. This is called a **relative cell reference**. When you move or copy a formula Excel adjusts relative cell references in the formula to reflect the new position. For example when you replicated the formula **=SUM(B14:D14)** in cell **B14** Excel automatically adjusted the cell references so that the formulae in the cells underneath became **=SUM(B15:D15)**, **=SUM(B16:D16)** and **=SUM(B17:D17)**.

Sometimes situations occur where a particular cell reference in a formula must remain the same when the formula is replicated. Suppose you had entered the formula **=A1*(B1+B2)** but needed any replicated versions of the formula to keep the cell reference **A1**. You can stop Excel from automatically adjusting column or row references by putting a dollar sign (**$**) in front of the parts of the cell reference that must stay the same. For the formula in this example, you would enter **=$A$1*(B1+B2)**. This type of cell reference is called an **absolute cell reference**.

> **TIP**
>
> If a dollar sign is placed in front of just the column letter, e.g. **$A1**, the column letter will never be changed but the row number will. If a dollar sign is placed in front of just the row number e.g. **A$1**, the row number will never be changed but the column letter will. If a dollar sign is placed in front of both the column letter and row number, e.g. **$A$1**, neither will be changed. If you position the cursor in the Formula bar where you need an absolute reference and then press F4, dollar signs will be inserted automatically. Press the F4 key again to switch between the different types of absolute reference.

Now you need to enter a formula in cell **G14** to calculate a figure for **Income** in **Week 1**. This formula will need to use absolute references to refer to the **Weekly Rental Rate** amounts in **Column C**.

- Click in cell **G14**.
- Type **=C7** and press the **F4** key to set **C7** as an absolute reference.
- Type ***B14+**
- Type **C8** and press the **F4** key to set **C8** as an absolute reference.
- Type ***C14+**
- Type **C9** and press the **F4** key to set **C9** as an absolute reference.
- Type ***D14**

The formula bar at the top of the screen should look like the example below.

f_x =$C$7*B14+$C$8*C14+$C$9*D14

- Press **Enter**. The result of the calculation will appear in cell **G14**.

- Use the **fill handle** to copy the formula in cell **G14** down as far as cell **G17**.

This section of your spreadsheet should now look like the example below.

13		ST	PR	CV	Vehicles Out	Availability	Income
14	Week 1	26	10	2	38	Low	4816
15	Week 2	22	6	4	32	OK	4264
16	Week 3	16	7	7	30	OK	4500
17	Week 4	26	7	6	39	Low	5336

Formatting data

Next you need to format the numbers on the spreadsheet. You are going to start by formatting the figures for **Weekly Rental Rate** in **Column C** so they're displayed with **2 decimal places**.

- Highlight cells **C7** to **C9**.

- Click **Format**, then **Cells** on the menu bar.

    The **Format Cells** dialogue box will be displayed.

- Click the **Number** tab if it isn't already selected.

- Click **Number** in the **Category** list.

- The value in the box next to **Decimal places** will already be set to **2**.

- Click **OK**.

Next you need to format the figures for **Number of vehicles** in **Column B** so they're displayed with **no decimal places**.

- Highlight cells **B7** to **B9**.

- Click **Format**, then **Cells** on the menu bar.

▶ Click the **Number** tab in the **Format Cells** dialogue box if it isn't already selected.

▶ Click **Number** in the **Category** list.

▶ Change the value in the **Decimal places** box to **0** by clicking the small down arrow <u>twice</u>.

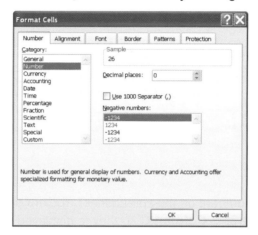

▶ Click **OK**.

Undo button

TIP

You won't see any obvious change in the appearance of the spreadsheet at this stage. Check this formatting by clicking in any cell from **B7** to **B9** and entering a number containing a decimal place. The digits after the decimal point will disappear when you press **Enter**. The value you entered will be rounded up or down to the nearest whole number. Click the undo button on the **Standard toolbar** once you've tried this.

Next you need to format the figures for **Income** in **Column G** so they're displayed with a **currency symbol and no decimal places**.

▶ Highlight cells **G14** to **G17**.

▶ Click **Format**, then **Cells** on the menu bar.

▶ Click the **Number** tab in the **Format Cells** dialogue box if it isn't already selected.

▶ Click **Currency** in the **Category** list.

▶ Change the value in the **Decimal places** box to **0** by clicking the small down arrow <u>twice</u>.

▶ The **Symbol** box should contain a **£** sign (click the down arrow on the right of the box and choose **£** from the list if any other symbol is displayed).

▶ Click **OK**.

Finally you need to format all the other numbers on the spreadsheet to be displayed with **no currency symbol and no decimal places**.

- Highlight cells **B14** to **E17**.
- Click **Format**, then **Cells**.
- Click **Number** in the **Category** list on the **Number** tab.
- Change the number of **Decimal places** to **0**.
- Click **OK**. Your spreadsheet should look like the example below.

	A	B	C	D	E	F	G
1			**Sunshine State Car Rental**				
2							
3	August						
4							
5	Fleet						
6	Vehicle Type	Number of vehicles	Weekly Rental Rate				
7	Standard	26	108.00				
8	Premium	12	152.00				
9	Convertible	9	244.00				
10	Total vehicles	47					
11							
12	Rentals						
13		ST	PR	CV	Vehicles Out	Availability	Income
14	Week 1	26	10	2	38	Low	£4,816
15	Week 2	22	6	4	32	OK	£4,264
16	Week 3	16	7	7	30	OK	£4,500
17	Week 4	26	7	6	39	Low	£5,336

Adding a header

Now we'll add some information to the header section of the workbook and save it.

- Click **View** on the menu bar, and then click **Header and Footer**.

  The **Page Setup** dialogue box will be displayed with the **Header/Footer** tab selected.

- Click the **Custom Header** button. The **Header** dialogue box will be displayed.
- Click in the **Left section** and type your name.
- Click in the **Center section** and type your centre number.
- Click in the **Right section**.
- Click the **Filename** button.

  Your **Header** dialogue box should look something like the example below.

Filename button

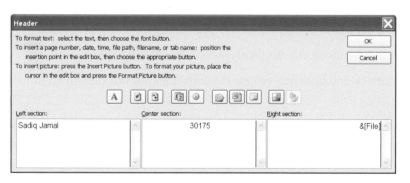

Click **OK** to return to the **Page Setup** dialogue box.

Click **OK** to exit.

Now you need to save the workbook.

Save button

Click the **Save** button on the **Standard** toolbar to save the workbook keeping the same name **reservations**.

> **TIP**
>
> You can place this information in the page footer if you prefer – just click the **Custom Footer** button and follow the same steps.

Hiding columns and printing

Next you need to produce a printout showing the formulae on the spreadsheet. The data for the different vehicle types in the **Rentals** section contains no formulae and does need to be included on the printout. This data can be temporarily removed from view by hiding columns **B to D**.

Click the column header for **column B** and hold the left mouse button.

Drag to the right as far as **column D**. Columns B to D will be highlighted.

	A	B	C	D	E	F	G
1		**Sunshine State Car Rental**					
2							
3	August						
4							
5	Fleet						
6	Vehicle Type	Number of vehicles	Weekly Rental Rate				
7	Standard	26	108.00				
8	Premium	12	152.00				
9	Convertible	9	244.00				
10	Total vehicles	47					
11							
12	Rentals						
13		ST	PR	CV	Vehicles Out	Availability	Income
14	Week 1	26	10	2	38	Low	£4,816
15	Week 2	22	6	4	32	OK	£4,264
16	Week 3	16	7	7	30	OK	£4,500
17	Week 4	26	7	6	39	Low	£5,336

Click **Format**, **Column** on the menu bar, and then click **Hide**.

Columns **B**, **C** and **D** will be hidden.

Next you need to use the **Options** dialogue box to reveal the formulae.

Click **Tools**, and then **Options** on the menu bar.

The **Options** dialogue box will appear.

Click the **View** tab if it isn't already selected.

In the **Window options** section click the check box next to **Formulas**.

Click **OK**. All the formulae will be displayed on the worksheet.

Adjust the width of any columns where the formulae are not displayed in full.

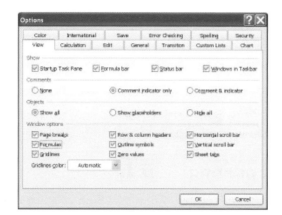

The printout needs to be on one page in **landscape orientation** with the gridlines and row and column headings visible. You need to use the **Page Setup** dialogue box to make sure the printout is correctly formatted.

▶ Click **File** on the menu bar, and then click **Page Setup**.

The **Page Setup** dialogue box will appear.

▶ Click the **Page** tab if it isn't already selected.

▶ In the **Orientation** section click the radio button next to **Landscape**.

▶ In the **Scaling** section click the radio button for **Fit to:** and leave the other options as **1 page wide by 1 page tall**.

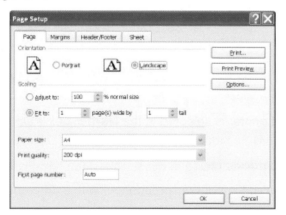

▶ Click the **Sheet** tab.

▶ In the **Print** section click the check boxes next to **Row and column headings** and **Gridlines**.

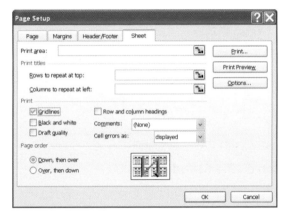

▶ Click the **Print Preview** button.

The spreadsheet will be displayed exactly as it will be printed – it should look something like the example below.

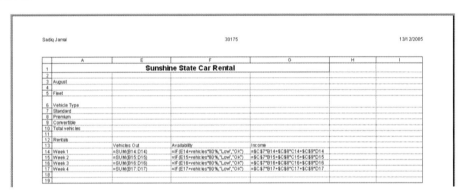

▶ Click the **Print** button at the top of the screen. The **Print Preview** will be closed and the **Print** dialogue box will appear.

▶ Check that the correct printer is selected in the **Name:** box – ask your tutor if you're not sure about this.

▶ Click **OK** to print the spreadsheet.

Finally you need to save this version of the spreadsheet with a different name.

▶ Click **File** on the menu bar, and then click **Save As...**

▶ Type the new name, **resforms**

▶ Click the **Save** button.

▶ Close **Excel**.

Task 2   Exploded pie charts

You have been asked to use a pre-prepared datafile to produce an exploded pie chart showing the proportion of rentals for each vehicle type from May to October. This task describes how to do this using the **Chart Wizard** tool.

Opening and saving the datafile

The datafile you need to use is called **summary**. In the example below it is in the user's **My Documents** folder. Your tutor will tell you where to find this file if it is stored in a different location.

- Load **Excel**.
- Click **File** on the menu bar, and then click **Open**.
- *Or* click the **Open** button on the **Standard** toolbar.

Open button

- Click the **My Documents** icon on the left of **Open** dialogue box.
- Click the down arrow next to the **Files of type:** box and select **Text Files**.
- Click on the text file called **summary**, and then click **Open**.
- Increase the width of any columns where the data cannot be seen in full. Your spreadsheet should now look like the example below.

	A	B	C	D	E	F	G	H
1	Vehicle Rental Summary							
2								
3	Vehicle Type	May	June	July	August	September	October	Total
4	Standard	97	99	102	103	80	81	562
5	Premium	37	48	39	32	35	38	229
6	Convertible	16	17	34	26	32	19	144
7								

- Click **File** on the menu bar, and then click **Save As...**
- Type the new name, **rentdists**
- Double-click the **Unit 2 PT** subfolder in your **My Documents** folder.
- Click the down arrow next to the **Files of type:** box and select **Microsoft Office Excel Workbook** file type.
- Click **Save**.

Highlighting the chart data

The exploded pie chart needs to display the proportion of rentals for each vehicle type. You need to highlight the relevant data in columns **A** and **H** before using the **Chart Wizard** to create the chart.

- Highlight cells **A4** to **A6**.
- Press and hold the **Ctrl** key.
- Highlight cells **H4** to **H6**.

	A	B	C	D	E	F	G	H
1	Vehicle Rental Summary							
2								
3	Vehicle Type	May	June	July	August	September	October	Total
4	Standard	97	99	102	103	80	81	562
5	Premium	37	48	39	32	35	38	229
6	Convertible	16	17	34	26	32	19	144

Creating the pie chart

▶ Click the **Chart Wizard** button.

▶ Click **Pie** in the **Chart type** list.

▶ Click the first **Exploded Pie** chart in the second row of the **Chart sub-type** section.

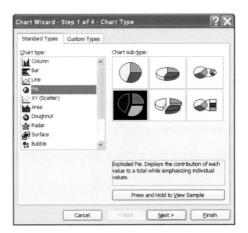

▶ Move to **Step 3** of the Chart Wizard by clicking the **Next** button <u>twice</u>.

▶ Click the **Titles** tab if it isn't already selected.

▶ Click in the **Chart title** box and type **Total Vehicle Rentals**

Chart legends and labels

Next you need to remove the legend from the pie chart and replace it with labels showing the vehicle types and the percentage of total rentals represented by each segment.

▶ Click the **Legend** tab.

▶ Uncheck the **Show Legend** box.

▶ Click the **Data labels** tab.

▶ Check **Category name** and **Percentage** boxes in the **Label Contains** list.

▶ Uncheck the **Show leader lines box**. This option generates a line connecting the segments and their labels when they are moved away from each other. You do not need any of these connecting lines on this pie chart.

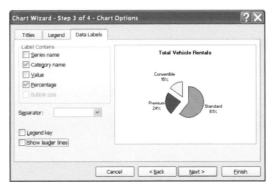

Click **Next**.

Click **As new sheet** to place the pie chart in a separate chart sheet.

Click **Finish**. The pie chart will appear in a new **Chart Sheet** – it should look like the one below.

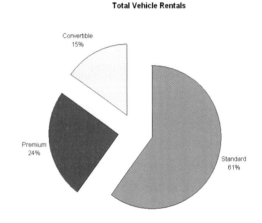

Total Vehicle Rentals

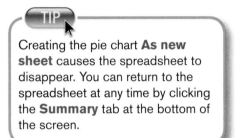

> **TIP**
>
> Creating the pie chart **As new sheet** causes the spreadsheet to disappear. You can return to the spreadsheet at any time by clicking the **Summary** tab at the bottom of the screen.

Formatting chart labels

Now you need to format the percentage figures on the segment labels so that they are displayed with **one decimal place**.

Click on any segment label. The segment labels will be highlighted.

Click **Format** on the menu bar, and then click **Selected Data Labels...**

The **Format Data Labels** dialogue box will appear.

Click the **Number** tab.

Change the value in the **Decimal places** box to **1** by clicking the small up arrow <u>once</u>.

Click **OK**. The percentage figures will be displayed with one decimal place.

Recolouring pie chart segments

Next you need to make the smallest segment on the pie chart for **Convertible** vehicles stand out more by changing the fill colour and moving it away from the other segments.

▶ Click <u>once</u> anywhere on the pie chart.

▶ Hold the **Shift** key and click <u>once</u> on the **Convertible** segment.

This segment of the pie chart will be selected.

▶ Double-click anywhere on the selected **Convertible** segment.

The **Format Data Series** dialogue window will appear.

▶ Click on a colour in the area section that will stand out from the other colours on the pie chart segments.

▶ Click **OK**. The pie chart will be displayed with the **Convertible** segment recoloured.

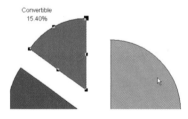

> **TIP**
>
> Make sure that all of the segments on a pie chart stand out by changing the fill colours on any segments that are too similar.

Moving pie chart segments

Now you are ready to move this segment away from the other segments.

▶ Position the mouse pointer over the centre of the **Convertible** segment.

▶ Click and hold the left mouse button.

▶ Drag up and across to the left. As you drag an outline will show where the segment will be placed when you let go of the mouse button. Let go of the mouse button when the segment outline is in roughly the same position as the example below.

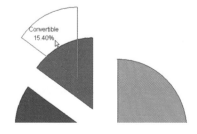

Adding a footer and printing

Now you need to add some information to the footer section of the chart.

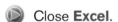 Click **View** on the menu bar, and then click **Header and Footer**.

The **Page Setup** dialogue box will be displayed with the **Header/Footer** tab selected.

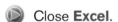 Click the **Custom Footer** button to display the **Footer** dialogue box.

 Click in the **Left section** and type your name.

 Click in the **Center section** and type your centre number. Your **Footer** dialogue box should look something like the one below.

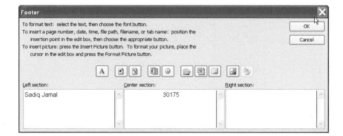

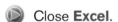 Click **OK** to return to the **Page Setup** dialogue box.

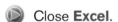 Click **OK** to exit.

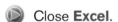 Click the **Print** button. The **Print** dialogue box will appear.

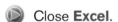 Check the correct printer is selected – ask your tutor if you're not sure about this – and then click **OK** to print the pie chart.

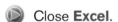 Click the **Save** button on the **Standard** toolbar to save the entire workbook (spreadsheet and chart) keeping the same name **rentdists**.

 Close **Excel**.

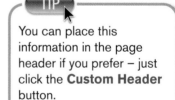

TIP

You can place this information in the page header if you prefer – just click the **Custom Header** button.

Save button

Task 3   Sorting and filtering data

You have been asked to update the records for rental fleet vehicles. One vehicle has been written off following an accident so its details need to be deleted. The management are considering charging more for low mileage vehicles. They need a report on the vehicles that would be affected. This task describes the steps you need to follow to update, filter and sort data in a pre-prepared datafile.

Opening and saving the datafile

The datafile you need to use is called **vehicles**. In the example below it is in the user's **My Documents** folder. Your tutor will tell you where to find this file if it is stored in a different location.

Open button

▶ Load **Excel**.

▶ Click **File** on the menu bar, and then click **Open**.

▶ *Or* click the **Open** button on the **Standard** toolbar.

▶ Click the **My Documents** icon on the left of **Open** dialogue box.

▶ Click the down arrow next to the **Files of type:** box and select **Text Files**.

▶ Click on the text file called **vehicles**, and then click **Open**.

▶ Increase the width of any columns where the data cannot be seen in full. Your spreadsheet should now look like the one below.

	A	B	C	D
1	Registration	Vehicle Type	Mileage	Colour
2	H 7493 LE	ST	1785	Red
3	K 3922 DE	ST	5464	Blue
4	J 3878 SX	CV	2139	Red
5	J 3982 XS	PR	8803	Green
6	J 7823 JU	ST	8052	Silver
7	J 9382 PL	ST	1085	Red
8	J 8939 KP	ST	7573	Green
9	K 3844 LX	ST	6467	Blue

▶ Click **File** on the menu bar, and then click **Save As...**

▶ Type the new name, **fleet**

▶ Double-click the **Unit 2 PT** subfolder in your **My Documents** folder.

▶ Click the down arrow next to the **Files of type:** box and select **Microsoft Office Excel Workbook** file type.

▶ Click **Save**.

Deleting a row

The entire row for the vehicle with registration **J 9832 PL** must be deleted. Before you can delete this row you need to locate the registration in the list. You could do this by reading through the list but this might prove to be quite time-consuming. The **Find and Replace** facility offers a much more efficient way to find data items in spreadsheets like this containing a large amount of data.

▶ Click **Edit** on the menu bar, and then click **Find...** The **Find and Replace** dialogue box will appear.

▶ Type **J 9832 PL** in the **Find what:** box.

▶ Click **Find Next**. The registration will be located in **row 38**.

Click **Close**.

36	H 3882 SE	CV	7590	Silver
37	K 3892 PT	ST	7699	Silver
38	J 9832 PL	ST	1470	Black
39	J 9832 PX	ST	6678	Green

Now you can delete this row.

Right-click the label for **row 38**. The row will be highlighted.

38	J 9832 PL	ST		1470	Black
3	✂ Cut			6678	Green
4	🗐 Copy			5378	Silver
4	🗐 Paste			3251	Red
4		Paste Special...		6453	Green
4				6555	Blue
4		Insert		3955	Black
4		Delete		5021	Silver
4				2478	Green

Click **Delete** in the drop-down list of options. The row will be deleted.

Click on any blank part of the spreadsheet.

Deleting a column

Next you need to delete a column. The information about the colour of the vehicles is not required. This means that **Column D** must be deleted.

Right-click the header for **Column D**.

The column will be highlighted.

	A	B	C	D	E
21	J 8932 KE	ST	1038	Green	✂ Cut
22	H 7383 JY	PR	8080	Silver	🗐 Copy
23	J 7483 UX	ST	7627	Red	Paste
24	J 3923 CD	ST	5486	Green	
25	H 3992 PN	PR	4204	Blue	Paste Special...
26	H 9309 KI	ST	1344	Black	Insert
27	H 3992 VY	CV	6913	Silver	Delete
28	K 2392 DE	ST	5876	Black	Clear Contents
29	J 7383 FT	ST	1396	Silver	
30	K 3892 YT	PR	7278	Green	Format Cells...
31	H 5631 JK	ST	5066	Silver	Column Width...
32	J 3822 UE	ST	1667	Silver	Hide
33	J 3892 CV	CV	7440	Blue	Unhide
34	K 3822 ZX	ST	7938	Blue	
35	H 7823 JT	PR	8549	Red	
36	H 3882 SE	CV	7590	Silver	

Click **Delete** on the shortcut menu. The column and all its contents will disappear.

TIP

You could be asked to insert a new column rather than a new row. The technique is almost the same – just right-click the column label in front of where you want the new column to be inserted, and then click **Insert** on the shortcut menu.

Inserting a row

Now you need to add some information about a new vehicle to the spreadsheet. This information must be added in a new row at the top of the spreadsheet.

 Right-click the header for **row 2**.

 Click **Insert** on the shortcut menu.

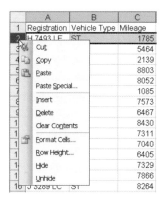

A new row will appear.

 Add the information shown below in the new row.

Registration	Vehicle Type	Mileage
H 2164 LX	ST	1207

Filtering and sorting data

Next you need to filter the data in the spreadsheet to find all the vehicles with **Mileage** less than **2000**. Once you have filtered the data it must be sorted into ascending order of **Vehicle Type**.

 Highlight cells **A1** to **C1**.

 Click **Data, Filter** on the menu bar, and then click **Auto Filter**.

Filter arrows will appear on the right of cells **A1**, **B1** and **C1**.

	A	B	C
1	Registrati ▼	Vehicle Typ ▼	Mileage ▼
2	H 2164 LX	ST	1207

 Click the filter arrow in cell **C1**. A drop-down list of filter options will appear.

 Click **(Custom...)** in the list. The **Custom AutoFilter** dialogue box will appear.

 Click the down arrow on the box under **Mileage**.

 Click **is less than or equal to** in the list of options.

 Click in the next box along and type **2000**. Your **Custom AutoFilter** dialogue box should look like the example below.

⊙ Click **OK**. The data will be filtered – you should have a list of records like the example below.

	A	B	C
1	Registration ▾	Vehicle Type ▾	Mileage ▾
2	H 2164 LX	ST	1207
3	H 7493 LE	ST	1785
8	J 9382 PL	ST	1085
18	H 3092 LK	CV	1132
19	K 3782 DC	ST	1098
20	H 8040 HS	ST	1797
22	J 8932 KE	ST	1038
27	H 9309 KI	ST	1344
30	J 7383 FT	ST	1396
33	J 3822 UE	ST	1667
47	H 8392 LE	PR	1313
50			

Next you need to sort the filtered data into ascending order of **Vehicle Type**.

⊙ Click the filter arrow in cell **B1**.

⊙ Click **Sort Ascending** in the list of options. The data will be sorted. Your spreadsheet should look like the example below.

	A	B	C
1	Registrati ▾	Vehicle Typ ▾	Mileage ▾
2	H 3092 LK	CV	1132
3	H 8392 LE	PR	1313
8	H 2164 LX	ST	1207
18	H 7493 LE	ST	1785
19	J 9382 PL	ST	1085
20	K 3782 DC	ST	1098
22	H 8040 HS	ST	1797
27	J 8932 KE	ST	1038
30	H 9309 KI	ST	1344
33	J 7383 FT	ST	1396
47	J 3822 UE	ST	1667

Adding a footer and saving

Now you need to add some information to the header section of the spreadsheet and save it.

⊙ Click **View** on the menu bar, and then click **Header and Footer**.

⊙ Click the **Custom Footer** button to display the **Footer** dialogue box.

⊙ Click in the **Left section** and type your name.

⊙ Click in the **Center section** and type your centre number.

⊙ Click in the **Right section** and click the **Filename** button.

Your **Footer** dialogue box should look something like the one below.

Filename button

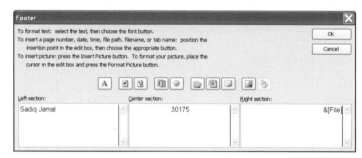

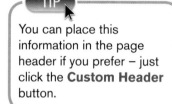

⊙ Click **OK** to return to the **Page Setup** dialogue box.

⊙ Click **OK** to exit.

Save button

⊙ Click the **Save** button on the **Standard** toolbar to save the workbook keeping the same name, **fleet**.

TIP

You can place this information in the page header if you prefer – just click the **Custom Header** button.

Printing

Now you need to print a copy of the filtered spreadsheet with the row and column headings visible.

⊙ Click **File**, and then **Page Setup...** on the menu bar to display the **Page Setup** dialogue box.

⊙ Click the **Sheet** tab.

⊙ Click the check box next to **Row and column headings** in the **Print** section.

⊙ Click the **Print Preview** button to check that all the data will be visible on the printed page.

⊙ Click the **Print** button at the top of the screen. The **Print Preview** will be closed and the **Print** dialogue box will appear.

⊙ Check that the correct printer is selected in the **Name:** box – ask your tutor if you're not sure about this.

⊙ Click **OK** to print the spreadsheet.

⊙ Close **Excel**.

Task 4   Linking spreadsheets

A new tax has been placed on holiday car rental companies. The Manager has asked you to check that the increase in operating costs will still be covered by the income from car rentals. To do this you will need to update a pre-prepared datafile and save it in Excel workbook format. The updated spreadsheet must then be linked to the spreadsheet called **reservations** that you created in Task 1.

Opening and saving the datafile

The datafile you need to use is called **income**. In the example below it is in the user's **My Documents** folder. Your tutor will tell you where to find this file if it is stored in a different location.

Load **Excel**.

Click **File** on the menu bar, and then click **Open**.

Or click the **Open** button on the **Standard** toolbar.

Open button

Click the **My Documents** icon on the left of the **Open** dialogue box.

Click the down arrow next to the **Files of type:** box and select **Text Files**.

Click on the text file called **income**, and then click **Open**.

Increase the width of any columns where all the data cannot be seen in full. Your spreadsheet should now look like the example below.

	A	B
1	Sunshine State Car Rental	
2		
3	August	
4		
5	Operating Costs	
6		
7	Item	Total
8	Administration	1047
9	Advertising	940
10	Staff	4218
11	Vehicle Maintenance	2394
12		
13		
14	Total Operating Costs	8599
15	Total Operating Costs (inc. Taxes)	
16		
17		
18	Income	
19		
20	Profit from rentals	

Click **File** on the menu bar, and then click **Save As…**

Type the new name, **overheads**

Double-click the **Unit 2 PT** subfolder in your **My Documents** folder.

Click the down arrow next to the **Files of type:** box and select **Microsoft Office Excel Workbook** file type.

Click **Save**.

Adding a new standard formula

You need to add a formula in **cell B15** of the spreadsheet to calculate the **Total Operating Costs (inc. Taxes)** by multiplying the amount in cell **B14** by **120%**.

Click in **cell B15**.

Type **=B14*120%** and press **Enter**. The result of the calculation will be displayed in **cell B15**.

Next you need to format the figure in cell **B15** to **2 decimal places**.

Click back in **cell B15**.

Increase Decimal button

Click the **Increase Decimal** button on the **Formatting toolbar** to add a second decimal point to the figure. This part of your spreadsheet should look like the example below.

13		
14	Total Operating Costs	8599
15	Total Operating Costs (inc. Taxes)	10318.80

Increase Decimal
button

Adding a formula to link spreadsheets

Next you need to add a formula in **cell B20** of the spreadsheet to calculate the **Profit from rentals** by subtracting the figure for **Total Operating Costs (inc. Taxes)** from the **Total Rental Income**. The figure for **Total Rental Income** can be calculated using data in the **reservations** spreadsheet created in **Task 1**.

▶ Open the workbook called **reservations**.

▶ Click the **overheads** workbook icon at the bottom of the screen.

▶ Click in **cell B20**.

▶ Type **=sum(**

▶ Click the **reservations** workbook icon at the bottom of the screen.

▶ Click in **cell G14** and hold the left mouse button.

▶ Drag down as far as cell **G17**, and then let go of the mouse button.

▶ Click the **overheads** workbook icon at the bottom of the screen.

▶ Type **)-B15**

The formula in the formula bar should look like the example below.

fx =SUM([reservations.xls]august!$G$14:$G$17)-B15

▶ Press **Enter**. The result of the calculation will be displayed in **cell B20**.

▶ Format the figure in cell **B20** to **2 decimal places**.

Date button

Printing and saving the spreadsheet

▶ Add your **name**, **centre number** and an **automatic date** to the header or footer of the spreadsheet.

- Print the spreadsheet on **one page** in **landscape orientation**.

- Click the **Save** button on the **Standard** toolbar to save the workbook keeping the same name **overheads**.

Save button

- Display the formulae on the spreadsheet.

- Print the spreadsheet on **one page** in **landscape orientation** with the **gridlines, row and column headings** visible.

- Save the spreadsheet with the new name **overforms**

- Close **Excel**. Click **No** if you are prompted to save changes to the **reservations** workbook.

Task 5   XY scatter graphs and bar graphs

Your manager has asked you to analyse some data by using data in pre-prepared datafiles and spreadsheets to create and format an **XY scatter graph** and a **bar graph**. This task describes how to do this using the **Chart Wizard** tool.

Opening and saving the datafile

The datafile you need to use is called **usage**. In the example below it is in the user's **My Documents** folder. Your tutor will tell you where to find this file if it is stored in a different location.

- Click **File** on the menu bar, and then click **Open**.

- *Or* click the **Open** button on the **Standard** toolbar.

Open button

- Click the **My Documents** icon on the left of **Open** dialogue box.

- Click the down arrow next to the **Files of type:** box and select **Text Files**.

- Click on the text file called **usage**, and then click **Open**.

This file should look like the example below.

	A	B
1	Vehicle Use	
2		
3	Mileage	Rentals
4	10345	63
5	11568	72
6	7670	48
7	4322	19
8	4529	22
9	10856	78
10	7051	37
11	11174	62
12	9121	92
13	10697	88

- Click **File** on the menu bar, and then click **Save As...**

- Type the new name, **milerents**

- Double-click the **Unit 2 PT** subfolder in your **My Documents** folder.

▶ Click the down arrow next to the **Files of type:** box and select **Microsoft Office Excel Workbook** file type.

▶ Click **Save**.

Creating an XY scatter graph

The XY scatter graph needs to plot the mileage for the selected vehicles against the reported number of breakdowns for them.

You need to start by highlighting the relevant data in columns **A** and **B** before using the **Chart Wizard** to create the chart.

▶ Click the **usage** tab at the bottom of the screen if it is not already selected.

▶ Highlight cells **A4** to **B13**.

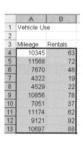

	A	B
1	Vehicle Use	
2		
3	Mileage	Rentals
4	10345	63
5	11568	72
6	7670	48
7	4322	19
8	4529	22
9	10856	78
10	7051	37
11	11174	62
12	9121	92
13	10697	88

Chart Wizard
button

▶ Click the **Chart Wizard** button on the **Standard** toolbar.

The **Chart Wizard** dialogue box will be displayed.

▶ Click **XY (Scatter)** in the **Chart type** list.

▶ Leave the first **Chart sub-type** selected. You do not need to join the data points on this graph.

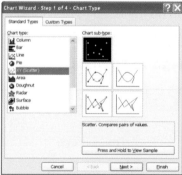

▶ Click **Next**. You'll be moved on to **Step 2** of the Chart Wizard. You don't need to do anything else at this stage.

▶ Click **Next**. You'll be moved on to **Step 3** of the Chart Wizard. You need to enter a title for the graph and labels for the axes.

▶ Click in the **Chart title** box and type **Sunshine State Car Rentals**

▶ Click in the **Category (X) axis** box and type **Mileage**

▶ Click in the **Value (Y) axis** box and type **Reported Breakdowns**

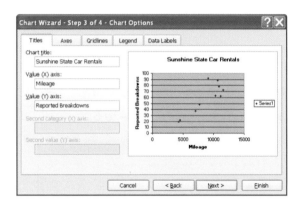

The legend on this chart doesn't provide any useful information about the data – so you can remove it.

▶ Click the **Legend** tab and uncheck the **Show Legend** box.

▶ Click **Next**. You'll be moved on to the final step of the Chart Wizard process.

▶ Click **As new sheet** to display the finished graph on a sheet of its own.

▶ Click **Finish**. The line graph will appear in a new **Chart Sheet**. It should look like the example below.

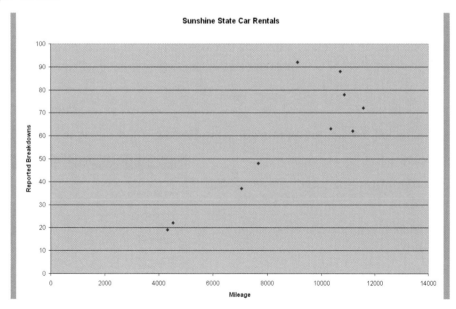

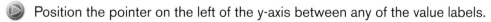

Changing axes scales

Next you need to change the scales on both the X and Y axes of the graph.

▶ Position the pointer on the left of the y-axis between any of the value labels.

▶ Double-click the left mouse button.

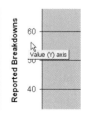

The **Format Axis** dialogue box will be displayed.

▶ Click the **Scale** tab.

▶ Click in the **Minimum** box and change the value to **20**

▶ Click in the **Maximum** box and change the value to **95**

▶ Click in the **Major** unit box and change the value to **5**

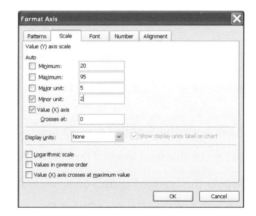

▶ Click **OK**.

Now you need to format the x-axis in the same way.

▶ Position the pointer on the left of the x-axis between any of the value labels.

▶ Double-click the left mouse button to display the **Format Axis** dialogue box.

▶ Click the **Scale** tab.

▶ Click in the **Minimum** box and change the value to **4000**

▶ Click in the **Maximum** box and change the value to **12000**

▶ Click in the **Major** unit box and change the value to **1500**

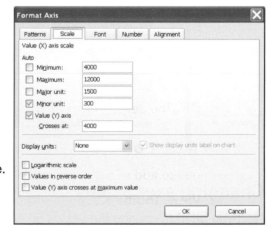

Your graph should look like the example opposite.

Formatting data points

Next you need to make the data points on each line stand out more by increasing their size.

▶ Position the pointer on one of the data points.

▶ Double-click the left mouse button.

The **Format Data Series** dialogue box will be displayed.

▶ The **Patterns** tab should be selected – if it isn't click on it.

▶ Click the small up arrow next to **Size** in the marker section to change the value displayed to **8 pts**.

TIP

Double-clicking on a data point to show the **Format Data Series** dialogue box can be quite difficult. If you have problems with this click once anywhere on the line, and then click **Format**, **Selected Data Series** on the menu bar. Click the **Data Labels** tab if you need to label data points with X or Y axis values at this stage.

TIP

Click the **Data Labels** tab and use the check boxes in the **Label Contains** section if you need to label data points with their X or Y axis values at this stage.

▶ Click **OK**. The data points on the graph will be enlarged.

Adding a text box to the graph

Now you need to add a label to the graph by inserting a text box.

▶ Click **View**, **Toolbars** and then click **Drawing**. The **Drawing** toolbar will appear at the bottom of the screen.

▶ Click the **Text Box** button on the **Drawing** toolbar.

The mouse pointer will change to a thin cross shape ⌐

Text Box button

▶ Position the pointer at the top of the graph away from the data points.

▶ Click and hold the left mouse button.

▶ Drag down and across to the right. As you drag an outline will show what size the text box will be when you let go of the mouse button. When the outline is roughly the same size as the text box shown below, let go of the mouse button.

▶ Click in the text box and type **BREAKDOWNS AND MILEAGE**

Now you need to format this text so that it stands out on the graph.

▶ Click at the end of the text, hold the mouse button and drag left to highlight the text.

▶ Click the small arrow on the right of the **Font Size** box and change the font size to **16**.

B

Bold button

▶ Click the **Bold** button.

▶ Click anywhere on the graph away from the text box. The text label should now look like the example below.

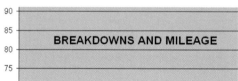

Text labels on graphs must be displayed in full and not overlap or touch any data points or lines. You can adjust the width of a text box using the round sizing handles on either side if any of the text is not clearly visible. You can reposition a text box by positioning the mouse pointer on the edge of the text box until it changes shape into a cross with four arrow heads, then click and hold the mouse button and drag the text box to a new location.

Inserting a footer and printing

Now you need to add some information to the page footer and print the graph.

▶ Click **View** and **Header and Footer** on the menu bar to view the **Page Setup** dialogue box.

▶ Click the **Custom Footer** button.

▶ Click in the **Left section** and type your name.

▶ Click in the **Center section** and type your centre number.

▶ Click the **Page** tab and make sure **Landscape** is selected in the **Orientation** section.

▶ Click the **Print** button, check the correct printer is selected in the **Print** dialogue, and then click **OK**.

▶ Save the spreadsheet keeping the filename **milerents**.

Creating a bar graph

Next you need to create a **bar graph** to show the distribution of vehicle rentals in May. You will need to use the workbook called **rentdists** that you created in Task 2.

▶ Open the workbook called **rentdists**.

▶ Click the **summary** tab at the bottom of the screen if it is not already selected.

▶ Highlight cells **A4** to **B6**.

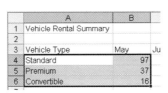

▶ Click the **Chart Wizard** button.

▶ Click **Bar** in the **Chart type** list.

▶ Leave the first **Chart sub-type** selected.

▶ Move to **Step 3** of the Chart Wizard by clicking the **Next** button twice.

▶ Click the **Titles** tab.

▶ Click in the **Chart title** box and type **MAY RENTAL DISTRIBUTION**

▶ Click in the **Category (X) axis** box and type **Vehicle Type**

▶ Click in the **Value (Y) axis** box and type **Number of rentals**

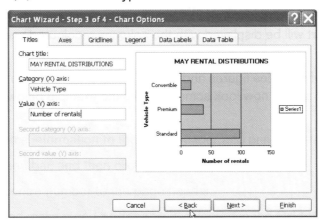

▶ Click the **Print** button, check the correct printer is selected in the **Print** dialogue, and then click **OK**.

▶ Save the workbook keeping the filename **rentdists**.

▶ Close **Excel**.

That's the end of the practice tasks. Now try the full New CLAiT Plus assignment that follows.

- Click in the **Left section** and type your name.
- Click in the **Center section** and type your centre number.
- Click the **Page** tab and make sure **Landscape** is selected in the **Orientation** section.
- Click the **Print** button, check the correct printer is selected in the **Print** dialogue, and then click **OK**.
- Save the spreadsheet keeping the filename **milerents**.

Creating a bar graph

Next you need to create a **bar graph** to show the distribution of vehicle rentals in May. You will need to use the workbook called **rentdists** that you created in Task 2.

- Open the workbook called **rentdists**.
- Click the **summary** tab at the bottom of the screen if it is not already selected.
- Highlight cells **A4** to **B6**.

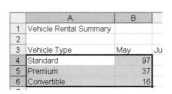

- Click the **Chart Wizard** button.
- Click **Bar** in the **Chart type** list.
- Leave the first **Chart sub-type** selected.
- Move to **Step 3** of the Chart Wizard by clicking the **Next** button <u>twice</u>.
- Click the **Titles** tab.
- Click in the **Chart title** box and type **MAY RENTAL DISTRIBUTION**
- Click in the **Category (X) axis** box and type **Vehicle Type**
- Click in the **Value (Y) axis** box and type **Number of rentals**

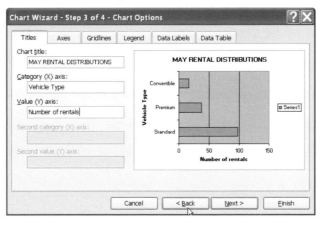

The legend on this chart doesn't provide any useful information about the data – so you can remove it.

▶ Click the **Legend** tab and uncheck the **Show Legend** box.

▶ Click **Next**.

▶ Click **As new sheet** to place the chart in a separate chart sheet.

▶ Click **Finish**. The bar chart will appear in a new **Chart Sheet** – it should look like the example below.

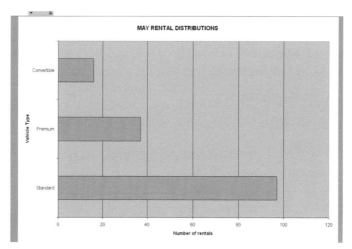

Recolouring and labelling bars

Next you need to change the colour of the bars on the chart and add labels to show the actual income represented by each one.

▶ Double-click any bar. The **Format Data Series** dialogue window will appear.

▶ Click the **Patterns** tab if it isn't already selected.

▶ Click on a colour in the area section that will stand out from the chart background.

▶ Click the **Data labels** tab.

▶ Check the **Value** box in the **Label contains** list.

▶ Click **OK**. The chart will be displayed with the columns recoloured and labelled with the sales figures.

▶ Click on any one of the sales figures and format the text as **bold** with a font size of **14 points**. Your chart should now look something like the example below.

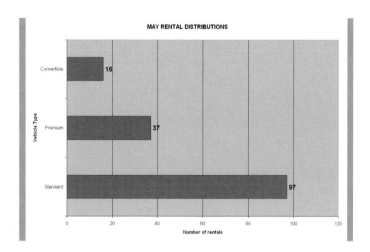

Changing the y-axis scale

Next you need to change the scale of the y-axis.

▶ Position the pointer on the left of the y-axis between any of the value labels.

▶ Double-click the left mouse button to display the **Format Axis** dialogue box.

▶ Click the **Scale** tab.

▶ Click in the **Maximum** box and change the value to **100**

▶ Click in the **Major** unit box and change the value to **10**

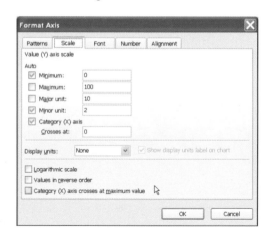

▶ Click **OK**.

Printing the chart

Finally you need to add some information to the page header and print the graph.

▶ Click **View** on the menu bar, and then click **Header and Footer**.

▶ Add your name and centre number to the page header.

▶ Click the **Page** tab and make sure **Landscape** is selected in the **Orientation** section.

▶ Click the **Print** button, check the correct printer is selected in the **Print** dialogue, and then click **OK**.

▶ Save the workbook keeping the filename **rentdists**.

▶ Close **Excel**.

That's the end of the practice tasks. Now try the full New CLAiT Plus assignment that follows.

Practice assignment

Scenario

You are working in the office of a holiday village. Your Manager has created some outline spreadsheets. You have been asked to complete the spreadsheets and produce reports and graphs for your Manager.

You will need the following files which have been provided in .CSV format:

TASK	FILENAME	DATAFILE INFORMATION
Task 1	**summer**	details of one week summer reservations
Task 2	**facilities**	data on usage of facilities
Task 3	**damage**	details of repair costs in chalets
Task 4	**weekly**	details of weekly operating costs
Task 5	**excursions**	data on excursions

To perform your tasks, you will need to use application software that will allow you to:

▶ manipulate and format numeric data

▶ use live data from one spreadsheet in another

▶ produce graphs and charts.

Assessment Objectives	TASK 1
	You will need the file **summer** to complete this task.
	You have been asked to produce a report on income from one week only reservations in the summer season of the year running from May to August. Unless otherwise instructed you may use any readable font and size to suit the data.
1	1 Open the file **summer** and save it in your software's normal file type using the filename **mayaug**
4a	2 a) Use text wrap to display the column labels below on 2 lines; do not split words: Number of chalets One week rate b) Ensure that all data is displayed in full.

c) Format the data items listed as follows:

LABEL	SIZE	COLUMNS
Green Vale Holiday Village	Large	Columns A – H Centred across all columns containing data.
Summer	Medium	Column A
Chalets	Medium	Column A
One week reservations	Medium	Column A

2a
2f

3 a) In the **Chalets** section use a function to calculate the **Total** of the **Number of chalets**.

   b) This figure must be displayed in the **Number of chalets** column next to the cell containing the word **Total**.

   c) Name this cell, **chalets**

2a
2c

The **Reservations** figure is calculated by adding together the figures for **SL**, **TW**, **FA** and **PR**.

In the **One week reservations** section, in the **Reservations** column, use a function to calculate the **Reservations** for each of the months **May** to **August**.

2a
2b
2c
2f
2h

5 Capacity is considered to be low if the **Reservations** are greater than 90% of the total number of chalets available.

   a) In the **One week reservations** section, use a function to calculate whether the **Capacity** for **May** is low:

   If the **Reservations** for **May** are greater than the result of the named cell **chalets** multiplied by 90% then **Low** should be displayed in the cell, otherwise it should be left empty.

   b) Replicate this formula for the other days.

2a
2b
2c
2d
2f
2h

6 You need to calculate the **Income** in the **One week reservations** section.

   a) In the Income column, in the May row, calculate the income for May:

   - in the **Chalets** section multiply the figure for **One week rate** for **Single SL** chalets by the figure for **SL May** from the **One week reservations** section
   - then add this figure to the **One week rate** for **Twin TW** multiplied by the figure for **TW May** from the **One week reservations** section
   - then add this figure to the **One week rate** for **Family FA** multiplied by the figure for **FA May** from the **One week reservations** section
   - add this figure to the **One week rate** for **Premium PR** multiplied by the figure for **PR May** from the **One week reservations section**.

   You will need to use absolute and relative cell references.

   b) Replicate this formula for the other months.

4a	7	a)	Format the figures in the **Income** column as integer with a currency symbol.
		b)	Format the figures in the **One week rate** column to 2 decimal places.
		c)	Display all other figures to 0 decimal places with no currency symbol.
5a	8	a)	Insert your name, centre number, and an automatic filename as a header or footer.
5b		b)	Save your spreadsheet keeping the filename **mayaug**.
5c		c)	Ensure all data is displayed in full. Print a copy of the spreadsheet mayaug showing all the figures.
5a	9		You have been asked for a printout of the formulae of your spreadsheet mayaug.
5d		a)	In the **One week reservations** section, hide all the information in the columns containing the data for **SL**, **TW, FA** and **PR** (columns B to E).
5e			
5f		b)	Display the formulae.
		c)	Set the page orientation to landscape.
		d)	Display gridlines and row and column headings.
		e)	Ensure that all formulae are fully displayed on one page and clearly legible.
		f)	Save the file with the filename **sumform**
		g)	Print the formulae on one page.
5a	10		Close the files **mayaug** and **sumform**.

Assessment Objectives	**TASK 2**

You will need the file **facilities** to complete this task.

Your manager has asked you to produce an exploded pie chart showing the guests usage of the holiday village facilities.

1	1		Open the datafile **facilities** and save it in your software's normal file type using the
5a			filename **usage**
3a	2		Using the **Total** number of guests for each **Facility** create an **exploded pie chart**.
3b		a)	Title the chart: **Use of Facilities**
4a		b)	Each sector must be clearly labelled with the **Facility** and **percentage**.
4b		c)	Do not display a legend.
4d		d)	Create the chart on a sheet that is separate from the data source.
4e		e)	Format the percentages to 1 decimal place.
		f)	Pull out the smallest sector of the pie chart so that it is further away from the rest of the chart.
5g	3	a)	Insert your name and centre number as a header or footer.
		b)	Print one copy of the chart.
		c)	Ensure that all data is distinctive and can be clearly identified when printed.
5a	4		Save and close the file.

Two　Manipulating Spreadsheets and Graphs

Assessment Objectives	TASK 3

You will need the file **damage** to complete this task.

You have been asked to update the maintenance records for estimated chalet repair costs. One chalet has been demolished so its details need to be deleted. Repairs on chalets requiring minimal maintenance will not be carried out until late winter. The management need a report on the chalets that would be affected.

1 5a	1　a)　Open the datafile **damage** and save it in your software's normal file type using the filename **repairs**
	b)　Ensure that all data is fully displayed.
	c)　Delete the entire row for chalet **2017A**.
2i	2　Filter the data to find all chalets where the **Repairs** cost less than **£30**.
2i	3　Sort the data in ascending order of **Chalet Type** ensuring that the corresponding data is sorted correctly.
5b	4　Insert your name, centre number and an automatic filename as a header or footer.
5a	5　Save your spreadsheet keeping the filename **repairs**.
5d	6　a)　Display row and column headings.
5e	b)　Print a copy of the filtered spreadsheet showing all the filtered data in full.

Assessment Objectives	TASK 4

You will need the file **weekly** and the file **mayaug** (that you created in Task 1) to complete this task.

An increase in the rate of company taxes will increase the weekly operating costs. Your Manager would also like you to check that the increased costs will still be covered by income from weekly chalet reservations. You will need to link the two spreadsheets to make the calculations.

1 5a	1　Open the datafile **weekly** and save it in your software's normal file type using the filename **sumweek**
2a 4a	2　In the **Weekly Outgoing** section, you need to calculate the figure for **Total (including Company Taxes)**.
	a)　In the **Total** column, next to the cell labelled **Total (including Company Taxes)** use a formula to calculate this figure by multiplying the **Total Outgoing** figure by **117%**.
	b)　Display this figure to **2** decimal places with no currency symbol.
2a 2e	3　You need to use a formula that will link the **sumweek** spreadsheet to the **mayaug** spreadsheet.

2g	a)	Open the file **mayaug** (that you created in Task 1).
	b)	In the **sumweek** spreadsheet, locate the **Weekly Profit** section. Locate the cell labelled **One week reservation profit**. In the cell next to **One week reservation profit** use a formula to calculate the total profit from the **mayaug** spreadsheet.
		This figure is calculated by adding all the figures in the **Income** column in the **mayaug** spreadsheet and then subtracting the figure for **Total (including Company Taxes)** in the **sumweek** spreadsheet.
	c)	Display this figure to **2** decimal places with no currency symbol.
5b	4	Insert your name, centre number and an automatic date as a header or footer.
5a	5 a)	Set the page orientation to landscape.
5b	b)	Ensure that all data is fully displayed on one page and clearly legible.
5c	c)	Save the spreadsheet keeping the filename **sumweek**.
	d)	Print the **sumweek** spreadsheet, showing the figures, on one page.
5e	6 a)	Display the formulae.
5f	a)	Display gridlines and row and column headings.
	b)	Ensure that all formulae are fully displayed on one page and clearly legible.
	c)	Save the file with the filename **prformulae**
	d)	Print the formulae on one page.
5a	7	Save and close any open spreadsheet files.

Assessment Objectives	**TASK 5**
	You will need the file **excursions** to complete this task.
	The Marketing Manager has asked you to analyse some data on recent excursions offered to village guests.
1	1 Open the datafile **excursions** and save it in your software's normal file format using
5a	the filename **trips**
3a	2 Create an **XY scatter graph** to plot the data for **Guests Purchasing** against
3b	**Running Cost**. Do not join the data points.
4b	a) Title the graph: **Green Vale Holiday Village**
4c	b) Label the x-axis: **Running Cost**
4f	c) Label the y-axis: **Guests Purchasing**
	d) Create the graph on a sheet that is separate from the data source.

e) Format the x-axis as follows:

minimum value: **200**

maximum value: **900**

interval: **50**

f) Format the y-axis as follows:

minimum value: **0**

maximum value: **220**

interval: **30**

g) In the plot area, insert a text box with the words:

TAKE UP ON EXCURSIONS

Ensure the text box does not overlap/touch any lines or data points.

5b	3	Insert your name and centre number as a header or footer.
5a	4	Save the file keeping the filename **trips**.
5g	5	Print one copy of the graph.
5a	6	Close the file and exit the software securely.
	7	Check all your printouts and files for accuracy.

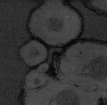

To pass this unit you must be able to:

- create a database file, set up fields and enter a range of information
- import datafile, update and interrogate database using complex search criteria
- plan and produce database reports in a variety of report formats
- print database reports.

Before you start this chapter, you or your tutor should download a zipped file called **Resources for Chapter 3** from **www.payne-gallway.co.uk/claitplus**. It will automatically unzip. Specify that the contents are to be saved in your **My Documents** folder.

The practice tasks that follow cover all the techniques you need to learn in order to pass a New CLAiT Plus Unit 3 CREATING AND USING A DATABASE assignment.

Practice tasks

Task 1   Creating a new database

Scenario

You are working for Seabridge Property Services as an office assistant. Your duties include providing database support to colleagues including database design, development, modifications and data manipulation.

 Create a subfolder called **Unit 3 PT** in your **My Documents** folder or network home directory folder where files created as you work through these practice tasks can be stored.

Creating a new database

You have been asked to create a small database of properties available for rent.

To get started you need to load Access. This can be done in one of two ways:

 either double-click the **Microsoft Access** icon on the main screen in Windows,

Microsoft Office
Access 2003

 or click the **Start** button at the bottom left of the screen, then click **Programs**, then click

 Microsoft Office Access 2003 .

> **TIP**
>
> The steps you need to follow to create a subfolder are described in **Chapter 1** on **page 5**.

The main **Access** window will be displayed with the **Task pane** visible.

TIP

If you can't see the **Task pane** click **View** and **Task pane** on the menu bar.

▶ Click **Create a new file...** in the **Task pane**. The **New File pane** will appear.

▶ Click **Blank database...** in the list of new file options. The **File New Database** window will be displayed.

▶ Click the **My Documents** icon on the left of the window if the contents of your **My Documents** folder are not already displayed.

▶ Double-click the **Unit 3 PT** subfolder.

▶ Click in the **File name:** box and type the name, **lettings**

▶ Click **Create**.

A window with the heading **lettings : Database** at the top will appear – this is called the **Database Window**. The **Objects bar** on the left lists the different types of object such as tables, queries, forms and reports that an Access database can contain.

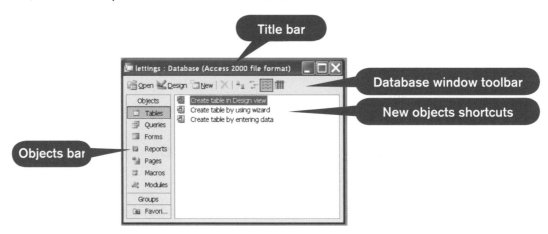

Clicking on an object name in the **Objects bar** will list all the objects of that type that are currently in the database. Clicking on an object type in the **Objects bar** then double-clicking on an object shortcut will create a new object. The **Database Window** contains an icon that will switch to **Design View** so that objects can be changed. This window also contains icons that can be used to open existing objects or create new ones.

Creating a new table

Access databases store information as a collection of **records** in a **table**. Each record contains individual items of data called **fields**. When you create a new table a **Field Name** and **Data Type** must be entered for each field. The Field Names and Data Types needed in the **lettings** database records are given in the table below.

FIELD NAME	DATA TYPE
PROPERTY NUMBER	Numbers, 0 decimal places
TYPE	Text
AREA	Text
BEDS	Numbers, 0 decimal places
BATHS	Numbers, 0 decimal places
MONTHLY RENT	Currency, with currency symbol, 2 decimal places
GARAGE	Logic field

TIP

Field Names might be referred to as **Field Headings** in a New CLAiT Plus assignment.

▶ Click on the **Table** object type in the Database Window.

▶ Double-click the **Create table in Design View** icon. A blank table will appear in which you can enter the Field Headings and Data Types.

▶ Type the first Field Name, **PROPERTY NUMBER**

▶ Press the **Tab** key to move to the **Data Type** column.

▶ Click the down arrow and select the data type **Number**.

▶ Click in the **Decimal Places** box in the bottom half of the window.

▶ Click the down arrow and select **0**.

The first row of your table design window should look like this:

Field Name	Data Type	
PROPERTY NUMBER	Number	

▶ Type the second Field Name, **TYPE**

▶ Press the **Tab** key to move to the **Data Type** column. **Text** will be automatically selected as the data type so you don't need to do anything else for this field.

▶ Enter the information for the third field, **AREA** in exactly the same way.

▶ Enter the information for the next two fields, **BEDS** and **BATHS**. Your table design should look like this:

Field Name	Data Type
PROPERTY NUMBER	Number
TYPE	Text
AREA	Text
BEDS	Number
BATHS	Number

▶ Type the next Field Name, **MONTHLY RENT**

▶ Click the down arrow and select the field type **Currency**.

▶ Set **Decimal Places** for this field to **2**.

Type the last Field Name, **GARAGE** and tab across to the **Data Type** column.

The data type **Logic** is specified for this field. In Access this data type appears in the list as **Yes/No**. Click the down arrow and select **Yes/No**. Your table design window should look like this:

Field Name	Data Type
PROPERTY NUMBER	Number
TYPE	Text
AREA	Text
BEDS	Number
BATHS	Number
MONTHLY RENT	Currency
GARAGE	Yes/No

Defining a primary key

Every table in an Access database must have a primary key (also known as the key field). The field that you choose as the primary key must have a different value for each record. You need to set the field **PROPERTY NUMBER** as the primary key for the **lettings** database.

Click anywhere in the row for **PROPERTY NUMBER**.

Click the **Primary Key** button on the **Standard** toolbar. A key symbol will appear in the left-hand margin next to the field name.

Primary Key button

	Field Name
🔑	PROPERTY NUMBER
	TYPE

Using codes in fields

Using coded values for fields helps to speed up data entry and cuts down on data errors. The **TYPE** and **AREA** fields need to be set up to use the following codes:

The **primary key** is usually the first field in any record. If you are not sure which field to use look through the records you need to enter and identify the field that has a different value for every record.

TYPE

DETACHED	**DET**
SEMI-DETACHED	**SEM**
TOWN HOUSE	**TWH**
FLAT	**FLA**
BUNGALOW	**BUN**

AREA

CLIFTON	**CL**
EASTLEIGH	**EL**
HAMPTON	**HA**

We will deal with the codes for the **TYPE** field first.

Click in the **Data Type** box for **TYPE**.

Click the down arrow and select **Lookup Wizard...** at the bottom of the list. The **Lookup Wizard** window will appear.

 Click the radio button next to **I will type in the values that I want**, then click **Next**.

 Click in the empty box under the heading **Col1** and type **DET**

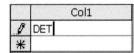

 Press the **Tab** key to move to the next empty box and type **SEM**

 Carry on entering the **TYPE** field codes until the contents of **Col1** are the same as the example below.

 Click **Next**, then click **Finish**.

 Click in the **Data Type** box for **AREA** and use the same technique to enter the codes for this field.

> **TIP**
>
> If you click the **Lookup** tab at the bottom of the Table Design Window any codes set for a field will be listed next to **Row Source**. You can make changes to the codes by clicking in this box.

Setting text field lengths

Field Name and **Data Type** are the only field characteristics you will be given in a Unit 3 assignment. Choosing and setting sensible **Lengths** for any text fields will help to reduce the amount of time you will need to spend modifying report layouts during an assignment.

 Click anywhere in the row for the **TYPE** field.

The default **Field Size** for this field shown at the bottom of the window is **50** characters. This field has been set to use codes that are only **3** characters in length so this default **Field Size** is far too large.

 Click in the **Field Size** box and type **3**

The **AREA** field has been set to use codes that are only **2** characters in length.

 Click anywhere in the row for the **AREA** field and change the **Field Size** to **2**

Saving the table structure

Now you are ready to close the table and save changes to the design.

- Click the **Close** icon (**X**) in the top right-hand corner of the table design window.
- Click **Yes** to save changes to the table design.
- You will be asked to enter a name for the table. Type the name **tblLettings** and click **OK**.

The Database Window will reappear with the name **tblLettings** listed.

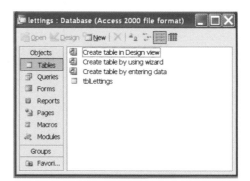

TIP

It is normal to add the prefix **tbl** to the name of a table when it is saved. You do not have to do this to meet the requirements of New CLAiT Plus but it is good practice.

Entering records in table view

Now you are ready to enter some records into the database. We will start by entering the records shown below in **Table View**.

PROPERTY NUMBER	TYPE	AREA	BEDS	BATHS	MONTHLY RENT	GARAGE
121	SEMI-DETACHED	EASTLEIGH	3	1	675.00	YES
123	DETACHED	CLIFTON	6	3	980.00	YES
125	SEMI-DETACHED	CLIFTON	4	2	795.00	NO
129	TOWN HOUSE	EASTLEIGH	4	2	760.00	YES
131	FLAT	HAMPTON	2	1	495.00	NO

- Click on the **Table** object type if it is not already selected in the Database Window.

- Double-click the **tblLettings** icon. A blank table will appear in which you can enter the new records.

- Type the **PROPERTY NUMBER** for the first record, **121**

- Press the **Tab** key to move to the **TYPE** field for this record, then click the small down arrow and choose **SEM** from the list.

- Tab to the **AREA** field, click the small down arrow and choose **EL** from the list.

- Tab to the **BEDS** field and type **3**

- Tab to the **BATHS** field and type **1**

- Tab to the **MONTHLY RENT** field and type **675** – you do not need to type the £ sign. Access will add this automatically because this field is formatted as currency.

- Tab to the **GARAGE** field and press the **SPACEBAR** to check the box to represent the **YES** value. The first record in your table should look like the example below.

PROPERTY NU	TYPE	AREA	BEDS	BATHS	MONTHLY REN	GARAGE
121	SEM	EL	3	1	£675.00	☑

TIP

If you want to display a field heading in full for a table column position the pointer on the line separating it from the next column and double-click the left mouse button. This technique is covered in more detail in Task 3.

- Now add the rest of the records shown in the table above.

- Click the **Close** icon (**X**) in the top right-hand corner of the table window to close the table and save the new records.

Creating and using a data entry form

Data entry forms provide an alternative method of entering new records in a database table. You are going to create and use a data entry form to add some more records to the lettings database.

- Click on the **Forms** object type in the **Database Window**.

- Click the **New** button at the top of the **Database Window**. The **New Form Window** will appear.

- Click **AutoForm: Columnar** in the list of options.

- Click the down arrow on the right of the box underneath and select **tblLettings**.

Click **OK**. A data entry form will appear with the first record in the data table displayed on it.

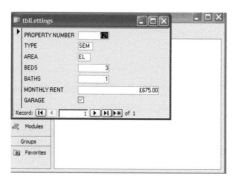

New Record
button

Click the **New Record** button at the bottom of the form. You will be presented with a blank version of the form. The cursor will be flashing in the **PROPERTY NUMBER** box.

Enter the first new record shown in the table below. Press the **Tab** key or point and click to move between the boxes on the form.

PROPERTY NUMBER	TYPE	AREA	BEDS	BATHS	MONTHLY RENT	GARAGE
134	BUNGALOW	CLIFTON	3	1	680.00	NO
135	FLAT	HAMPTON	2	1	545.00	YES
137	DETACHED	EASTLEIGH	5	2	975.00	YES
141	DETACHED	HAMPTON	5	3	910.00	YES
143	SEMI-DETACHED	CLIFTON	4	2	755.00	NO

New Record
button

Click the **New Record** button again when you have finished. The record you have just entered will be added to the table and saved automatically.

Now carry on and enter the rest of the records in the table above.

Click the **Close** icon (**X**) in the top right-hand corner of the form window when you have finished entering all of the records.

TIP

You can enter records using either **Table View** or a Data Entry Form during a New CLAiT Plus assignment. Use whichever method you prefer.

Click **Yes** when you are prompted to save changes to the form.

Type the name, **frmLettings** and click **OK**.

Now reopen the table in **Table View** to see what the finished data table looks like.

▶ Click on the **Table** object type in the Database Window.

▶ Double-click the **tblLettings** icon. The data table will be displayed. Check each record carefully to make sure your table is the same as the example below.

PROPERTY NUMBER	TYPE	AREA	BEDS	BATHS	MONTHLY RENT	GARAGE
121	SEM	EL	3	1	£675.00	☑
123	DET	CL	6	3	£980.00	☑
125	SEM	CL	4	2	£795.00	☐
129	TWH	EL	4	2	£760.00	☑
131	FLA	HA	2	1	£495.00	☐
134	BUN	CL	3	1	£680.00	☐
135	FLA	HA	2	1	£545.00	☑
137	DET	EL	5	2	£975.00	☑
141	DET	HA	5	3	£910.00	☑
143	SEM	CL	4	2	£775.00	☐

TIP

Always check new records carefully to make sure they match those given in the table in your assignment. Mistakes made when creating new records are a common reason for candidates failing Unit 3 assignments.

Task 2   Tabular reports and labels

Your have been asked to use the **lettings** database to print a **tabular report** displaying all records and a set of labels. This task describes how to do this using the **Report Wizard** and **Label Wizard** tools.

Opening an existing database

To get started you need to open the **lettings** database created in the last task.

▶ Load **Access**.

▶ Click **File** on the menu bar, and then click **Open**.

▶ *Or* click the **Open** button on the **Standard** toolbar.

Open button

▶ Click the **My Documents** icon on the left of the window if the contents of your **My Documents** folder are not already displayed.

▶ Double-click the **Unit 3 PT** subfolder.

▶ Click on the database file called **lettings**, and then click **Open**.

The **Database window** will appear.

Creating a tabular report

You need to produce a **tabular report**, in **landscape orientation**, displaying <u>all</u> records.

▶ Click on the **Reports** object type in the **Database Window**.

▶ Double-click the **Create report by using wizard** icon. The **Report Wizard** window will appear with the question **Which fields do you want on your report?**

All the fields need to be displayed for each record in the following order:

PROPERTY NUMBER
MONTHLY RENT
TYPE
AREA
BEDS
BATHS
GARAGE

▶ Click **PROPERTY NUMBER** in the list of available fields if it is not already selected.

▶ Click the single right arrow between the **Available fields:** and **Selected fields:** boxes. The **PROPERTY** field will be added to the **Selected fields:** box.

▶ Add the **MONTHLY RENT** field in exactly the same way.

▶ Now click the double right arrow to add the remaining fields. Your **Selected fields:** box should look like the example below.

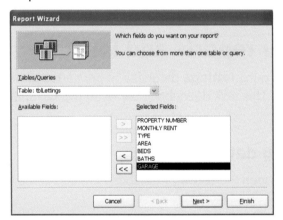

TIP

If you need to remove a field from the **Selected fields:** box click on the single left arrow between the boxes. Click the double left arrow to remove all the fields if you need to start again.

▶ Click **Next**. You will be presented with a window asking if you want to add any grouping levels. We will deal with grouped reports later in the chapter so you can ignore this for now.

▶ Click **Next**. You will be presented with a window asking what sort order you want for your records. The data need to be sorted in descending order of **PROPERTY NUMBER**.

- Click the small down arrow on the right of the first box and select **PROPERTY NUMBER** from the list of fields.

- Click the **Ascending** button next to the box, it will change to **Descending**.

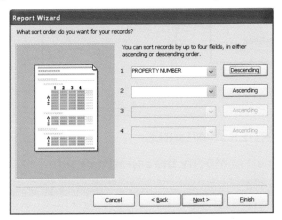

- Click **Next**. You will be presented with a window asking how you would like to lay out your report.

- Click the radio button next to **Tabular** in the **Layout** section if it is not already selected.

- Click the radio button next to **Landscape** in the **Orientation** section if it is not already selected.

- Click the check box next to **Adjust the field width so all fields fit on a page** at the bottom of the window if it is not already selected.

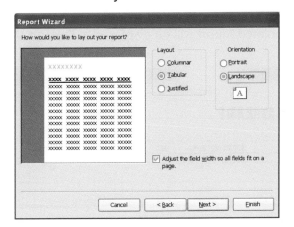

- Click **Next**. You will be presented with a window asking what style you would like.

- Click the **Compact** style in the list, and then click **Next**. You will be presented with a window asking what title you want for your report.

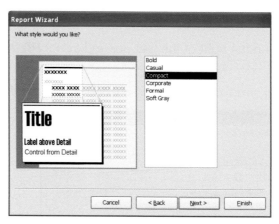

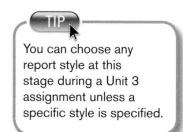

TIP

You can choose any report style at this stage during a Unit 3 assignment unless a specific style is specified.

▶ Type the title, **PROPERTIES AVAILABLE**

▶ Click the radio button next to **Modify the report's design**.

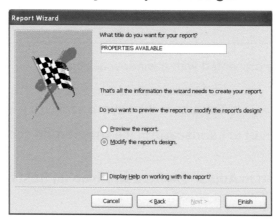

▶ Click **Finish**. The completed report will be displayed in **Design View**. It should look like the example below.

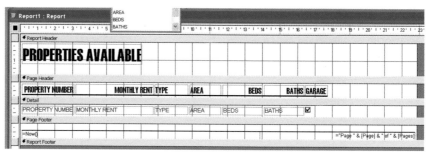

Modifying the report layout

Now you need to modify the report layout so that the information in each column will be displayed in centre alignment.

▶ Position the pointer on the left of the **Page Header** section in the dashed ruler area. The pointer will change into a small right pointing horizontal arrow.

▶ Click the left mouse button to select all the **Page Header** contents.

- Click the **Center** button on the Formatting toolbar at the top of the screen. The contents of each **Page Header** text box will be centre aligned.

- Centre align the contents of the **Detail** section in exactly the same way. When you have finished the **Page Header** and **Detail** sections your report should look like the example below.

Centre aligning the **Page Header** and **Page Detail** sections is a quick way to improve the appearance of a report. You do not have to do this unless it is specifically asked for in an assignment.

Center button

PROPERTY NUMBER	MONTHLY RENT	TYPE	AREA	BEDS	BATHS	GARAGE
PROPERTY NUMBER	MONTHLY RENT	TYPE	AREA	BEDS	BATHS	☑

If any column heading is not displayed in full in **Print Preview** you will need to adjust the size of the text box in the **Page Header** section. Click the text box to select it, then position the mouse pointer over the centre left or right sizing handle until it changes into a two-headed arrow. Click and hold the left mouse button and drag to the left or right until the text box is the size you want, then let go of the mouse button.

Modifying the report page footer

Next you need to modify the **report page footer** so that an **automatic date** and **your name** and **centre number** will be displayed at the bottom of the page.

The left side of the **Page Footer** section of the report has a text box with *=Now()* displayed in it. This generates the automatic date that you need so this part of the **Page Footer** can be left alone. The right side of the **Page Footer** section of the report has a text box with *="Page "* & *[Page]* & *" of "* & *[Pages]* displayed in it. This generates an automatic page number and total number of pages. This information is not required so you can edit the contents of this text box to make it add your name and centre number to the **Page Footer** instead.

- Click once in the right text box to select it, and then click again to edit the text inside.

- Delete all of the text and type *="*

- Type **your name**

- Press the **Spacebar** <u>twice</u>.

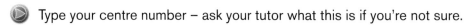

- Type your centre number – ask your tutor what this is if you're not sure.

- Type **"** then click anywhere in the grey area to the right of the **Page Footer**.

Your **Page Footer** section should now look something like the example below.

Printing the tabular report

View button

Maximize button

Now you need to print the report.

- Click the **View** button on the **Standard** toolbar to view the report in **Print Preview**.

- Click the **Maximize** button in the top right corner of the report window if it does not completely fill the screen. Your report should look like the example below.

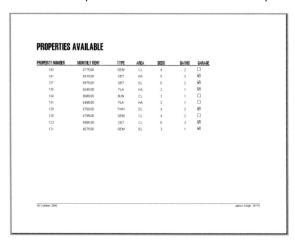

Print button

- Click the **Print** button on the standard toolbar to print the report.

- Click the **Close** icon (**X**) in the top right-hand corner of the report window.

- Click **Yes** at this stage if you're asked to save any changes.

Using the Label Wizard

Next you need to use the **Label Wizard** to produce a set of labels, sorted in ascending order of **PROPERTY NUMBER** for each property to display the following fields:

PROPERTY NUMBER
TYPE   AREA (Separated by at least two spaces on <u>one</u> line)
MONTHLY RENT

- Click on the **Reports** object type in the **Database Window** if it is not already selected.

New icon

- Click the **New** icon at the top of the **Database Window**. The **Report Window** will appear.

- Click **Label Wizard** in the list of options.

▷ Click the down arrow on the right of the box underneath and select **tblLettings**.

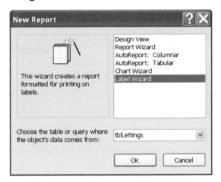

▷ Click **OK**.

▷ You will be presented with a window asking what label size you want. We're going to use an **Avery** size of **52 mm x 70 mm** with **2** labels across the page.

▷ Click the drop-down arrow next to the box labelled **Filter by manufacturer:** and select **Avery**.

▷ Click the **Product** number **52 mm x 70 mm** if it is not already highlighted.

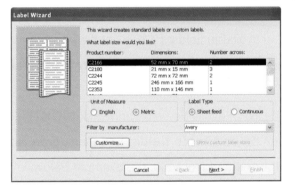

Change the options in this window if you are asked to use a specific label size or generate a certain number of labels across the page.

▷ Click **Next**. You will be presented with some options to change the appearance of the text on the labels. We will change just the font size in this example.

▷ Click the down arrow next to the box labelled **Font size:** and select **12** from the list of options.

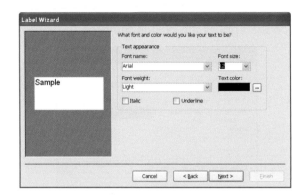

- Click **Next**. You will be presented with a window asking what you would like on the labels.

- Click **PROPERTY NUMBER** in the list of available fields if it is not already selected.

- Click the arrow between the **Available fields:** and **Prototype label:** boxes.

- Press **Enter**.

- Click **TYPE** in the list of available fields if it has not been automatically selected.

- Click the arrow between the **Available fields:** and **Prototype label:** boxes.

- Press the **Spacebar** <u>twice</u>.

- Click **AREA** in the list of available fields if it has not been automatically selected.

- Click the arrow between the **Available fields:** and **Prototype label:** boxes.

- Press **Enter**.

- Scroll down through the list of available fields and click **MONTHLY RENT**.

- Click the arrow between the **Available fields:** and **Prototype label:** boxes.

  Your **Prototype label:** box should look like the example below.

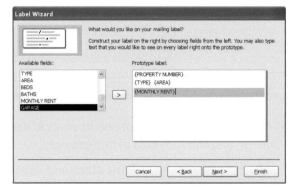

- Click **Next**. You will be presented with a window asking which fields you would like to sort by.

- Click **PROPERTY NUMBER** in the list of available fields if it is not already selected.

- Click the single arrow between the **Available fields:** and **Sort by:** boxes.

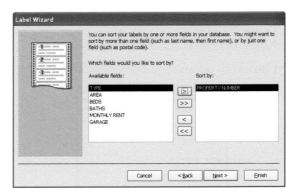

Click **Next**. You will be presented with a window asking what name you would like for your report.

Type the name **IbsLettings**

Click the radio button next to **Modify the label design**.

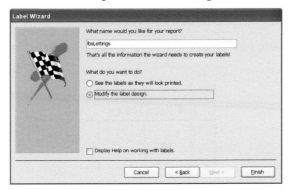

Click **Finish**. The completed labels report will be displayed in **Design View**.

Modifying the labels page footer

Next you need to modify the report's design so that the **date** and **your name** and **centre number** appear in the **page footer**.

Double-click the grey bar labelled **Page Footer** at the bottom of the screen. A window labelled **Section: PageFooterSection** will appear.

○ Click the **Format** tab in this window if it is not already selected.

○ Click inside the **Height** box and replace the current value with **2**.

○ Click the **Close** icon (**X**) in the top right-hand corner of the **Section Window**. The **Page Footer** section will expand giving enough room to add a text label containing the **date** and **your name** and **centre number**

Label button

○ Click the **Label** icon on the **Toolbox**. The mouse pointer will change to a small cross with a letter A attached to it.

○ Position the pointer in the top left corner of the **Page Footer** section.

> **TIP**
>
> Click **View** and **Toolbox** on the **Menu bar** if the **Toolbox** is not visible.

○ Click and hold the left mouse button.

○ Drag down and across to the right. As you drag an outline will show what size the text label box will be when you let go of the mouse button. When the outline is roughly the same size as the text box shown below, let go of the mouse button.

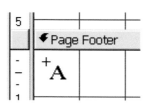

○ Click in the text label box and type **today's date**

○ Hold the **Shift** key down and press **Enter** <u>twice</u> to move down two lines.

○ Type **your name** followed by your **centre number**. Your text label box should now look something like the example below.

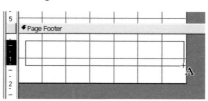

Printing the labels report

Now you need to print the labels report.

-  Click the **View** button on the **Standard** toolbar to view the labels in **Print Preview**.

- Click the **Maximize** button in the top right corner of the report window if it does not completely fill the screen. Your labels should look like the example below.

View button

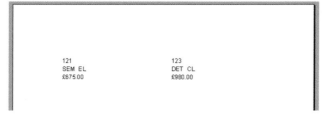

121	123
SEM EL	DET CL
£675.00	£980.00

- 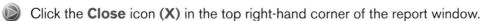 Click the **Print** button on the standard toolbar to print the report.

- Click the **Close** icon (**X**) in the top right-hand corner of the report window.

- Close **Access** down.

Print button

Task 3   Creating a database from existing data

You have been asked to create a database of all the properties currently being rented out using some existing data.

Importing a datafile

To start setting up this database you need to create a blank access database and import a datafile called **properties**.

First create the blank database:

- Load **Access**.

- Click **Create a new file...** in the **Task pane**.

- Click **Blank database...** in the list of new file options.

- Click the **My Documents** icon on the left of the window if the contents of your **My Documents** folder are not already displayed.

- Double-click the **Unit 3 PT** subfolder.

- Click in the **File name:** box and type the name, **properties**

- Click **Create**.

Next import the datafile:

- Click **File, Get External Data** and **Import...** on the **Menu bar**. The **Import** window will appear.

- Click the **My Documents** icon on the left of the window to view the contents of your **My Documents** folder.

- Click the small down arrow on the right of the box labelled **Files of type:** and scroll down to select **Text Files (*.txt;*.csv;*.tab;*.asc)**.

- Click the file called **properties** which should now be visible in your list of files.

- Click **Import. The Import Text Wizard** will start up.

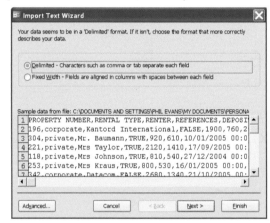

- Click the radio button next to **Delimited** if it is not already selected, then click **Next**. You will be presented with another window asking what delimiter separates your fields.

- Click the radio button next to **Comma** if it is not already selected as the delimiter in the first row of options.

- Click the check box next to **First Row Contains Field Names**.

- Click the small down arrow on the right of the box labelled **Text Qualifier:** and select the first option of double quotation marks (").

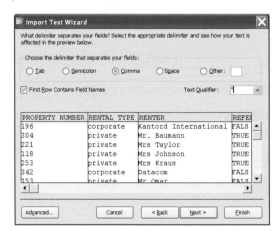

- Click **Next**.

- Click the radio button next to **In a New Table** if it is not already selected, then click **Next**.

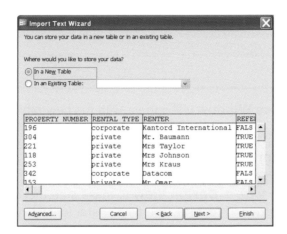

You will be presented with another window asking you to choose field options. It will save time to modify the field options in **Design View** once the data has been imported so you can skip this stage without making any changes.

▶ Click **Next**. You will be presented with another window asking you to define a primary key for the new table.

▶ Click the radio button next to **Choose my own primary key**. The **PROPERTY NUMBER** field will be automatically selected.

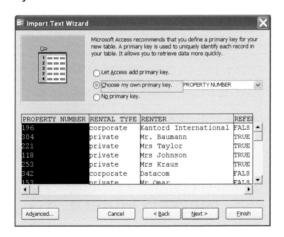

 TIP

You do not need to choose a primary key at this stage. Click the **No primary key** radio button if you are not sure which field to use or want to add a primary key later on. Remember that the primary key must have a different value in each record.

The final window of the **Import Wizard** will appear.

▶ Type the table name **tblProperties** in the box labelled **Import to Table:** then click **Finish**. You should see a message like the one below.

Import Text Wizard

ⓘ Finished importing file 'C:\Documents and Settings\CLAIT\My Documents\properties.csv' to table 'tblProperties'.

OK

▶ Click **OK**. The **Database Window** will appear with the new table **tblProperties** highlighted.

Modifying field characteristics

Next you need to modify the table in **Design View** to make sure that each field has an appropriate **data type**, **length** and **format**. The field characteristics you need to use for this table are shown below. You should also set some sensible **lengths** for the text fields at this stage.

FIELD NAME	DATA TYPE
PROPERTY NUMBER	Numbers, 0 decimal places
RENTAL TYPE	Text
RENTER	Text
REFERENCES	Logic field
DEPOSIT PAID	Currency, with currency symbol, 0 decimal places
MONTHLY RENT	Currency, with currency symbol, 0 decimal places
DATE RENTED	English date (day, month, year) in any format
DURATION	Numbers, 0 decimal places

Design icon

Property Update Options icon

▶ Click the **Design** icon at the top of the **Database Window**. The table will be displayed in **Design View**.

▶ Click in the **Data Type** box for **PROPERTY NUMBER**.

▶ Set the data type to **Number** with **0 Decimal Places**.

▶ Click in the **Data Type** box for **RENTAL TYPE**. **Text** will be automatically selected as the data type for this field.

▶ Set the **Field Size** at the bottom of the window to **15**

TIP

The **Property Update Options** icon will appear at the bottom of the screen at this stage. Ignore this and carry on with making the changes to the table structure.

TIP

If you looked through the records in **Table View** you would see just two values in the **RENTAL TYPE** field – **private** and **corporate**. The longest of these values, **corporate**, is **9 characters** long. We have used **15** as the **Field Size** for this field because it is large enough for the longest current value and allows some extra characters for any new longer values. This is the technique that you should use when deciding on **Field Sizes** for uncoded text fields.

Click in the **Data Type** box for **RENTER**. **Text** will be automatically selected as the data type for this field.

Set the **Field Size** at the bottom of the window to **40**

Carry on and set the characteristics for the remaining fields as specified in the table above. Your table design should look like the example below when you have finished.

Field Name	Data Type
PROPERTY NUMBER	Number
RENTAL TYPE	Text
RENTER	Text
REFERENCES	Yes/No
DEPOSIT PAID	Currency
MONTHLY RENT	Currency
DATE RENTED	Date/Time
DURATION	Number

Click the **Close** icon (**X**) in the top right-hand corner of the **Table Design** window.

Click **Yes** to save changes to the table design.

Click **Yes** when the warning message below appears.

Microsoft Office Access

Some data may be lost.

The setting for the FieldSize property of one or more fields has been changed to a shorter size. If data is lost, validation rules may be violated as a result.
Do you want to continue anyway?

[Yes] [No]

Adjusting table column widths

Next you need to adjust the width of some columns in the table so that the field names and data can been seen in full.

Open **tblProperties** in **Datasheet View**.

Click the **Maximize** button in the top right corner of the table window if it does not completely fill the screen.

Position the mouse pointer on the line between the **PROPERTY NUMBER** and **RENTAL TYPE** columns. The pointer will change to a double-headed arrow.

Double-click the left mouse button. The **PROPERTY NUMBER** column will automatically widen so that the field name can be seen in full.

Repeat this process for any other columns where the field names or data cannot be seen in full. The top portion of your table should look like the example below when you have finished.

PROPERTY NUMBER	RENTAL TYPE	RENTER	REFERENCES	DEPOSIT PAID	MONTHLY RENT	DATE RENTED	DURATION
290	private	Mrs Johnson	☑	£810	£540	27/12/2004	14

Amending data

You need to make the following changes to the table:

Enter a **RENTAL TYPE** of **corporate** for **PROPERTY NUMBER 309** rented by **DataCom**.

You need to start by finding the record for **PROPERTY NUMBER 309** in the table. You could do this by looking through the records but this might prove to be quite time-consuming. The **Find and Replace** facility offers a much more efficient way to locate specific data items in large data tables.

▶ Click anywhere in the **PROPERTY NUMBER** column. This will set **PROPERTY NUMBER** as the field to search.

▶ Click **Edit** on the menu bar, and then click **Find…** The **Find and Replace** dialogue box will appear. **PROPERTY NUMBER** will already be selected as the field next to **Look In:**

▶ Type **309** in the **Find what:** box.

▶ Click **Find Next**. The record will be located with **309** highlighted in the **PROPERTY NUMBER** field.

▶ Click **Cancel**.

▶ Click in the **RENTAL TYPE** field.

▶ Delete the current value using the backspace key and type **corporate**

Enter a **MONTHLY RENT** of **£760** for **PROPERTY NUMBER 326** rented by **Mr. Le Blanc**.

▶ Find property number **326** in the table.

▶ Replace the current value for **Monthly Rent** with **760** – this field is formatted to automatically display numbers in currency format so you don't need to type the **£** sign.

Delete the record for **PROPERTY NUMBER 339**.

▶ Find property number **339** in the table and click anywhere in the row for this record.

▶ Click the **Delete Record** icon on the **Table Datasheet** toolbar. You will see this message:

Delete Record icon

▶ Click **Yes** to delete the record.

These new records need adding to the table:

PROPERTY NUMBER	RENTAL TYPE	RENTER	REFERENCES	DEPOSIT PAID	MONTHLY RENT	DATE RENTED	DURATION
343	private	Mr. Searle	YES	1460	975	14/10/2006	16
347	corporate	FlexiCorp	NO	1320	880	17/10/2006	24
349	private	Ms Byrne	NO	1035	690	11/10/2006	18

To add these records:

⊳ Click in the blank row at the end of the table and enter the data for the first new record.

⊳ Repeat this process for the rest of the new records.

That's all of the changes to the table completed – now you can close it.

⊳ Click the **Close** icon (**X**) in the top right-hand corner of the **Table** window.

⊳ Click **Yes** to save changes to the table design.

Creating a query

Searching, or interrogating a database, involves looking for an individual record or group of records that match certain conditions or **criteria**. To start a search the user must enter a search command or **query**. This tells the database software which fields to look at in each record and what to look for. The results of a query can be displayed on screen or printed out as a list or report.

Due to a recent change in the law Seabridge Property Services must pay a 75% refund of the initial deposit to any companies renting properties. Some companies do not pay deposits on properties so they do not need to be included. You have been asked to create a query to find only those **corporate RENTERS** of properties that <u>have</u> paid a deposit.

⊳ Click on the **Queries** object type in the **Database Window**.

⊳ Double-click the **Create query by using wizard** icon.

The **Simple Query Wizard** window will appear with the question, **Which fields do you want in your query?** The table **tblProperties** will already be selected in the box headed **Tables/ Queries**.

⊳ Click the double right arrow between the **Available fields:** and **Selected fields:** boxes. All of the fields will be added to the **Selected fields:** box.

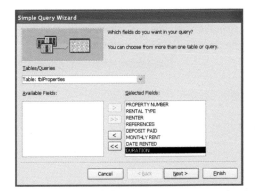

You could create a tailored list of individual fields in the **Selected fields:** box at this stage by highlighting fields in the **Available fields:** box one at a time and clicking the single right pointing arrow. Adding all the fields at this stage is not a problem because fields can be left out of the query later on by making changes in **Design View**.

⊚ Click **Next**. You will be presented with a window asking if you want a detail or summary query.

⊚ Click the radio button next to **Detail** if it is not already selected.

⊚ Click **Next**. You will be presented with a window asking what title you want for your query.

⊚ Type the name, **qryCorpRefunds**

⊚ Click the radio button next to **Modify the query design**, and then click **Finish**. The **Query Design Table** will be displayed.

Entering search criteria

Next you need to enter the **criteria** that specify which fields to search and the values to search for. This query needs to search the **RENTAL TYPE** field for **corporate** and the **DEPOSIT PAID** column for amounts *greater than* 0.

⊚ Click in the criteria row in the **RENTAL TYPE** column and type **corporate**

⊚ Click in the criteria row in the **DEPOSIT PAID** column and type **>0** Your query design table should look like the example below.

Field:	PROPERTY NUMBER	RENTAL TYPE	RENTER	REFERENCES	DEPOSIT PAID	MONTHLY RENT	DATE RENTED	DURATION
Table:	tblProperties	tblProperties	tblProperties	tblProperties	tblProperties	tblProperties	tblProperties	tblProperties
Sort:								
Show:	☑	☑	☑	☑	☑	☑	☑	☑
Criteria:		"corporate"			>0			
or:								

Run button

⊚ Click the **Run** button on the **Query Design** toolbar at the top of the screen to run the query and view the results.

⊚ Click the **Maximize** button in the top right corner of the query window if it does not completely fill the screen. Your query results should look like the example below.

TIP

In this example you are using the **greater than** symbol (>) to set the search criteria for **DEPOSIT PAID**. The other symbols that you might need to use are listed below.

=	equal to
<	less than
<=	less than or equal to
>=	greater than or equal to
<>	not equal to

PROPERTY NUMBER	RENTAL TYPE	RENTER	REFERENCES	DEPOSIT PAID	MONTHLY RENT	DATE RENTED	DURATION
196	corporate	Kantord International	☐	£1,900	£760	26/10/2005	29
342	corporate	Datacom	☐	£2,680	£1,340	21/10/2005	9
124	corporate	FlexiCorp	☐	£1,500	£375	27/11/2005	12
242	corporate	FlexiCorp	☐	£1,425	£570	09/12/2004	7
324	corporate	Baymar Portford	☐	£1,490	£990	01/12/2004	16
298	corporate	Kantord International	☐	£1,590	£1,055	03/12/2004	15
217	corporate	Mr Ojay	☐	£770	£510	20/12/2005	31
142	corporate	Kantord International	☐	£1,538	£615	19/06/2005	30
309	corporate	Datacom	☐	£1,890	£1,260	01/07/2005	32
303	corporate	Datacom	☐	£1,850	£1,230	08/06/2005	35
316	corporate	FlexiCorp	☐	£1,680	£1,115	30/08/2005	9
240	corporate	Baymar Portford	☐	£2,180	£1,450	18/11/2005	7
252	corporate	Kantord International	☐	£1,412	£565	03/11/2005	20
220	corporate	Kantord International	☐	£1,338	£535	14/02/2006	16
288	corporate	FlexiCorp	☐	£1,440	£955	29/01/2005	12
219	corporate	Datacom	☐	£2,620	£1,260	13/11/2005	11
292	corporate	FlexiCorp	☐	£1,760	£1,170	06/12/2004	26
122	corporate	Kantord International	☐	£2,200	£880	07/09/2005	17
347	corporate	FlexiCorp	☐	£1,320	£880	17/10/2006	24

▶ Click the **Close** icon (**X**) in the top right-hand corner of the **Query** window.

▶ Click **Yes** to save changes to the query.

Adding a calculated field to a query

Next you need to create a new field called **REFUND** in your query that will calculate the 75% deposit refund due to corporate renters of properties. The new field needs to multiply the **DEPOSIT PAID** by 0.75.

▶ Open **qryCorpRefunds** in **Design View**.

▶ Click the **Maximize** button in the top right corner of the table window if it does not completely fill the screen.

▶ Click in the **Field:** row of the blank column immediately after **DURATION**.

▶ Type **REFUND:0.75*[DEPOSIT PAID]**

REFUND: 0.75*[DEPOSIT PAID]

▶ Click the **Run** button to run the query and view the results.

▶ Maximize the query window if it does not completely fill the screen. Your query results should now look like the example below.

 TIP

You might also need to use the divide (/), minus (-) or addition (+) symbols in a calculated field. Enclose existing field names in brackets [ ] and do not place any spaces in the calculated field.

Run button

PROPERTY NUMBER	RENTAL TYPE	RENTER	REFERENCES	DEPOSIT PAID	MONTHLY RENT	DATE RENTED	DURATION	REFUND
196	corporate	Kantord International	☐	£1,900	£760	26/10/2005	29	1425
342	corporate	Datacom	☐	£2,680	£1,340	21/10/2005	9	2010
124	corporate	FlexiCorp	☐	£1,500	£375	27/11/2005	12	1125
242	corporate	FlexiCorp	☐	£1,425	£570	09/12/2004	7	1068.75
324	corporate	Baymar Portford	☐	£1,490	£990	01/12/2004	16	1117.5
298	corporate	Kantord International	☐	£1,590	£1,055	03/12/2004	15	1192.5
217	corporate	Mr Ojay	☐	£770	£510	20/12/2005	31	577.5
142	corporate	Kantord International	☐	£1,538	£615	19/06/2005	30	1153.5
309	corporate	Datacom	☐	£1,890	£1,260	01/07/2005	32	1417.5
303	corporate	Datacom	☐	£1,850	£1,230	08/06/2005	35	1387.5
316	corporate	FlexiCorp	☐	£1,680	£1,115	30/08/2005	9	1260
240	corporate	Baymar Portford	☐	£2,180	£1,450	18/11/2005	7	1635
252	corporate	Kantord International	☐	£1,412	£565	03/11/2005	20	1059
220	corporate	Kantord International	☐	£1,338	£535	14/02/2006	16	1003.5
288	corporate	FlexiCorp	☐	£1,440	£955	29/01/2005	12	1080
219	corporate	Datacom	☐	£2,620	£1,260	13/11/2005	11	1965
292	corporate	FlexiCorp	☐	£1,760	£1,170	06/12/2004	26	1320
122	corporate	Kantord International	☐	£2,200	£880	07/09/2005	17	1650
347	corporate	FlexiCorp	☐	£1,320	£880	17/10/2006	24	990
			☐					

▶ Click the **Close** icon (**X**) in the top right-hand corner of the **Query Design** window.

▶ Click **Yes** to save changes to the query design.

▶ Close **Access** down.

Task 4   Grouped reports

You have been asked to use the **qryCorpRefunds** query to prepare a report with the title **CORPORATE DEPOSIT REFUNDS**. The fields **RENTER**, **PROPERTY NUMBER**, **DEPOSIT PAID** and **REFUND** need to appear on the report in this order. The report needs to be grouped by **RENTER** and include a **sub total** of the **REFUND** amounts for each renter and an **overall total** of the **REFUND** amounts at the end.

Creating a grouped report

You need to use the **Report Wizard** to prepare this report and then format it in **Design View**.

- ▶ Load **Access** and open the **properties** database.

- ▶ Click on the **Reports** object type in the **Database Window**.

- ▶ Double-click the **Create report by using wizard icon**. The **Report Wizard** window will appear with the question, **Which fields do you want on your report?**

- ▶ Click the down arrow on the right of the box headed **Tables/Queries** and select **qryCorpRefunds** from the list if it is not already selected.

  These fields need to be displayed for each record found by the query in the order shown:

  RENTER
  PROPERTY NUMBER
  DEPOSIT PAID
  REFUND

- ▶ Click **RENTER** in the list of available fields.

- ▶ Click the single right arrow between the **Available fields:** and **Selected fields:** boxes. The **RENTER** field will be added to the **Selected fields:** box.

- ▶ Add the rest of the fields listed above in the order shown in exactly the same way. Your **Selected fields:** box should look like the example below.

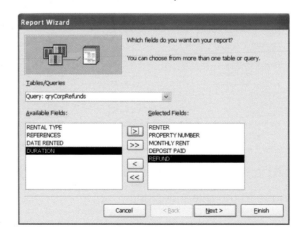

- ▶ Click **Next**. You will be presented with a window asking if you want to add any grouping levels. This report needs to be grouped by **RENTER**.

- Click **RENTER** if it is not already selected in the list of fields on the left.

- Click the single right arrow between the two boxes.

- Click **Next**. You will be presented with a window asking what sort order you want for your records. The data need to be sorted in ascending order of **PROPERTY NUMBER** then in ascending order of **DEPOSIT PAID**.

- Click the small down arrow on the right of the first box and select **PROPERTY NUMBER** from the list of fields.

- Click the small down arrow on the right of the second box and select **DEPOSIT PAID**.

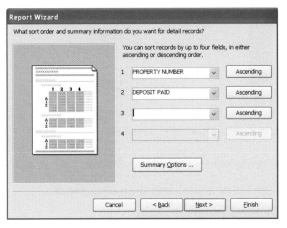

- This is also the stage in the **Report Wizard** that you need to specify that sub totals and an overall total are required for the calculated **REFUND** field. Click the **Summary Options** button. The **Summary Options** window will appear asking, **What summary values would you like calculated?**

- Click the check box next to **REFUND** in the **Sum** column.

- Click the radio button next to **Detail and Summary** if it is not already selected.

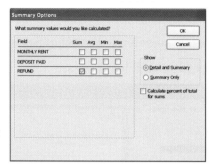

▶ Click **OK** then click **Next**. You will be presented with a window asking how you would like to lay out your report.

▶ Click the radio button next to **Stepped** in the **Layout** section if it is not already selected.

▶ Click the radio button next to **Portrait** in the **Orientation** section if it is not already selected.

▶ Click the check box next to **Adjust the field width so all fields fit on a page** at the bottom of the window if it is not already selected.

> **TIP**
>
> You could be asked to use any of the **Avg** (average), **Min** (minimum) or **Max** (maximum) summary values at this stage.

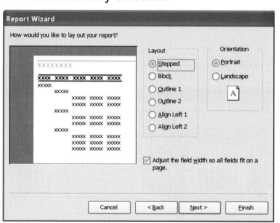

▶ Click **Next**. You will be presented with a window asking what style you would like.

▶ Choose **Formal** from the list of styles, and then click **Next**.

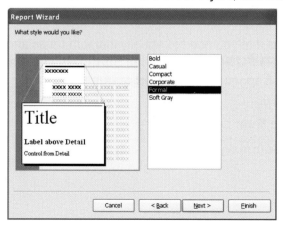

> **TIP**
>
> You can choose any style at this stage unless a specific one is specified. We are using **Formal** this time so that your report will look exactly the same as the examples that follow.

- Click **Next**. You will be presented with a window asking what title you want for your report.
- Type the title **CORPORATE DEPOSIT REFUNDS**
- Click the radio button next to **Preview the report** if it is not already selected.
- Click **Finish**. The report will be opened in **Print Preview**. It should look something like the example below.
- Click the **Maximize** button in the top right corner of the report window if it does not completely fill the screen.

CORPORATE DEPOSIT REFUND

RENTER	PROPERTY NUMBER	DEPOSIT PAID	REFUND
Baymar Portford			
	240	£2,180	1635
	324	£1,490	1117.5
Summary for 'RENTER' = Baymar Portford (2 detail records)			
Sum			2752.5

Modifying the report in Design View

Next you need to improve the appearance of the report by modifying it in **Design View**.

- Open the report in **Design View**. It should look like the example below with the **Toolbox** visible.

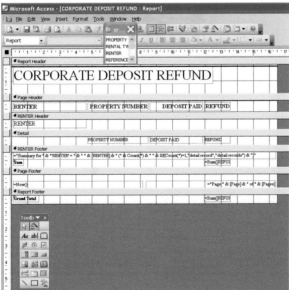

TIP

Click **View**, **Toolbars**, and then **Toolbox** if the **Toolbox** does not appear. You might also see other small windows such as the **Field List** window shown in the example above. Click the **Close** icon (**X**) in the top right-hand corner to close any window like this.

You need to start by removing the text box that generates the text beginning **Summary for 'RENTER' =** for each group of records.

▶ Click the text box at the top of the **RENTER Footer** section to select it.

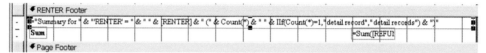

Cut button

▶ Click the **Cut** button on the **Report Design** toolbar to remove the text box.

Next you need to edit the text box that generates the text **Sum** on the row containing the **REFUND** total for each group of records.

▶ Click inside the text box and delete the text **Sum**, then type **REFUND DUE**

Next you need to move this text box closer to the text box **=Sum([REF...** that generates the total **REFUND** amount for each group of records.

▶ Click the right edge of the text box to select it.

▶ Position the mouse pointer over the bottom edge of the text box until it changes into a hand shape.

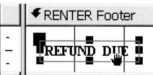

▶ Click and hold the left mouse button.

▶ Drag across to the right until the text box is in the position shown below, then let go of the mouse button.

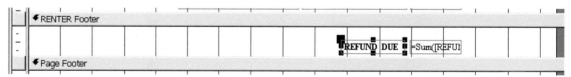

▶ Click the **View** button to preview the report. Your report should look like the example below.

RENTER	PROPERTY NUMBER	DEPOSIT PAID	REFUND
Baymar Portford			
	240	£2,180	1635
	324	£1,490	1117.5
	REFUND DUE		2752.5

> **TIP**
>
> If a text label is not displayed in full on a report you must increase the size of the text box containing the label. Click the **View** button to return to **Design View**, and then click the text box. Position the pointer over the left centre sizing handle of the text box until it turns into a double horizontal arrow. Click and hold the left mouse button and drag slightly left, then let go of the mouse button. Click the **View** button to preview the report – if any of the text is still missing repeat this process.

Next you need to format the **=Sum([REF** text box so that the total **REFUND** amounts will be displayed in **currency format** with **2 decimal places**.

- Return to **Design View**.

- Select the **=Sum([REF** text box in the **Renter Footer** section.

- Position the mouse pointer over the bottom edge of the text box until it changes into the hand shape.

- Double-click the left mouse button. A window labelled **Text Box: Sum Of REFUND** will appear.

- Click the **All** tab.

- Click in the **Format** box, click the small down arrow, scroll down the list of options and select **Currency**.

- Click in the **Decimal Places** box, click the small down arrow and select **2** from the list of options.

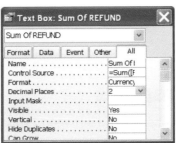

- Close the **Text Box** properties window.

- Format the **REFUND** text box in the **Detail** section in exactly the same way so that the individual **REFUND** amounts will be displayed in **currency format** with **2 decimal places**.

- Preview these changes to the report.

Next you need to edit and format the text boxes in the **Report Footer** section.

- Click inside the **Grand Total** text box, delete the text and type **TOTAL REFUNDS DUE**.

- Preview the report and adjust the size of this text box if the label cannot be seen in full.

- Move this label next to the **=Sum([REF** text box.

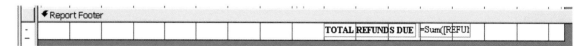

▶ Format the **=Sum([REF** text box so that the figure will be displayed in **currency format** with **2 decimal places**.

That's the last of the design changes this report needed. Now you can view and print the report.

▶ Click the **View** button on the **Report Design** toolbar to return to **Print Preview**. Your report should look like the example below.

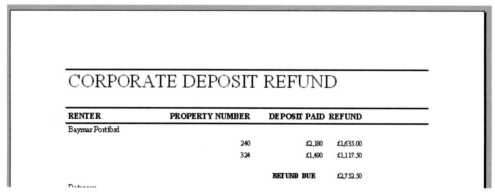

Print button

▶ Click the **Print** button on the **Print Preview** toolbar to print the report.

▶ Close the report saving any changes to the design.

▶ Close **Access** down.

TIP

You might need to click **File** and **Print...** on the menu bar to make sure the correct printer is selected at this stage. Ask your tutor if you're not sure about which printer to use.

Task 5   Columnar reports

The **MONTHLY RENT** for all properties rented between **January 2005** and **March 2005** is going to be reviewed. You have been asked to create a query to find all properties rented during this period. The information found by this query needs to be presented in a **columnar report**.

Creating a new query

You need to use the **Query Wizard** to create the query before using it to generate the report.

▶ Load **Access**.

▶ Open the **properties** database.

▶ Click on the **Queries** object type in the **Database Window**.

▶ Double-click the **Create query by using wizard** icon.

▶ Click the down arrow on the right of the box headed **Tables/Queries** and select **tblProperties** from the list.

These fields need to be displayed for each record found by the query in the order shown:

PROPERTY NUMBER
RENTER
MONTHLY RENT
DATE RENTED

⊳ Add the fields listed above in the order shown to the **Selected fields:** box, then click **Next**.

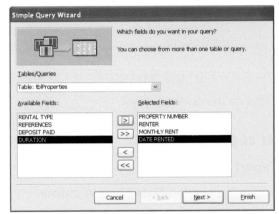

⊳ Click the radio button next to **Detail** if it is not already selected.

⊳ Click **Next**.

⊳ Type the name **qryJanMar05**

⊳ Click the radio button next to **Modify the query design**, and then click **Finish**. The **Query Design Table** will be displayed.

Entering the search criteria

This query needs to search the **DATE RENTED** field for dates <u>between</u> **01/01/2005** <u>and</u> **31/03/2005**.

⊳ Click in the criteria row in the **DATE RENTED** column and type **between #01/01/2005# and #31/03/2005#**.

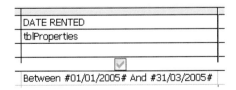

The search criteria in this example uses the **AND** operator. Your might also need to use the **OR** operator in a query. You could, for example, search the **DURATION** field in this database for values of **12 OR 24** rather than a range. You should also note that dates in search criteria must be enclosed in **#** symbols. Text values should be enclosed in double quotes **""**.

Run button

Click the **Run** button to run the query and view the results.

Maximize the query window if it does not completely fill the screen. Your query results should look like the example below.

PROPERTY NUMBER	RENTER	MONTHLY RENT	DATE RENTED
304	Mr. Baumann	£610	10/01/2005
253	Mrs Kraus	£530	16/01/2005
153	Mr Omar	£700	14/01/2005
243	Cornwallis Imports	£1,415	07/02/2005
288	FlexiCorp	£955	29/01/2005

Click the **Close** icon **(X)** in the top right-hand corner of the **Query Design** window.

Click **Yes** to save changes to the query design.

Creating a columnar report

Now you need to use the **Report Wizard** to prepare a columnar report based on the new query.

Click on the **Reports** object type in the **Database Window**.

Double-click the **Create report by using wizard** icon.

Click the down arrow on the right of the box headed **Tables/Queries** and select **qryJanMar05** from the list.

Click the double right arrow between the **Available fields:** and **Selected fields:** boxes to add all the fields, then click **Next**.

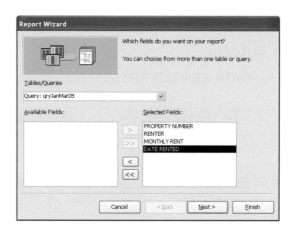

This report does not need any grouping levels, so you can click **Next**.

The data need to be sorted in ascending order of **MONTHLY RENT**. Click the small down arrow on the right of the first box and select **MONTHLY RENT** from the list of fields.

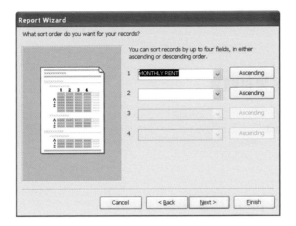

▶ Click **Next**.

▶ Click the radio button next to **Columnar** in the **Layout** section.

▶ Click the radio button next to **Portrait** in the **Orientation** section if it is not already selected.

▶ Click the check box next to **Adjust the field width so all fields fit on a page** at the bottom of the window if it is not already selected.

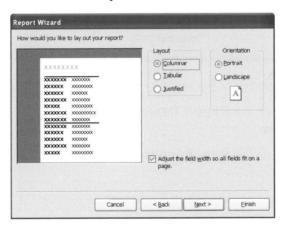

▶ Click **Next**. You will be presented with a window asking what style you would like.

▶ Choose **Compact** from the list of styles, and then click **Next**.

▶ Click **Next**. You will be presented with a window asking what title you want for your report.

▶ Type the title, **RENTS TO REVIEW**

▶ Click the radio button next to **Preview the report** if it is not already selected.

▶ Click **Finish**. The report will be opened in **Print Preview**. It should look something like the example below.

TIP

You can choose any style at this stage unless a specific one is specified. We are using **Compact** this time so that your report will look exactly the same as the examples that follow.

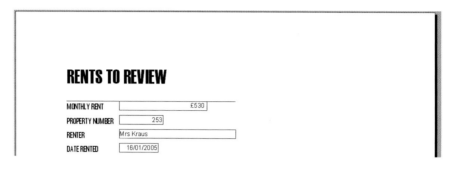

RENTS TO REVIEW

MONTHLY RENT	£530
PROPERTY NUMBER	253
RENTER	Mrs Kraus
DATE RENTED	16/01/2005

Adding a footer and printing the report

Next you need to modify the report footer in **Design View** before printing the report.

 Open the report in **Design View**.

Maximize the report window if it does not completely fill the screen.

Reduce the size of the **date** and **page number** text boxes in the **Page Footer** section.

Use the **Label** tool to add your **name** and **centre number** to the space you have just created in the centre of the **Page Footer** section.

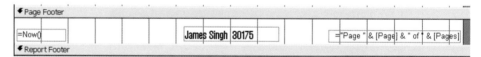

Page Footer					
=Now()			James Singh	30175	="Page " & [Page] & " of " & [Pages]
Report Footer					

Now you are ready to view and print the report.

Click the **View** button on the **Report Design** toolbar to return to **Print Preview**.

Click the **Print** button on the **Print Preview** toolbar to print the report.

Close the report saving any changes to the design.

Close **Access** down.

Print button

> **TIP**
>
> The steps you need to follow to modify the **Page Footer** section of the report in this way are described in **Task 2** on page **109**.

That's the end of the practice tasks. Now try the full New CLAiT Plus assignment that follows.

Practice assignment

Scenario

You are employed by Premier DVD Rentals as an Office Assistant. Your duties include providing database support to branch outlets including database design, development, modifications and data manipulation.

Assessment Objectives	TASK 1

TASK 1

You have been asked to create a small database of ex-rental DVDs that are going to be offered for sale in the branch outlets.

1a   1   a)   Open a database software application.

1b   b)   Create a new database called **sales** using the field headings and data types below.

1c   c)   Ensure that field lengths are long enough to display all the information in full.

FIELD HEADING	DATA TYPE
DVD	Numbers, 0 decimal places
BRANCH	Text
PRICE	Currency, with a currency symbol, 2 decimal places
CATEGORY	Text
LENGTH	Numbers, 0 decimal places
SPECIAL EDITION	Logic field

For the fields **BRANCH** and **CATEGORY** use the following codes:

BRANCH

BUCKLEY	**BK**
GRANGEFORTH	**GR**
WHITEFIELD	**WH**

CATEGORY

ACTION	**ACT**
COMEDY	**COM**
SCIENCE FICTION	**SCF**
ANIMATED	**ANM**

1d

2   Enter the records below into your database.

You may use a data entry form to enter data.

Note: the currency symbol must also display in the PRICE field.

DVD	BRANCH	PRICE	CATEGORY	LENGTH	SPECIAL EDITION
1242	GRANGEFORTH	4.99	ACTION	143	YES
1249	BUCKLEY	4.75	SCIENCE FICTION	121	YES
1251	BUCKLEY	4.75	ACTION	141	NO
1267	GRANGEFORTH	4.99	SCIENCE FICTION	124	NO
1272	WHITEFIELD	5.99	ANIMATED	119	YES
1281	GRANGEFORTH	5.99	COMEDY	113	NO
1289	GRANGEFORTH	4.99	COMEDY	109	YES
1291	WHITEFIELD	4.75	SCIENCE FICTION	107	NO
1293	WHITEFIELD	4.99	ANIMATED	112	NO
1294	BUCKLEY	3.75	COMEDY	102	NO
1299	GRANGEFORTH	5.99	ACTION	118	YES

1f

3   Check your data for accuracy and save the database.

Assessment Objectives

TASK 2

1e
1f
1g
3a
3b
3c
4a
4b

1   Using the database saved in Task 1 produce a **tabular** report, in **landscape** orientation, displaying all records, presented as follows:

a)   Display all fields in the following order:

DVD

BRANCH

PRICE

CATEGORY

LENGTH

SPECIAL EDITION

b)   Title the report: **DVDS FOR SALE**

c)   Sort the data in ascending order of **DVD**.

d)   In the footer display:

an automatic date field

your name

your centre number

do not display the page number

e) Ensure all data will be fully displayed on the printout.

f) Save and print the report in one page in landscape orientation.

2 Produce labels for each DVD to display the following fields:

PRICE BRANCH (separated by at least two spaces, on one line)

CATEGORY

LENGTH

a) Sort the data in descending order of **PRICE**.

b) Do not display field headings on the labels.

c) In the footer display:

the date

your name

your centre number

d) Ensure all data will be fully displayed on the printout.

e) Print the labels on one page.

3 Save and close the database.

1e
1g
3a
3b
3c
4a
4b

1f

Assessment Objectives

TASK 3

Premier DVD Rentals branches keep records of DVDs rented out to members and have asked for a database to be created from their existing data.

1 Create a new database using the name **rentals**

2a
1f
2b

2 Import the datafile called **rentals** and save it in your database software's file format.

3 Check that the field characteristics are as shown in the following table, modify them if necessary:

FIELD HEADING	DATA TYPE
DVD	Numbers, 0 decimal places
BRANCH	Text
RATE	Numbers, 2 decimal places
CERTIFICATE	Text
NEW RELEASE	Logic field
MEMBER	Numbers, 0 decimal places
DATE RENTED	English date (day, month, year) in any format
NIGHTS	Numbers, 0 decimal places

Note: the currency symbol must also display in the **RATE** field.

2c	4	You need to amend the following data:

a) Enter a **RATE** of **£3.75** for DVD **1659**.

b) Amend the **CERTIFICATE** for DVD **2082** to be **PG**.

c) Delete the **entire record** for DVD **2046**.

d) Create **2 new records** for the following DVDs:

DVD	BRANCH	RATE	CERTIFICATE	NEW RELEASE	MEMBER	DATE RENTED	NIGHTS
4001	BK	£4.99	18	YES	1041	19/10/06	3
4002	GR	£2.99	12	NO	1073	21/10/06	2

1f	5	Save the database keeping the filename **rentals**.
1f	6	A 75% refund of the **RATE** for one night is going to be paid to customers of BRANCH
2d		**GR** who have rented DVDs for more than 2 nights.
2e		a) In a query, find only those customers of BRANCH **GR** who have rented DVDs for more than 2 nights.

b) In the same query, create a new field called **REFUND** and calculate the **REFUND** by multiplying the **RATE** by **0.75**.

c) Save the query as **REFUND**

Assessment Objectives	TASK 4	
1e	1	Use the query **REFUND** to produce a grouped report in portrait orientation titled:
3a		**GRANGEFORTH RENTAL REFUNDS**
3b		a) Display the **MEMBER, DVD, RATE, NIGHTS** and **REFUND** fields only, in this
3c		order.
3d		b) Group the report by **MEMBER**.
3e		c) Display a **sub total** of the REFUND amounts due to each MEMBER and an
3f		**overall total** of the REFUND amounts at the end of the report.
4a		d) Give the sub totals the label **REFUND**
4b		e) Give the overall total the label **TOTAL REFUNDS FOR GRANGEFORTH**

f) Display the values in the **REFUND** field including the sub totals and overall total as currency, with a currency symbol and to 2 decimal places.

g) Sort the report in ascending order by **MEMBER** and then in ascending order of **DVD**.

h) In the footer display:

   an automatic date field

   automatic page numbers

   your name

   your centre number

i) Save and print the report in portrait orientation to fit onto no more than **2** pages.

Assessment Objectives	TASK 5
1f	1 The condition of DVDs last rented between June and July 2006 needs to be checked.
2d	a) In a query, find all the DVDs with a **DATE RENTED** between **1st June** and **31st**
1e	**July 2006**.
1f	b) Save the query as **JUNEJULY**
1g	2 Use the query **JUNEJULY** to produce a columnar report in portrait orientation titled:
3a	**DVDS TO BE CHECKED**
3b	a) Display the **DVD**, **BRANCH** and **DATE RENTED** fields only, in this order.
3c	b) Sort the report in ascending order of **DVD**.
4a	c) In the footer display:
4b	**an automatic date field**
	automatic page numbers
	your name
	your centre number
	d) Save and print the report in portrait orientation to fit onto no more than **2** pages.
	3 Close the database and exit the software.

To pass this unit you must be able to:

- ✓ set up and use master page/template according to a design brief
- ✓ set up page layout grids/guides
- ✓ import and manipulate text and image files
- ✓ amend publication content using proof correction symbols
- ✓ produce professional publications/documents
- ✓ prepare a publication for press.

Before you start this chapter, you or your tutor should download a zipped file called **Resources for Chapter 4** from **www.payne-gallway.co.uk/claitplus**. It will automatically unzip. Specify that the contents are to be saved in your **My Documents** folder.

The practice tasks that follow cover all the techniques you need to learn in order to pass a New CLAiT Plus Unit 4 E-PUBLICATION DESIGN assignment.

Practice tasks

Task 1   Creating a new publication

Scenario

You are working as an administrative assistant in the head office of Stateside Cars, an importer of classic American vehicles based in the North East of England. One of your jobs is to prepare promotional material.

▶ Create a subfolder called **Unit 4 PT** in your **My Documents** folder or network home directory folder where files created as you work through these practice tasks can be stored.

The steps you need to follow to create a subfolder are described in **Chapter 1** on page **5**.

You have been asked to prepare an advertising leaflet:

▶ the text has been prepared for you

▶ you will be asked to make some amendments to this text

▶ the approximate positioning of the page items and text is shown on the Page Layout Sketches and text flow diagrams on pages 141 and 144.

Creating a blank publication

To get started you need to load **Publisher**. This can be done in one of two ways:

Microsoft Office
Publisher 2003

 either double-click the **Microsoft Publisher** icon on the main screen in Windows,

 or click the **Start** button at the bottom left of the screen, then click **Programs**, then click
 Microsoft Office Publisher 2003

The main Publisher window will be displayed. You now have the options of creating a new publication or opening and working on an existing publication.

 Click **Blank print publication** in the **Task pane**. The **Publication Designs pane** will appear – you don't need to use this so click **(x)** in the top right-hand corner of the pane to close it.

 TIP

Publisher offers a wide range of publication templates and layouts to choose from. These can save time when setting up a publication but make a lot of decisions about layout and style for you. To meet the requirements for this unit you must create publications and templates from scratch to match specified page layouts.

Setting page orientation and margins

Next you need to specify the paper size, page orientation and margin settings on the **master page**.

 Click **View** on the menu bar, and then click **Master Page**. The master page will look like the one shown below with the **Edit Master Pages** toolbar displayed at the bottom of the screen.

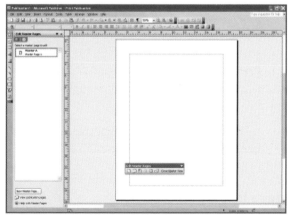

 TIP

The first thing you'll be asked to do during a New CLAiT Plus Unit 4 assignment is format a new document by setting the paper size, page orientation and margins. You could also be asked to specify a number of columns per page and adjust the amount of space between the columns.

We'll start by setting the page orientation for the publication to **Landscape**.

▶ Click **File** on the menu bar, and then click **Page Setup**. The **Page Setup** dialogue box will appear.

▶ Click the **Layout** tab if it isn't already selected.

▶ The Publication type should already be set as **Full page** – if it isn't scroll through the list and click on this option.

▶ Click the radio button next to **Landscape** under **Orientation**.

Next we'll set **A4** as the **Paper size** for the publication.

▶ Click the **Printer and Paper** tab.

▶ Click the down arrow in the box next to **Size:** in the **Paper** section and choose **A4** in the list of options if it is not already selected.

▶ Click **OK**.

Next we'll set the page margins for the publication.

Layout Guides
button

▶ Click the **Layout Guides** button on the **Edit Master Pages** toolbar. The **Layout Guides** dialogue box will appear.

▶ Click the **Margin Guides** tab if it isn't already selected.

The left and right margins for this publication must be **2 cm**.

▶ Click inside the boxes for the **left** and **right** margins. Replace each value with **2 cm**

The top and bottom margins for this publication must be **3 cm**.

 Click inside the boxes for the **top** and **bottom** margins. Replace each value with **3 cm**

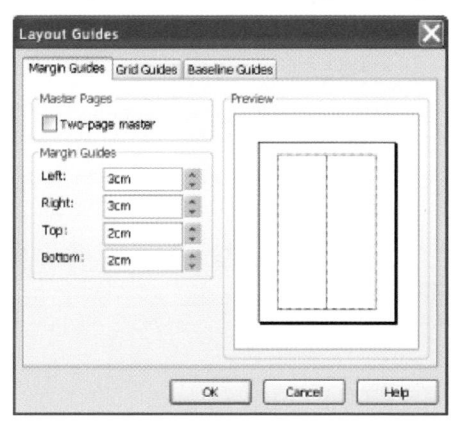

Setting up columns

Next you need to set up a three column layout for each page. The amount of empty space between the columns must be exactly 1 cm.

 Click the **Grid Guides** tab.

 Change the value next to **Columns** to **3** by clicking the small up arrow <u>twice</u>.

 Change the value next to **Spacing** to **1 cm** by clicking the small up arrow <u>twice</u>. This will leave 1 cm of empty space between the columns.

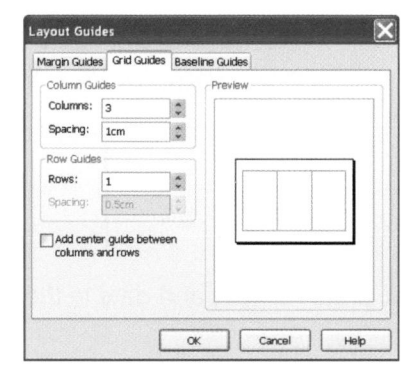

 Click **OK**. Your master page should look like the example below.

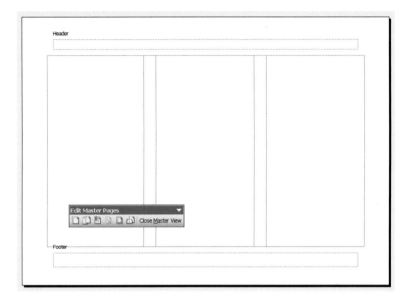

Inserting headers and footers

Next you need to add your name and centre number in the margin area at the top of the page.

▶ Click **View** on the menu bar, and then click **Header and Footer**. The **Header and Footer** toolbar will appear. The cursor will be flashing in the left of the header section.

▶ Type **your name** and **centre number**.

Align Right button

▶ Click the **Align Right** button on the **Formatting** toolbar. Your name and centre number will move flush to the right margin.

Now you need to add an automatic page number and date in the margin area at the bottom of the page.

Show Header and Footer button

▶ Click the **Show Header/Footer** button on the **Header and Footer** toolbar. The cursor will start flashing in the footer section.

First we'll add an automatic page number.

▶ Click the **Insert Page Number** button on the **Header and Footer** toolbar. A **#** symbol will appear to show that a page number will be automatically inserted on each page of the publication.

▶ Click the **Center** button on the **Formatting** toolbar. The **#** symbol will move to the centre of the page.

Next we'll add the date on a new line underneath the page number.

> Press **Enter** and click the **Insert Date** button on the **Header and Footer** toolbar. The **Footer Text Box Overflow** icon will appear to indicate that there is not enough room in the page footer for another line of text. This problem can be solved by slightly increasing the size of the Footer Text Box.

Overflow button

> Position the pointer over the bottom centre sizing handle of the text box until it changes into a double-headed vertical arrow.

> Click and hold the left mouse button.

> Drag down towards the bottom of the page, let go of the mouse button when the date appears.

> Click the **Align Left** button on the **Formatting** toolbar. The date will move flush to the left margin. Your page footer should now look something like the one below.

Align Left button

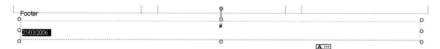
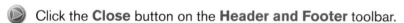

> Click the **Close** button on the **Header and Footer** toolbar.

Close

> Click the **Close Master View** button on the **Edit Master Pages** toolbar.

Close button

Close Master View

Close Master View button

Setting up the first page layout

Next you need to set up the layout for the first page of the publication as shown in the Page Layout Sketch below.

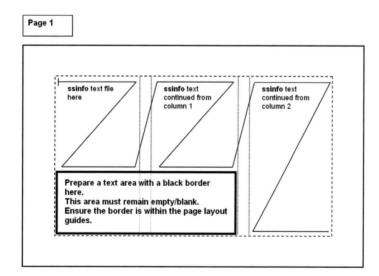

We'll start by creating a text box that takes up the top two-thirds of the first column as shown on the Page Layout Sketch.

> Click the **Text Box** button in the **Objects** toolbar on the left of the screen.

Text Box button

The mouse pointer will change to a thin cross shape

▶ Position the pointer on the top left corner of the first column.

▶ Click and hold the left mouse button.

▶ Drag down and across to the right side of the right column. As you drag an outline will show what size the text box will be when you let go of the mouse button. When the text box is roughly the same size as the one shown below, let go of the mouse button.

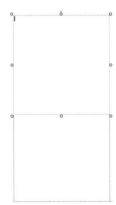

Now we need to create an identical text box in the second column. The quickest way to do this is by copying and pasting the first text box.

▶ Click the text box in the first column if it is not already selected with the round sizing handles visible.

▶ Click the **Copy** button on the **Standard** toolbar at the top of the screen.

▶ Click the **Paste** button. A second text box will appear slightly offset from the first.

▶ Position the mouse pointer on the edge of the text box until it changes shape into a cross with four arrow heads.

▶ Click and hold the left mouse button.

▶ Drag right towards the second column. As you drag a dotted outline will show you where the text box will be when you let go of the mouse button. When the text box is in the same position as the example below, let go of the mouse button.

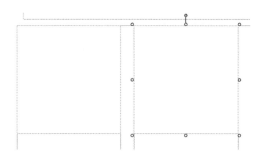

Next we need to create a text box that takes up the whole of the third column.

▶ Click the **Text Box** button in the **Objects** toolbar.

Text Box button

▶ Position the cross pointer on the top left corner of the third column.

▶ Click and hold the left mouse button.

▶ Drag down and across to the bottom right corner of the column. When the text box is the same size as the one shown below, let go of the mouse button.

Finally we need to create a text box that takes up the bottom third of the first and second columns as shown on the Page Layout Sketch.

▶ Click the **Text Box** button in the **Objects** toolbar.

Text Box button

▶ Position the cross pointer on the left column guide of the first column just underneath the bottom border of the first text box.

▶ Click and hold the left mouse button.

▶ Drag down and across to the bottom right corner of the second column. Let go of the mouse button when the text box is the same size as the column.

This text box must have a black border.

▶ Click the **Line/Border Style** button on the **Formatting** toolbar.

Border button

▶ Select **3 pt** from the drop-down list of options.

The layout of your first page should be the same as the example below.

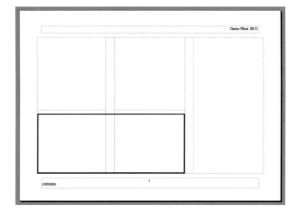

Creating a second page

Now you need to create a second page based on the Master Page.

▶ Click **Insert** on the menu bar, and then click **Page...**

The **Insert Page** dialogue box will appear.

▶ Click the radio button next to **After current page** if it is not already selected.

▶ Click the radio button next to **Insert blank pages** if it is not already selected.

▶ Click **OK**. The new page will be inserted and displayed.

Setting up the second page layout

Next you need to set up the layout for this page as shown in the Page Layout Sketch below.

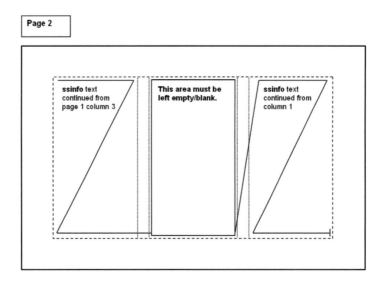

- Create a text box that takes up the entire first column.
- Create a text box that takes up the entire third column.

The layout of your second page should now be the same as the example below.

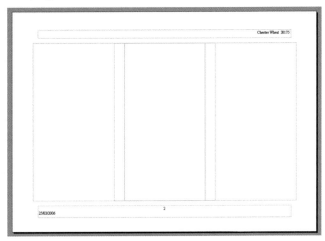

Creating text box links

Now you need to link the text boxes on both pages together. The text box links will make text inserted in the first column on the first page overflow automatically into the other columns as shown on the Page Layout Sketches.

- Click the tab for **Page 1** at the bottom of the **Publisher** window.
- Click inside the text box at the top of the first column.
- Click the **Create Text Box Link** button on the **Connect Text Boxes** toolbar at the top of the screen. The pointer will change shape to a jug symbol.
- Position the pointer over the text box at the top of the second column. The pointer will change into a pouring jug symbol, click the left mouse button. The **Go to Previous Text Box** symbol will appear at the top of the text box to show that a link has been created.

Next we need to link the text box at the top of the second column to the text box in the third column.

- Click the **Create Text Box Link** button.
- Position the pointer over the text box in the third column, and then click the left mouse button.

Now we need to link the text box in the third column to the text box in the first column on the second page.

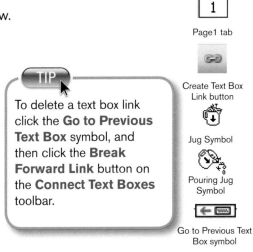

TIP

To delete a text box link click the **Go to Previous Text Box** symbol, and then click the **Break Forward Link** button on the **Connect Text Boxes** toolbar.

Page1 tab

Create Text Box Link button

Jug Symbol

Pouring Jug Symbol

Go to Previous Text Box symbol

Create Text Box Link button

Create Text Box
Link button

Page2 tab

▶ Click the **Create Text Box Link** button.

▶ Click the tab for **Page 2** at the bottom of the **Publisher** window to move to the second page.

▶ Position the pointer over the text box in the first column, and then click the left mouse button.

Finally we need to link the text box in the first column to the text box in the third column.

▶ Click the **Create Text Box Link** button.

▶ Position the pointer over the text box in the third column, and then click the left mouse button.

Go to Previous
Text Box button

Go to Next Text
Box button

> **TIP**
>
> Check text box links by clicking the **Go to Previous Text Box** button on each text box to work back through the links until you arrive back at the first text box. You can repeat this process with the **Go to Next Text Box** buttons until you arrive back at the last text box.

Importing a text file

Now the text boxes have been created and linked you can import the main **body text** for the publication. The body text is in a pre-prepared text file called **ssinfo**. Your tutor will tell you where to find this file. In the example below it is inside a network folder called **Resources**. Your tutor will tell you where to find this file if it is in a different location.

Page1 tab

▶ Click the tab for **Page 1** at the bottom of the **Publisher** window to move to the first page if it is not already displayed.

▶ Click in the text box at the top of the first column.

▶ Click **Insert** on the menu bar, and then click **Text File**.

The **Insert Text** dialogue box will appear.

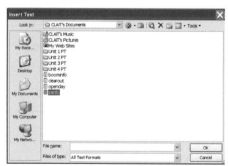

▶ Click on the file called **ssinfo**, and then click **OK**.

You might see the message below.

146

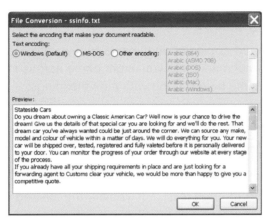

▶ Click the radio button next to **Windows (default)** if it isn't already selected.

▶ Click **OK**. The text file will be imported and overflow automatically into the linked text boxes. The two pages of your publication should now look like the example below.

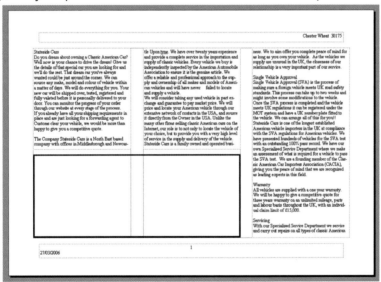

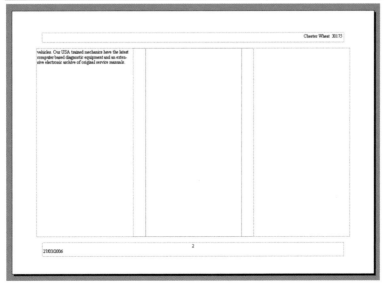

Correcting text using proof marks

Proof marks are used on printed copies of documents to give instructions about corrections that need to be made. The proof marks that you might come across in a Unit 4 CLAiT Plus assignment are show in the table below along with their meanings.

Instruction	Proof marks	Meaning
insert		insert additional words (shown above the symbol or in a balloon)
delete	———— through text	delete the marked text
close up		remove the space between the symbols
transpose vertically		swap words around vertically
transpose horizontally		swap words around horizontally
new paragraph		create a new paragraph
capitalisation	≡	change lower case text to upper case text
stet	– – – – – with ✓ in the margin	ignore a marked correction instruction

TIP

The corrections you'll need to make during a Unit 4 assignment will be shown on a copy of the text file. Any of the proof marks shown in the table above could be used.

The changes that need to be made to the text in this publication are shown below.

▶ Work through the publication and make these corrections before carrying on.

The Company // Stateside Cars is a North East based company with offices in American Middlesbrough and Newcastle Upon tyne. We have over twenty years experience and provide a complete service in the importation and supply of classic vehicles. Every vehicle we buy is independently inspected by the American Automobile Association to ensure it is the genuine article. We offer a reliable and professional approach to the supply and ownership of all makes and models of American vehicles and will have never ⌒ failed to locate and supply a vehicle. We will consider taking any used vehicle in part exchange and guarantee to pay market price. We will price and locate your American vehicle through our extensive network of contacts in the USA, and source it directly from the Owner in the USA. Unlike the many other firms selling classic American cars on the Internet, our role is to not only to locate the vehicle of your choice, but to provide you with a very high level of service in the supply and delivery of the vehicle.

✓ Stateside Cars is a family owned and operated business. We to aim offer you complete peace of mind for as long as you own your vehicle. As the vehicles we supply are unusual in the UK, the closeness of our relationship is a very important part of our service.

Formatting text

Next we need to format the body text and headings in the publication by changing the font style, font size, emphasis and alignment. We'll start with the body text and format it as follows:

style: **sans serif**
size: **12**
emphasis: **regular/normal**
alignment: **justified**

- Click anywhere in the first column.

- Hold down the **Ctrl** key, and then press the **A** key to select all the body text. The text will turn black.

- Click the down arrow in the **Font name** box at the top of the screen.

- Scroll up through the list of available fonts and click on the font called **Arial**.

- Click the small arrow on the right of the **Font Size** box.

- Scroll through the list of available sizes and click on **12**.

TIP

There are two basic types of font, called **Serif** and **Sans Serif**. Serif fonts have little tails – called serifs – at the top and bottom of each letter. This sentence is written in a Serif font called Times New Roman. Serif fonts are used for large amounts of text that will be read quickly, such as in newspapers or books. The serifs 'lead your eye' from one word to the next. Sans Serif fonts don't have any tails on the letters and are used in places where text needs to be clear and easy to read, such as road signs and text books. This book has been written in a Sans Serif font called Arial. You could also be asked to choose a **Serif** font for the body text – the technique is exactly the same. The **Serif** font – Times New Roman – is normally pre-selected for text by Publisher.

- Click the **Justify** button on the **Formatting** toolbar. The first page of your publication should now look like the example below.

Justify button

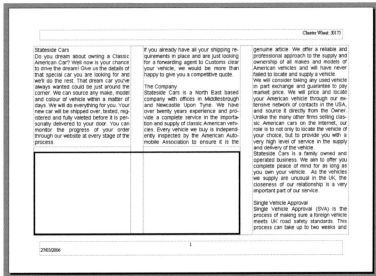

Next we'll format the heading **Stateside Cars** as follows:

style: **serif**
size: **22**
emphasis: **bold**
alignment: **centre**

⊙ Highlight the heading **Stateside Cars** by clicking it <u>three</u> times – you can click and drag if you prefer.

⊙ Use the **Font name** box to select the font called **Georgia**.

B

Bold button

⊙ Click the **Bold** button on the **Formatting** toolbar.

⊙ Use the **Font Size** box to select size **22**.

≡

Center button

⊙ Click the **Center** button on the **Formatting** toolbar.

⊙ Click anywhere away from the text to remove the highlighting. The heading should now look like the example below.

Now we'll format the four subheadings **The Company**, **Single Vehicle Approval**, **Warranty** and **Servicing** as follows:

style: **serif**
size: **16**
emphasis: **bold, italic**
alignment: **left**

⊙ Highlight the first subheading **The Company**.

⊙ Use the **Font name** box to select the font called **Georgia**.

B

Bold button

⊙ Use the **Font Size** box to select size **16**.

⊙ Click the **Bold** button on the **Formatting** toolbar.

I

Italic button

⊙ Click the **Italic** button on the **Formatting** toolbar. The first subheading should now look like the example below.

happy to give you a competitive quote.

The Company
Stateside Cars is a North East based

▤

Align Left button

⊙ Highlight the next subheading **Single Vehicle Approval**.

⊙ Apply the same formatting to this text.

⊡ 2

Page2 tab

⊙ Click the tab for **Page 2** at the bottom of the **Publisher** window to move to the second page.

⊙ Format the two remaining subheadings, **Warranty** and **Servicing**, in exactly the same way.

150

TIP

Left alignment is automatically selected for text by Publisher. If left alignment is specified and the **Align Left** button is already selected when text is highlighted you won't need to do anything.

Removing widows and orphans

Widows and orphans are single lines of text that appear at the top or bottom of a text box or column separated from the rest of the paragraph they belong to. You need to remove any widows or orphans from the publication.

- ▶ Click inside any text box, then hold down the **Ctrl** key, and then press the **A** key to select all the body text.

- ▶ Click **Format** on the menu bar, and then click **Paragraph**.

- ▶ Click the **Line and Paragraph Breaks** tab.

- ▶ Click **Widow/Orphan control** check box.

- ▶ Click **OK**.

- ▶ Leave the body text highlighted.

Removing hyphens

Publisher automatically adds hyphens to text where words meet the edge of a text box and cannot be displayed in full. We need to remove these hyphens from the publication.

- ▶ Click **Tools**, **Language** on the menu bar, and then click **Hyphenation...**

- ▶ Uncheck the box next to **Automatically hyphenate this story**.

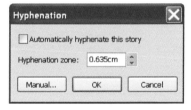

- ▶ Click **OK**.

- ▶ Leave the body text highlighted.

Adjusting leading

Next we are going to change the amount of empty space between lines by adjusting the **leading**. This term originates from the days when typesetters placed strips of lead (metal) between lines of text created from individual metal letters. The finished plate was then inked and used to print books and newspapers. You need to adjust the leading in your publication to balance the length of the columns so that there is no more than **10 mm** of empty space at the bottom of them. You also need to check and adjust the spacing between paragraphs to ensure that it is consistent.

▶ Select all the body text.

▶ Click **Format** on the menu bar, and then click **Paragraph**.

▶ Click the **Indents and Spacing** tab.

▶ Click in the **Between lines:** box and type **1.1**

▶ Click the small up arrow next to **Before paragraphs:** <u>twice</u> to display **2pt**.

▶ Click the small up arrow next to **After paragraphs:** <u>twice</u> to display **2pt**.

▶ Click **OK**.

The two pages of your publication should now look something like the examples below.

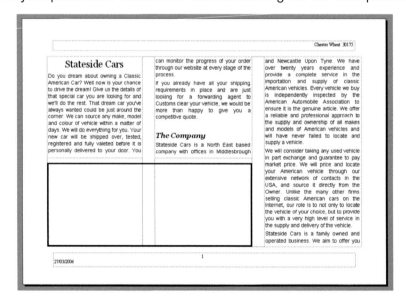

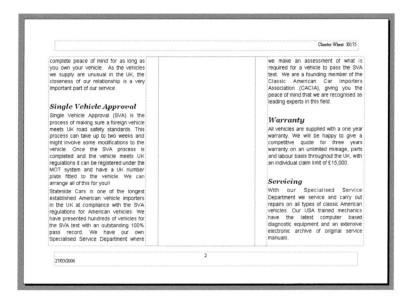

Saving the publication

Next you need to save the new publication.

▶ Click **File** on the menu bar, and then click **Save**.

▶ *Or* click the **Save** button on the **Standard** toolbar.

Save button

▶ The **Save** dialogue box will appear. The name highlighted in the **File name** box is the default filename which is normally something like **Publication1**. This can be changed to whatever you like.

▶ Double-click the **Unit 4 PT** folder if it is not already selected.

▶ Type the name **statesinfo** and click the **Save** button.

Printing a composite copy

Next you need to print a **composite copy** of the publication. This just means print a normal black and white copy of the page with all the text and images visible. If you were printing in colour it is possible to produce separate prints that show just the objects on a page that are a certain colour. This is a facility that you will use later on in this chapter.

▶ Click **File**, and then **Print** on the menu bar at the top of the screen. The **Print** dialogue window will appear.

▶ You might need to select a printer at this stage – check this with your tutor.

▶ Click the radio button next to **All** if it isn't already selected.

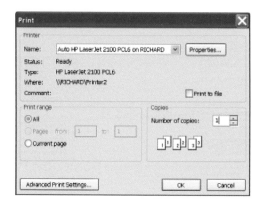

▶ Click **OK** to print the publication.

▶ Click **File** on the menu bar, and then click **Exit**, or click **(X)** in the top right-hand corner of the screen to close Publisher.

Task 2 Creating a template publication

This task takes you through the steps needed to create a new publication that can be used as a template.

You have been asked to create a template that can be used to produce flyers.

You will need to prepare the template in two colours, black and red.

The template will be used to produce two publications.

The Layout Sketch shows the approximate positioning of the text and images.

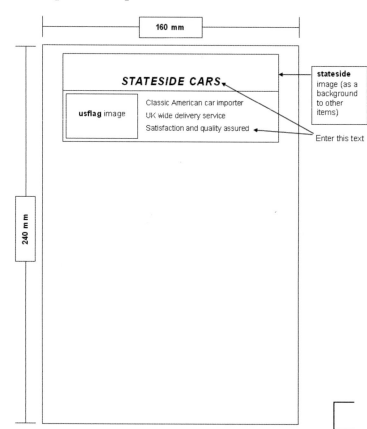

Creating a custom sized publication

To get started you need to create a blank publication using the measurements given in the Layout Sketch.

- Load **Publisher**.

- Click **Blank print publication** in the **Task pane**.

- Close the **Publication Designs pane**.

- Click **File** on the menu bar, and then click **Page Setup**. The **Page Setup** dialogue box will appear.

- Click the **Layout** tab if it isn't already selected.

- Click **Custom** in the list under **Publication type**.

- Click in the **Width:** box, delete the current value and then type **16 cm**

- Click in the **Height:** box, delete the current value and then type **26 cm**

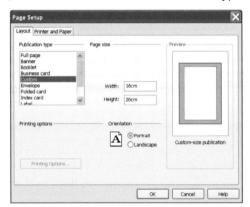

- Click the radio button next to **Portrait** under **Orientation** if it isn't already selected.

- Click the **Printer and Paper** tab and set the **Paper size** to **A4**.

- You might need to select a printer at this stage – check this with your tutor.

- Click **OK**.

TIP

If page measurements are given in mm divide them by 10 to work out the correct measurement in cm. In this example the page width is specified as 160 mm or 16 cm; the page height is 260 mm or 26 cm.

Adjusting page margins

The Layout Sketch shows the **stateside** image quite close to the top of the page edge with small margins on the left and right of the page. We need to slightly reduce the size of the page margins to make sure the finished publication most closely matches the Layout Sketch.

- Click **View** on the menu bar, and then click **Master Page**.

- Click the **Layout Guides** button on the **Edit Master Pages** toolbar. The **Layout Guides** dialogue box will appear.

Layout Guides button

- Click the **Margin Guides** tab if it isn't already selected.

- Click inside the boxes for the **left** and **right** margins. Replace each value with **1.5 cm**

- Click inside the boxes for the **top** and **bottom** margins. Replace each value with **1 cm**

- Click **OK**.

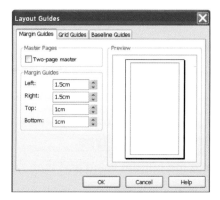

If a Layout Sketch does not give any information about margin settings you can just use the default settings for the publication. Look closely at the Layout Sketch before doing this. If the margins appear smaller or larger than the default settings you might need to make some changes to achieve the best result.

Importing an image

Next we need to insert and position the image shown on the Layout Sketch.

- Click **Insert** on the menu bar, and then click **Picture, From File**.

    The **Insert Picture** dialogue box will appear. The image file you need is called **stateside**. Your tutor will tell you where to find this file. In the example below the image file is in a shared network drive called **Resources**.

- Click on the file called **stateside**, and then click **Insert**.

The image will be inserted in the publication. It will be selected with the sizing handles and the **Picture** toolbar visible.

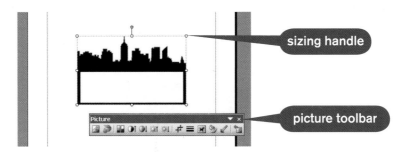

sizing handle

picture toolbar

Positioning an image

Next we need to position the image on the page so that it is in the position shown on the Layout Sketch.

⊳ Move the mouse pointer over the image until it changes shape into a cross with four arrow heads.

⊳ Click and hold the left mouse button.

⊳ Drag left and up towards the top of the page. As you drag a dotted line will show you where the image will be when you let go of the mouse button. When the picture is in the position shown below, let go of the mouse button.

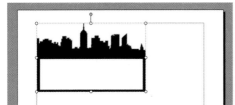

TIP

If you don't get an image in the correct position first time just try moving it again. Images should not overlap margins, columns or be placed over text unless you are specifically told to do this. You may need to 'fine tune' the position of the image by dragging and dropping it up and down or from left to right. Use the arrow keys on the keyboard to do this if you're not confident controlling the mouse.

Resizing an image

Now we need to resize the image so that it fills the area between the blue dashed page margin guides.

⊳ Click the image to select it if the sizing handles are not already visible.

⊳ Move the mouse pointer over the bottom right sizing handle until it changes shape into a diagonal two-headed arrow.

⊳ Click and hold the left mouse button.

Drag down and across towards the right of the page. As you drag a dotted line will show you how big the image will be when you let go of the mouse button. When the outlined area is the same size as the example below, let go of the mouse button.

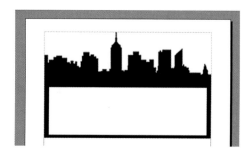

TIP

Never use the side or top and bottom sizing handles to resize an image – this will distort it. For Unit 4 assignments you should resize images so that they stay in proportion. Always use the corner sizing handles to resize images.

Placing an image in the background

The Layout Sketch tells us the **stateside** image needs to be in the background compared with the other items on the page. To make this happen we need to send the image to the back of the page.

Click **Arrange, Order** on the menu bar, and then click **Send to Back**.

You won't see any obvious change in the image at this stage but when we add the other items to the page they will appear in front of this image.

Adding and formatting text

Next we need to add the text **STATESIDE CARS** shown on the Layout Sketch to the publication.

Text Box button

Click the **Text Box** button in the **Objects** toolbar.

Position the cross pointer over the white area of the stateside image in the position shown below.

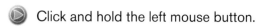

Click and hold the left mouse button.

Drag down and across to the bottom right corner of the second column. When the text box is the same size as the one shown below, let go of the mouse button.

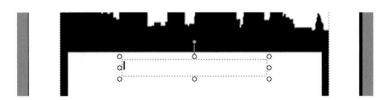

▶ Type **STATESIDE CARS**

Next we need to format the text.

▶ Highlight the text by clicking it <u>three</u> times – you can click and drag if you prefer.

▶ Use the **Font name** box to select the font called **Georgia**.

▶ Use the **Font Size** box to select size **20**

▶ Click the **Bold** button.

▶ Click the **Italic** button.

▶ Click the **Center** button.

▶ Click the small down arrow next to the **Font Color** button on the **Formatting** toolbar.

Resize the text box if all the text is not displayed in full once it has been formatted. Reposition the text box if it is overlapping the black area at the top of the **stateside** image after you have resized it.

Bold button

Italic button

Centre button

Font Color button

▶ Click **More Colors…** The **Colors** dialogue box will appear.

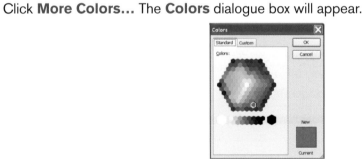

▶ Click a red colour on the palette.

▶ Click **OK**.

This text should now look like the example below.

STATESIDE CARS

Next you need to add the other three lines of text shown on the Layout Sketch.

▶ Click the **Text Box** button and position the cross pointer over the white area of the stateside image in the position shown below.

Text Box button

STATESII

▶ Create a text box the same size as the example below.

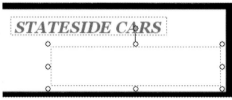

▶ Enter the text:

Classic American car importer
UK wide delivery service
Satisfaction and quality assured

▶ Format this text as follows:

style: **serif, Georgia**
size: **10**
emphasis: **normal, italic**
alignment: **left**
colour: **black**

This text should look like the example below when you have finished.

Classic American car importer
UK wide delivery service
Satisfaction and quality assured

Drawing lines

Next we need to draw a horizontal line between the two text boxes.

Line button

▶ Click the **Line** button in the **Objects** toolbar on the left of the screen.

▶ Position the cross-shaped pointer ╈ on the left edge of the stateside image between the two text boxes.

▶ Click and hold the left mouse button.

▶ Press the **Shift** key – this will keep the line straight.

▶ Drag across towards the right edge of the stateside image. Let go of the **Shift** key and mouse button when the line looks like the one shown below.

Click the **Line/Border Style** button on the **Formatting** toolbar.

Line/Border Style
button

Click **3 pt** in the list of line styles.

Your publication should now look like the example below.

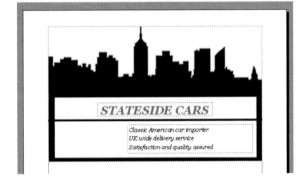

 TIP

Use the up and down arrow keys on the keyboard to 'fine tune' the position of the line if it is not midway between the text boxes.

Adding another image

Next you need to insert and position the image shown on the bottom left of the Layout Sketch.

Click **Insert** on the menu bar, and then click **Picture, From File**.

The image file you need is called **usflag**. Your tutor will tell you where to find this file. In the example below the image file is in a shared network drive called **Resources**.

Click on the file called **usflag**, and then click **Insert**.

Position and resize the image on the page so that it looks like the example below.

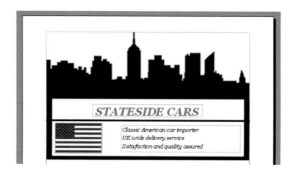

Saving the publication

Finally you need to save the new publication.

Save button

▶ Click **File** on the menu bar, and then click **Save**.

▶ *Or* click the **Save** button on the **Standard** toolbar.

▶ Type the name **templflyer** and click the **Save** button.

▶ Close **Publisher**.

Task 3 Modifying a template publication

Once you've created a template publication you'll be asked to make some changes to it by grouping and copying objects, and adding or replacing images. This task takes you through these techniques.

Opening an existing publication

▶ Load **Publisher**.

Open button

▶ Click **File** on the menu bar, and then click **Open**.

▶ *Or* click the **Open button** on the **Standard** toolbar. The Open dialogue box will appear.

▶ Click on **templflyer** and **Open**.

Your manager has asked you to make some additions to this template, and has provided the opposite Page Layout Sketch to help you.

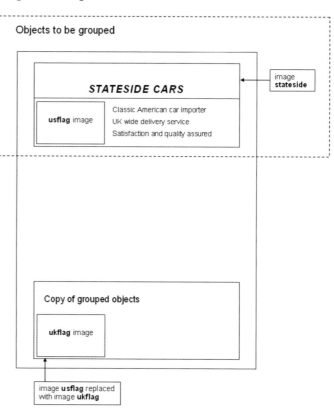

Grouping and copying objects

To get started you need to group and copy all the objects on the page as shown in the Layout Sketch.

▶ Click **View** on the menu bar, and then click **Master Page**.

▶ Hold down the **Ctrl** key, and then press the **A** key to select all the objects on the master page.

Objects can be selected to form a group by holding the shift key down and clicking on them one by one. To deselect a group of objects just click on a blank area of the page.

▶ Click the **Group Objects** icon that has appeared underneath the selected objects.

▶ Click the **Copy** button on the **Standard** toolbar.

▶ Click the **Paste** button on the **Standard** toolbar. A copy of the grouped objects will appear slightly offset from the original.

▶ Drag the copied group into the position shown below at the bottom of the screen.

Group Objects
icon

Copy button

Paste button

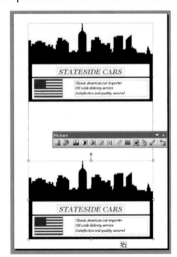

▶ Click the **Ungroup Objects** icon underneath the copied group.

Replacing an image

Next you need to delete the **usflag** image at the bottom of the page and replace it with the **ukflag** image as shown on the Layout Sketch.

▶ Click on a blank area of the page to deselect the objects at the bottom of the page.

▶ Click the **usflag** image to select it.

▶ Press either the **Backspace** or **Del** key to delete the image.

Click **Insert** on the menu bar, and then click **Picture, From File**.

The image file you need is called **ukflag**. Your tutor will tell you where to find this file. In the example below the image file is in a shared network drive called **Resources**.

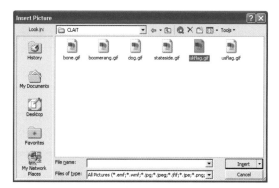

Click on the file called **ukflag**, and then click **Insert**.

Position and resize the image on the page so that it looks like the example below.

Adding a page footer

Next you need to add your name and centre number in the margin area at the top of the page.

Click **View** on the menu bar, and then click **Header and Footer**. The cursor will be flashing in the left of the header section.

Type **your name** and **centre number**.

Close button

Click the **Close** button on the **Header and Footer** toolbar.

That's the last change we needed to make to this publication. Now we need to print a composite copy of the publication and save it.

Printing with crop marks

This publication is set to print on A4 paper which is slightly larger than the custom page size. Setting **crop marks** to print will show where to trim printed pages to match the custom page size.

Click **File, Print** on the menu bar, and then click **Advanced Print Settings**.

Click the **Page Settings** tab.

 Click the check box next to **Crop marks** in the **Printer's marks** section if it is not already selected.

 Click **OK**.

 You might need to select a printer at this stage – check this with your tutor.

 Click **OK** to print the publication.

 Click the **Save** button to save the publication keeping the filename **templflyer**.

> **TIP**
>
> Crop marks will only print if the page size for a publication is smaller than the selected printer paper size.

> **TIP**
>
> You could click **File, Save As...** on the menu bar, then click the small down arrow next to **Save as type:** and select **Publisher Template** at this stage. Check with your tutor if it is OK to use this option.

 Close **Publisher**.

Task 4   Creating a publication from a template

You have been asked to prepare a flyer to advertise a stock clearance event.

Creating a new publication

To get started you need to create a new publication based on the template that you created in the last two tasks.

> **TIP**
>
> If you saved this publication as a **Publisher Template** in **Task 3** click **Templates** in the **New Publication** window of the **Task Pane**, and then double-click the preview of the template.

 Load **Publisher**.

 Open your copy of the publication **templflyer**.

To get started you need to save the publication with a new filename.

 Click **File** on the menu bar, and then click **Save As...**

 Type the new name, **clearflyer**

Applying special effects to text

To get started we need to add some text to the publication using a special effect called **WordArt**.

 Click the **Insert WordArt** button on the **Objects** toolbar at the left of the screen. The **WordArt Gallery** window will appear.

Insert WordArt button

165

Click the second WordArt style in the first row of options, and then click **OK**. The **Edit WordArt Text** dialogue window will appear.

Click in the first text box and type **STOCK CLEAROUT**

Click the small down arrow under **Size:** and select **24** from the list.

> **TIP**
>
> You do not need to create a text frame first if you are using WordArt to add text with a special effect.

Click **OK** to insert the WordArt into the publication.

Drag and drop the WordArt into the position shown in the example below.

Importing text from a file

Next we need to import and format some text from a pre-prepared text file.

Create a text box under the heading **STOCK CLEAROUT** like the one shown in the example below.

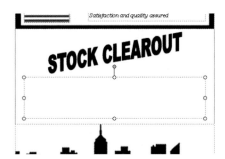

The text file you need to import is called **clearout**. Your tutor will tell you where to find this file. In the example below it is inside a network folder called **Resources**.

▶ Click in the second text box.

▶ Click **Insert** on the menu bar, and then click **Text File**. The **Insert Text** dialogue box will appear.

▶ Click on the file called **clearout**, and then click **OK** to import the text.

▶ Format the imported text as follows:

style: **serif, Georgia**
size: **14**
emphasis: **bold**
alignment: **centre**
colour: **red**

The centre section of your publication should now look like the example below.

Printing colour-separated copies

Next you need to print a set of colour-separated copies of the publication to see how colours are laid out.

▶ Click **File** on the menu bar, and then click **Print...** The **Print** dialogue window will appear.

▶ You might need to select a printer at this stage – check this with your tutor.

Colour-separated copies are used by commercial printers to see how colours are laid out. They'll appear in black and white even if they're sent to a colour printer. Publisher will print one page for each colour used in a publication. You'll need to write the name of the colour used on each page after printing.

⊙ Click **Advanced Print Settings**. The **Advanced Print Settings** dialogue window will appear.

⊙ Click the **Separations** tab if it is not already selected.

⊙ Click the small down arrow next to **Output:** and select **Separations** in the list.

⊙ Click the small down arrow next to **These plates:** and select **All defined inks** from the list if it is not already selected.

⊙ Click the check box next to **Don't print blank plates**. Your **Advanced Print Settings** should now look like the example below.

⊙ Click **OK**.

⊙ Click **OK** again to print the separations – remember to write the name of the colour used on each page.

⊙ Save the publication and close **Publisher**.

That's the end of the practice tasks. Now try the full New CLAiT Plus assignment that follows.

Practice assignment

Scenario

You are working as an office assistant for a chain of Boarding Kennels. Part of your job is to prepare advertising materials and information sheets for customers.

Assessment Objectives		TASK 1
		Before you begin this task make sure that you have the file **kinfo**.
	1	Create a new publication.
1a		Format the document as follows:
1b		Orientation: **Landscape**
1c		Top Margin: **30 mm (3 cm)**
1f		Bottom Margin: **30 mm (3 cm)**
1j		Left Margin: **20 mm (2 cm)**
		Right Margin: **20 mm (2 cm)**
		Columns: **3**
		Space between columns: **10 mm (1 cm)**

3b	2	Insert the following headers and footers:

	TEXT	ALIGNMENT
Header	your name and centre number	flush to right margin
Footer	automatic page number (starting at page 1)	centre
	the date	flush to left margin

(1e, 1g relate to item 2)

1d	3	Set up the page layout as shown in the Page Layout Sketch on page 171.
1g, 2a, 2c	4	Import the text file **kinfo** and position this text as shown in the Page Layout Sketch on page 171.
3a	5	Make the corrections shown on page 171.
2d	6 a)	Format the body text to be:

style: **sans serif**

size: **14**

emphasis: **regular/normal**

alignment: **justified**

b) Format the heading **BOOMERANG KENNELS** to be:

style: **serif**

size: **20**

emphasis: **bold**

alignment: **centre**

c) Format the 3 subheadings **Accommodation**, **Health** and **Opening**, to be:

style: **serif**

size: **16**

emphasis: **bold, italic**

alignment: **left**

3c

7 Copyfit the publication ensuring that:

a) the leading is adjusted so that there is no more than 10 mm of vertical space anywhere in the document, except where indicated in the Page Layout Sketch (the bottom of column 2 of page 2 and the whole of column 3 of page 2)

b) columns are balanced to within 10 mm

c) leading is consistent

d) paragraph spacing is consistent

e) there are no hyphenated line endings

f) subheadings are kept with at least two lines of related text

g) there are no widows or orphans

h) all material is displayed as specified

i) the text file is displayed in full.

4a

8 Save your publication using the filename **boominf**

4d

9 Print a composite copy of your publication.

Close any open documents.

Page Layout Sketch for Task 1

Page 1

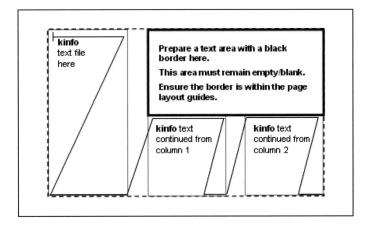

Page 2

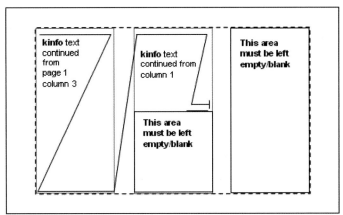

TEXT TO BE CORRECTED IN TASK 1

Boomerang Kennels

Accommodation
We have kennel units specifically designed for small, large and families of dogs
in addition to a separate kennel unit for animals in need of convalescence or
rest.
~~All kennels are built to the highest specification.~~ All kennels ⟨____⟩ are
⟨heated⟩ ⟨individually⟩, this provides warm, comfortable accommodation for all
breeds, ages and sizes of dogs. <u>r</u>aised sleeping benches, tiled floors and
thermal blankets all enable an ~~ext~~remely high standard of hygiene to be
maintained throughout.//Owners are welcome to bring along their own bedding, toys
and treats. Music is played 24 hours a day in both kennel blocks to relax the
dogs and minimise any anxiety.   *personal*
In addition to all dogs having their own/outside weatherproofed covered run, we
also exercise daily all dogs individually within our own two secure exercise
areas. All dogs are exercised morning and afternoon, Monday to Friday inclusive.
At weekends and bank holidays, the dogs are exercised ~~in the morning only~~.   ⊘
Health
All animals must be fully vaccinated; proof of this from your own veterinary
surgeon will be requested on arrival. Failure to provide this will mean that

Assessment Objectives	TASK 2

Before you begin this task ensure you have the files **boomerang** and **dog**.

You have been asked to create a template that can be used to produce notices.

You will need to prepare the template in two colours, **black** and **green**. The template will be used to produce two publications.

You may use any fonts, sizes and styles for the text in this template, but you must use the colours specified in the assignment.

A Layout Sketch is given on the next page to show the approximate positioning of the text and images:

1a 1b 1j	1 Using suitable software, create a new publication using the measurements given in the Layout Sketch. Use any margins and layout guides to suit your publication.
2b 2c	2 a) Import the image **boomerang** and position it at the top of your publication as shown in the Layout Sketch. b) The image may be resized, but must be kept in proportion.

1g
2c
2d
2f
3b
	3 a) Create a text area/frame and enter the text **Boarding Kennels**.
	    b) Position this text at the top of the white area on top of the **boomerang** image, as shown in the Layout Sketch.
	    c) **Centre** this text.
	    d) Colour this text **green**.
	    e) Make sure that the text is clearly visible and does not touch or overlap the black area of the **boomerang** image.

2e
2f
	4 a) Draw a thick black line next to the text **Boarding Kennels** as shown in the Layout Sketch.
	    b) Make sure the line touches, but does not extend beyond the line across the centre of the **boomerang** image.
	    c) Make sure the black line is clearly visible and does not touch or overlap the text.

1g
2c
2d
2f
3b
	5 a) Create a text area/frame and enter the text:
	
	       Individually heated kennels
	
	       Outside weatherproofed covered runs
	
	       Secure exercise areas
	    b) Position this text in the bottom centre of the white area on top of the image **boomerang**, as shown in the Layout Sketch.
	    c) **Centre** this text.
	    d) Colour this text **black**.

		e)	Make sure that the text is clearly visible and does not touch or overlap the black edges of the image **boomerang**.
2b	6	a)	Import the image **dog**.
2c		b)	Position the image **dog** on top of the image **boomerang**, in the top right-hand corner, as shown in the Layout Sketch.
2f		c)	The image may be resized, but must be kept in proportion.
		d)	Make sure that the image is clearly visible and does not touch or overlap the text, the black line or the black edges of the image **boomerang**.
1h	7		Save the template using the filename **noticetemplate**

Page Layout Sketch for Task 2

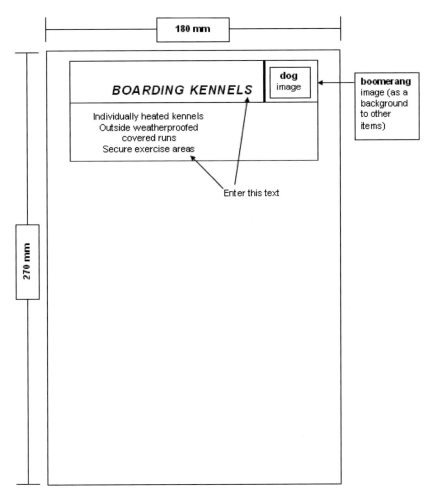

Assessment Objectives

TASK 3

Before you begin this task ensure you have the file **bone** and the template **noticetemplate** (that you created in Task 2).

Your Manager has requested some additions to the template, and has provided the following Page Layout Sketch shown below to help you.

Page Layout Sketch for Task 3

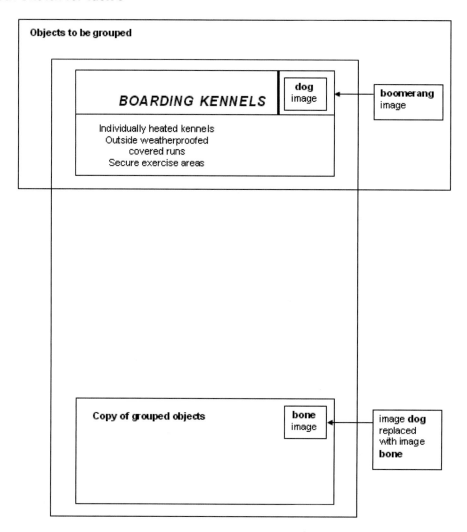

Continue working in the template **noticetemplate** that you created in Task 2.

2h	1	Group all the items in the publication.
2c	2	Copy the grouped items and paste the **copy** at the bottom of the template as shown in
2h		the Layout Sketch.

2i	3	Ungroup the **copy** of the grouped items.	
2b	4	Replace the image **dog** within the ungrouped items, with the image **bone**.	
2c			
1e	5	Insert your name and centre number as a header or footer.	
1h	6	a)	Make sure all items are clearly shown and that all items placed on
3c			top of the image **boomerang** are not touching or overlapping unless specified.
		b)	Save this template retaining the filename **noticetemplate**.
1h	7	a)	Set crop marks to print.
1k		b)	Print a composite copy of the template showing crop marks.
4c		c)	Save and close the template retaining the filename **noticetemplate**.
4d			

Assessment Objectives	**TASK 4**		
	Before you begin this task ensure you have the files **openday** and **noticetemplate** (that you saved in Task 3).		
	You have been asked to prepare a notice for an open day at the kennels.		
1a	1	Open a **copy** of the template **noticetemplate**.	
1i	2	a)	Import the text file **openday**.
2a		b)	Position this text in the white space in the centre of the publication.
2c		c)	**Centre** this text.
2d		d)	Colour this text **green**.
3c		e)	Display the text using fonts, styles and sizes to suit your publication.
		f)	Make sure that **all** the text is fully displayed and does not touch or overlap any page items.
4a	3	Save your publication using the filename **open12jul**	
4b	4	a)	Prepare colour-separated printouts.
		b)	Print a colour-separated copy of the publication.
		c)	Check that one print shows **only** the green items.
		d)	The colour of this printout must be shown on the print. You may need to handwrite the word **green** on this print.
		e)	Check that one print shows **only** the black items.
		f)	The colour of this printout must be shown on the print. You may need to handwrite the word **black** on this print.
4a	5	Save your publication keeping the filename **open12jul**.	

Assessment Objectives	TASK 5
	Before you begin this task ensure you have the files **locations** and **noticetemplate** (that you saved in Task 3).
	You have been asked to prepare a publication to advertise boarding kennel locations.
1a, i	1 Open a **copy** of the template **noticetemplate**.
1g	2 a) Create a text area/frame and enter the text:
3b	**Locations**
2g	b) Position this text at the top of the white space under the image **boomerang**.
	c) Apply a special effect to this text (for example WordArt or reverse text).
2a	3 a) Import the text file **locations**.
2c	b) Position this text in the white space in the centre of the publication.
2d	c) Format the text using fonts, styles, sizes and alignment to suit your publication.
3c	d) Make sure that **all** the text is fully displayed and does not touch or overlap any page items.
4a	4 Save your publication using the filename **kenlocs**
4d	5 a) Print a composite copy of your publication.
	b) Close the file and exit the application.

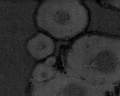
To pass this unit you must be able to:

- ☑ identify and use presentation software correctly
- ☑ set up a slide layout
- ☑ select fonts and enter text
- ☑ import and insert images correctly
- ☑ use the drawing tools
- ☑ format slides and presentation
- ☑ re-order slides and produce printed handouts
- ☑ manage and print presentation files.

Before you start this chapter, you or your tutor should download a zipped file called **Resources for Chapter 5** from **www.payne-gallway.co.uk/claitplus**. It will automatically unzip. Specify that the contents are to be saved in your **My Documents** folder.

The practice tasks that follow cover all the techniques you need to learn in order to pass a New CLAiT Plus Unit 5 DESIGNING AN E-PRESENTATION assignment.

Practice tasks

Task 1   Preparing a master slide

Scenario

You are an administrative assistant in White Lake Conference Centre. You have been asked to produce two presentations that will be used to promote the facilities and services offered by the Conference Centre.

 Create a subfolder called **Unit 5 PT** in your **My Documents** folder or network home directory folder where files created as you work through these practice tasks can be stored.

This task describes how to set up a master slide for the first presentation that will be used to promote the facilities and services offered by the Conference Centre.

The steps you need to follow to create a subfolder are described in **Chapter 1** on **page 5**.

Creating a new presentation

Microsoft Office PowerPoint

To get started you need to load **PowerPoint**. This can be done in one of two ways:

▶ *either* double-click the **PowerPoint** icon on the main screen in Windows,

▶ *or* click the **Start** button at the bottom left of the screen, then click **Programs**, then click Microsoft Office PowerPoint 2003:

The main **PowerPoint** window will be displayed. You now have the options of creating a new presentation or opening and working on an existing presentation.

▶ Click **Create a new presentation** in the **Task pane**. The **New Presentation pane** will appear.

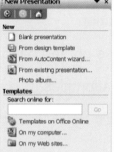

> **TIP**
>
> If you can't see the Task pane click **View, Task pane** on the menu bar.

▶ Click **Blank presentation**. The display will change to show the available **Slide Layout** options.

PowerPoint will automatically select the **Title Slide** layout which is not the one we want. The layout we need to use is **Title and Text** which will allow us to enter a title with different levels of bulleted text underneath.

▶ Click the **Title and Text** icon in the **New Presentation pane**.

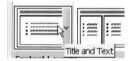

>
> **TIP**
>
> We're using the default slide orientation of **Landscape** for this presentation. If you're asked to use **Portrait** orientation click **File, Page Setup…** on the menu bar to open the **Page Setup** window. Click the radio button next to **Portrait** under **Slides** in the **Orientation** section, and then click **OK**.

Next we need to make sure the **Master Slide** is set up correctly. The master slide specifies how every slide in a presentation will look. For example, if you choose a particular background colour and font style for the master slide, this background colour and font style will be the same on every slide. The master slide for this presentation must be set up as follows:

Background	light blue
Text for all slides	sans serif (e.g. Arial, Gill Sans, Tahoma)

Item	Font Size	Enhancement
Header	small	your name and centre number
Footer	small	automatic date – any English format (day, month, year) slide number to be displayed on all slides

Item	Font Size	Enhancement
Slide headings	large	bold
First level bullet	medium	to include a bullet character
Second level bullet	smaller than first level bullets (legible)	italic to include a bullet character

Setting slide background colour

We'll start by setting the background colour for the slides to light blue.

▶ Click **View**, **Master**, **Slide Master** on the menu bar. The master slide will be displayed – it should look like the example below.

▶ Click **Format** on the menu bar, and then click **Background**.

The **Background** dialogue box will appear.

▶ Click the small arrow underneath **Background fill**. A choice of fill options will appear.

⊙ Click **More Colors**.

⊙ Click a light blue colour on the palette, then **OK**.

The default background colour for slides is white. If the background colour for slides is specified as white you won't need to do anything at this stage.

⊙ Click the **Apply to All** button. The new background colour will be shown on the master slide.

Formatting headings and bullets

Next we'll check that a Sans Serif font is selected for the slide headings and bullets. We can also set the font size and enhancements specified in the second table at this stage.

⊙ Click on the text **Click to edit Master title style** in the **Title Area**.

A large bold text is specified for the slide headings.

⊙ The font type in the **Font** box should be preset to **Arial**.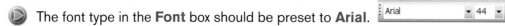

If this font is not selected or you want to use a different Sans Serif font click the small down arrow on the right of the **Font** box and select a font from the drop-down list.

⊙ The font size in the **Font Size** box should be preset to **44**. This is large enough so you can leave this as it is.

⊙ Click the **Bold button** on the **Formatting** toolbar.

Next we need to set the properties specified in the table for the first level bullet.

If this font size is not selected click the small down arrow on the right of the **Font Size** box and select **44** from the drop-down list.

▷ Click on the text **Click to edit Master text styles** in the **Object Area**.

▷ A medium size text is specified for this bullet. The preset text size of **32** shown in the **font size box** is fine compared with the size of the title text so you can leave this as it is.

Now we'll set the properties specified in the table for the second level bullet.

▷ Click on the text **Second level** in the main frame.

▷ A smaller italic text is specified for this bullet. The preset text size of **28** shown in the **font size box** is slightly large compared with the size of the first level bullet text so we'll reduce this.

▷ Click the small arrow on the right of the **Font Size** box.

▷ Scroll down the list of available sizes, and select **20**.

▷ Click the **Italic button** on the **Formatting** toolbar at the top of the screen.

Italic button

That's the text formatting completed. Next we need to add the information specified for the page header and footer.

Adding header and footer information

▷ Click the text **<date/time>** in the **Data Area** at the bottom of the screen.

▷ Click **Insert** on the menu bar, and then click **Date and Time**. The **Date and Time** dialogue box will appear.

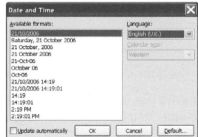

▶ Click the option in the list of available formats that shows just a date followed by the time with no seconds displayed.

▶ Click **OK**. The current date will be displayed in the **Date Area**.

▶ Click the text **<footer>** in the **Footer Area** at the bottom of the screen.

▶ Type your name followed by a few spaces and your centre number.

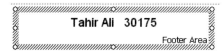

Tahir Ali   30175

Footer Area

The last thing we need to do is add the current slide number on the bottom right corner of each slide. A space is already set up for this in the **Number Area**. We need to close the master slide before activating the numbering.

▶ Click the **Close Master View** button on the **Slide Master View** Toolbar.

▶ Click **Insert** on the menu bar, and then click **Slide Number**. The **Header and Footer** dialogue box will appear.

▶ Click **Slide number**, and then click the **Apply to All** button.

The slide number will appear in the bottom right corner of the slide. The footer area of your first slide should now look like the one below.

21/10/2006 14:20   Tahir Ali   30175   1

Saving the presentation

Now we're ready to save the presentation.

Save button

▶ Click **File** on the menu bar, then click **Save**.

▶ Or click the **Save button** on the **Standard** toolbar. The **Save** dialogue box will appear.

The name highlighted in the **File name** box is the default filename which is normally something like **Presentation1** or **Presentation2**. This can be changed to whatever you like.

▶ Double-click the **Unit 5 PT** folder if it is not already selected.

▶ Type the name, **wlcmast**

▶ Click the **Save** button.

The **Save** dialogue window will disappear. The filename **wlcmast** will be displayed at the top of the screen. The presentation will now be saved with this name whenever the save button on the Standard toolbar is clicked.

Finally we need to close PowerPoint down.

▶ Click **File** on the menu bar, and then click **Exit**.

▶ Or click **(x)** in the top right-hand corner of the screen.

Task 2   Creating and working with slides

This task takes you through the steps needed to create slides, add text and insert images in a presentation.

▶ Load **PowerPoint**.

To work through this task you need to load your copy of the presentation called **wlcmast**.

▶ Click **File** on the menu bar, and then click **Open**.

▶ *Or* click the **Open button** on the standard toolbar. The **Open** dialogue box will appear.

▶ Double-click the **Unit 5 PT** folder.

▶ Click on **wlcmast** and **Open**. The presentation will open with a blank first slide like the example below.

Open button

Adding text to a slide

To get started you need to open a text file containing layout information and text for the presentation.

▶ Load **Word**.

The datafile you need to use is called **whitelake**. This file should be in your **My Documents** folder.

Open button

- ▶ Click **File** on the menu bar, and then click **Open**.

- ▶ Or click the **Open** button on the **Standard** toolbar.

- ▶ Click the down arrow next to the **Files of type:** box.

- ▶ Scroll down through the drop-down list of options and click **Text Files**.

- ▶ Click on the file called **whitelake**, and then click **Open**. The text file will be opened – it should look like the example below.

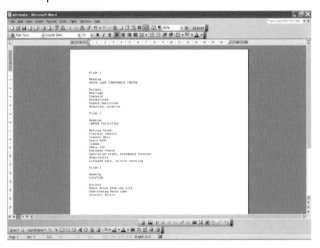

- ▶ Highlight the heading text for Slide 1 **WHITE LAKE CONFERENCE CENTRE**.

```
Slide 1

Heading
WHITE LAKE CONFERENCE CENTRE
```

- ▶ Click the **Copy** button on the **Standard** toolbar.

- ▶ Click the **PowerPoint** icon at the bottom of the screen. Microsoft Power...

- ▶ Click on the text **Click to add title** in the **Title Area**.

- ▶ Click the **Paste** button on the **Standard** toolbar. The title of your first slide should now look like the example below.

- ▶ Click the **Word** icon at the bottom of the screen. whitelake - Micr...

- ▶ Highlight the bullet text for **Slide 1**.

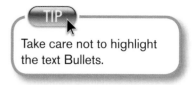

Take care not to highlight the text Bullets.

Click the **Copy** button on the **Standard** toolbar.

Click the **PowerPoint** icon at the bottom of the screen.

Click on the text **Click to add text** in the **Object Area**.

Click the **Paste** button on the **Standard** toolbar. The first slide of your presentation should now look like the example below.

Creating new slides

Next you need to add two new slides to the presentation.

Either click the **New Slide** button on the **Formatting** toolbar

New Slide button

Or click **Insert**, and then **New Slide** on the menu bar. A second blank slide will appear.

Repeat this process to create a third blank slide. The outline pane of your presentation should look like the example opposite.

Click **Slide 2** in the outline pane.

Copy and paste the Heading text for **Slide 2** from the **whitelake** text file into the **Title Area** of this slide.

Copy and paste the Bullets text for **Slide 2** from the **whitelake** text file into the **Object Area** of this slide.

Click **Slide 3** in the outline pane.

Copy and paste the Heading and Bullets text for **Slide 3** from the **whitelake** text file into the corresponding areas of this slide. The three slides of your presentation should look like the example below.

That's all the text added to the slides – now you can close the **whitelake** file.

▶ Click the **Word** icon at the bottom of the screen.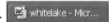

▶ Click **File** on the menu bar, and then click **Exit**.

▶ *Or* click **(x)** in the top right hand corner of the screen.

Inserting and formatting an image

Next we'll insert, resize and position an image on the first slide.

▶ Click **Slide 1** in the outline pane.

▶ Click **Insert** on the menu bar, and then click **Picture, From File**. The **Insert Picture** dialogue box will appear.

The image file you need is called **lake.jpg**. This file should be in your **My Documents** folder.

▶ Click on the file called **lake**, and then click **Insert**. The image will be inserted on the slide with round sizing handles visible.

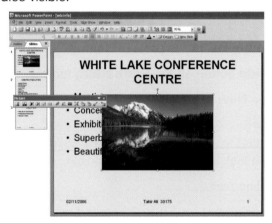

Now you need to reduce the size of the image.

▶ Move the mouse pointer over the bottom right sizing handle until it changes shape into a diagonal two-headed arrow.

▶ Click and hold the left mouse button.

Drag up towards the top left corner of the image. As you drag a dotted line will show you how big the image will be when you let go of the mouse button. When the picture is roughly the same size as the one shown in the example below, let go of the mouse button.

TIP

Never use the side handles to resize an image – this will distort it. For e-presentation assignments you should resize the images so that they stay in proportion. This means always use the corner handles for resizing.

Next we need to move the image into position next to the bulleted list.

Click once on the image to make sure it is selected and the handles are visible.

Move the mouse pointer over the image until it changes shape into a cross with four arrow heads.

Click and hold the left mouse button.

Drag across to the right of the slide. As you drag a dotted line will show you where the image will be when you let go of the mouse button. When the picture is in roughly the same position as the one shown below, let go of the mouse button.

TIP

If you don't get the image in the right position just try moving it again. Don't worry about getting the image exactly in the middle of the main frame. Just make sure it doesn't overlap the title or any of the information in the footer at the bottom of the slide.

That's the first slide finished. Now you need make some changes to the second slide.

Demoting bullets

We are going to demote some of the bullets on the second slide to become **second level bullets**.

▶ Click **View, Toolbars** and then **Outlining** on the menu bar. The **Outlining** toolbar will appear on the left of the screen.

▶ Click the **Outline** tab in the Outline pane.

▶ Click anywhere in the text **Flexible layouts** in the Outline pane.

Demote button

▶ Click the **Demote** button on the Outlining toolbar. The bullet will move to second Level.

▶ Repeat this process for the following bullets:

Seats 5000
Seats 300
Specialist staff, broadband Internet
Licensed bars, on-site catering

Your second slide should look now like the example below.

Promote button

TIP

Click the **Promote** button on the Outlining toolbar if you demote a bullet by accident or need to promote a bullet to a higher level.

Replacing text

Now we need to replace the word **Meeting** with the word **Conference** throughout the presentation. The **Replace** facility offers the quickest way to do this.

▶ Click **Edit** on the menu bar, and then click **Replace**.

The **Replace** dialogue box will appear.

▶ Click in the **Find what** box and type **Meeting**

▶ Click in the **Replace with** box and type **Conference**

▶ Click the check box next to **Match case**. Your **Replace** dialogue box should now look like the example below.

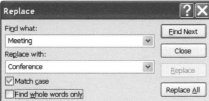

▶ Click **Replace All**. A message will appear telling you that **2** replacements have been made.

▶ Click **OK**.

▶ Click **Close**.

Printing slides as handouts

Finally we need to print the slides as **handouts** in **Portrait** orientation with **3** slides to a page.

▶ Click **File** on the menu bar, and then click **Page Setup**. The **Page Setup** dialogue box will appear.

▶ In the **Notes, handouts & outline** section click the radio button for **Portrait** if it is not already selected.

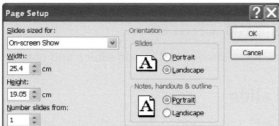

▶ Click **OK**.

▶ Click **File** on the menu bar, and then click **Print**. The **Print** dialogue box will appear.

▶ Click the radio button next to **All** in the **Print range** section if it is not already selected.

TIP

You might also need to choose a printer at this stage – if you do your tutor will tell you what to do.

⊳ Click the down arrow next to the **Print what** box in the **Handouts** section.

⊳ Click **Handouts** in the drop-down list of options.

⊳ Click the down arrow next to the **Slides per page** box in the **Handouts** section.

⊳ Click **3** in the drop-down list of options.

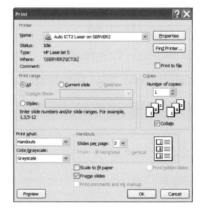

⊳ Click **OK**.

Saving with a new name

Finally we need to save the presentation with a new name.

⊳ Click **File**, and then **Save As...** on the menu bar. The **Save As** dialogue box will appear.

⊳ Double-click the **Unit 5 PT** folder if it is not already selected.

⊳ Type the new name, **wlcinfo1** and click **Save**.

⊳ Close **PowerPoint**.

Task 3   Tables and charts

This task takes you through the steps needed to add tables and charts to a presentation.

Creating a content slide

To get started you need to add a new slide to the presentation between **Slide 1** and **Slide 2**. This slide will have a table in the Object Area giving information about the capacity and cost of rooms in the conference centre.

⊳ Load **PowerPoint**.

⊳ Open your copy of the presentation called **wlcinfo1**.

⊳ Click **Slide 1** in the Outline pane.

⊳ Insert a new blank slide.

To create a table in the Object Area we need to use a different layout for this slide.

▶ Click the **Title and Content** icon in the **Content Layouts** section of the **Slide Layout pane**. An icon will appear in the Object Area with the message **Click icon to add content** underneath.

▶ Click on the text **Click to add title** in the **Title Area**.

▶ Type **CONFERENCE ROOMS**

Creating a table

Next we need to create a table with three columns and six rows in the Object Area of the slide.

Insert Table button

▶ Click the **Insert Table** icon in the centre of the Object Area. The **Insert Table** dialogue box will appear.

▶ Click the small up arrow under **Number of columns:** <u>once</u> to change the number in the box to **3**.

▶ Click the small up arrow under **Number of rows:** until the number in the box is **6**.

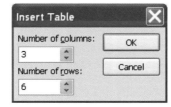

▶ Click **OK**. The table will appear in the Object Area of the slide – it should look like the example below.

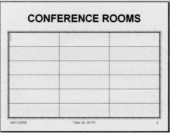

Copying text from a datafile

Now we need to copy and paste the text for this table from a datafile. We'll use Microsoft Excel to view the datafile.

▶ Load **Excel**.

The datafile you need to use is called **rooms**. This file should be in your **My Documents** folder.

Open button

▶ Click **File** on the menu bar, and then click **Open**.

▶ *Or* click the **Open button** on the **Standard** toolbar.

▶ Click the down arrow next to the **Files of type:** box.

191

Scroll down through the drop-down list of options and click **Text Files**.

Click on the file called **rooms**, and then click **Open**. The datafile will be opened.

Highlight cells **A1** to **C6**.

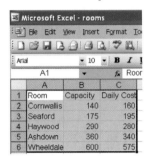

Click the **Copy** button on the **Standard** toolbar.

Close **Excel**.

Highlight the table in the object area of **Slide 2**.

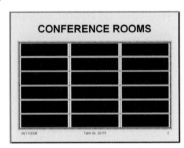

Click **Edit**, and then **Paste Special...** on the menu bar. The **Paste Special** dialogue box will appear.

Click **Unformatted Text** in the box labelled **As:**

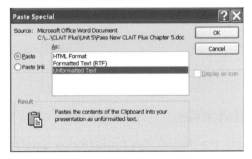

Click **OK**. The text will appear in the table – it should look like the example below.

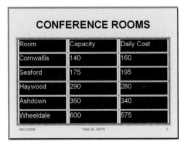

Formatting table text

Now we need to format the text in the table. We'll start by changing the font style and size.

▶ Click the small down arrow on the right of the **Font** box and select the Sans Serif font called **Verdana** from the drop-down list.

▶ Click the small arrow on the right of the **Font Size** box, scroll down the list of available sizes, and select **24**.

Next we'll format the column headings.

▶ Highlight the column headings **Room**, **Capacity** and **Daily Cost**.

Room	Capacity	Daily Cost

▶ Click the **Bold** button on the **Formatting** toolbar.

▶ Click the **Italic** button on the **Formatting** toolbar.

B

Bold button

Next we'll format the columns **Capacity** and **Daily Cost** to be centre aligned.

▶ Highlight the columns **Capacity** and **Daily Cost**.

I

Italic button

Capacity	Daily Cost
140	160
175	195
290	280
360	340
600	575

▶ Click the **Center** button on the **Formatting** toolbar.

Centre button

Formatting table borders

Now we need to format the table borders.

▶ Highlight the table contents.

Room	Capacity	Daily Cost
Cornwallis	140	160
Seaford	175	195
Haywood	290	280
Ashdown	360	340
Wheeldale	600	575

▶ Click **Format**, and then **Table...** on the menu bar. The **Format Table** dialogue box will appear.

▶ Click the small down arrow next to the box labelled **Width:** and select **3 pt** from the drop-down list of options. Click **OK**.

193

Your table should now look like the example below.

Room	Capacity	Daily Cost
Cornwallis	140	160
Seaford	175	195
Haywood	290	280
Ashdown	360	340
Wheeldale	600	575

Inserting an organisation chart

Next we need to add another new slide to the presentation between **Slide 3** and **Slide 4**. This slide will have an Organization Chart in the Object Area giving information about the conference centre event staff.

- Click **Slide 3** in the Outline pane.

- Click **Insert** on the menu bar, and then click **New Slide**.

- Select the **Title and Content** layout for this slide.

- Click on the text **Click to add title** in the **Title Area** and type **EVENT STAFF**

- Click the **Insert Diagram or Organization Chart** icon in the centre of the Object Area. The **Diagram Gallery** dialogue window will appear.

Organization Chart

- Click **Organization Chart** if it is not already selected, then click **OK**. A blank Organization Chart will appear along with the **Organization Chart** toolbar.

- Click in the box at the top of the chart and type **EVENTS COORDINATOR** – don't worry about the text overflowing the box, we'll deal with this shortly.

- Click in the bottom left box on the chart and type **CONCERT MANAGER**

- Click in the bottom centre box on the chart and type **CONFERENCE MANAGER**

- Click the **Fit Text** button on the **Organization Chart** toolbar. Your organisation chart should look like the example below.

Fit Text button

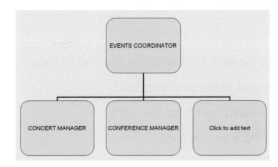

- Click the edge of the bottom right box to select it, and then press the **Backspace** key to delete it.

- Click on the **CONFERENCE MANAGER** box to select it.

- Click the small down arrow next to **Insert Shape** on the **Organization Chart** toolbar.

- Click **Subordinate** in the list of options – a new box will appear underneath the **CONFERENCE MANAGER** box.

- Click in the new box and type **ADMINISTRATION ASSISTANT**

- Click the small down arrow next to **Insert Shape** on the **Organization Chart** toolbar.

- Click **Coworker** in the list of options – a new box will appear alongside the **ADMINISTRATION ASSISTANT** box.

- Click in the new box and type **BOOKING ASSISTANT**

- Select the **CONCERT MANAGER** box.

- Add a **Subordinate** box with the text **ADMINISTRATION ASSISTANT**

- Click the **Fit Text** button on the **Organization Chart** toolbar.

- Click anywhere outside the Organization Chart. **Slide 4** of your presentation should now look like the example below.

Fit Text button

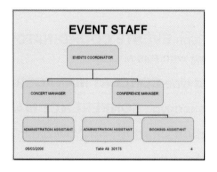

You could be asked to create other types of chart such as **column**, **bar** or **line** – the technique is exactly the same.

Creating charts

Next we need to add a new slide with a pie chart at the end of the presentation.

▶ Insert a new slide at the end of the presentation.

▶ Select the **Title and Content** layout for this slide.

▶ Add the title **EVENT TYPES** to this slide.

Insert Chart icon

▶ Click the **Insert Chart** icon in the centre of the Object Area. A sample chart and small spreadsheet will appear. Some of the icons on the **Standard** toolbar will also change. To get started we need to change the chart type.

▶ Right-click on the chart area outside the actual chart but within the chart boundary.

▶ Select **Chart Type...** from the menu that appears. The **Chart Type** dialogue box will be displayed.

If the Chart Type isn't on your menu, you probably clicked in the wrong place. PowerPoint brings up different menus depending on where you click.

▶ Click **Pie** in the left-hand window of the **Chart Type** dialogue box. You'll be given a choice of different pie charts, but the one already selected is fine so click **OK**.

To create the pie chart you need to add the following information to the spreadsheet:

Conferences	32
Concerts	47
Exhibitions	19
Meetings	84
Private	17

▶ Click in the cell labelled **1st Qtr**, type **Conferences** and press **Enter**.

▶ Work your way along the first row and add the rest of the events shown above.

▶ Click the left scroll bar arrow at the bottom of the window to move back to the start of the spreadsheet.

▶ Click in the cell labelled **East** and press **Delete** to delete this label.

▶ Click in the cell containing the value **20.4** and type **32**

▶ Work your way along the second row and add the rest of the values shown above.

We don't need the remaining rows, so they can be deleted.

▶ Click the row **2** column header to select the whole row.

▶ Press the **Delete** key to delete all the values in this row.

▶ Click column header **B** to select the whole column.

▶ Press the **Delete** key to delete all the values from this column.

▶ Delete all the values in row **3**. The spreadsheet should look like the example below.

		A	B	C	D	E	F
		Conferenc	Concerts	Exhibition	Meetings	Private	
1	Pie 1	32	47	19	84	17	
2							
3							

wlcinfo2 - Datasheet

Formatting a chart

Now we need to format the chart. We'll start by removing the legend and adding labels and percentages to the segments.

▶ Right-click on the chart area outside the actual chart but within the chart boundary.

▶ Select **Chart Options...** from the menu. The **Chart Options** dialogue box will be displayed.

▶ Click the **Legend** tab.

▶ Uncheck the box next to **Show Legend**.

▶ Click the **Data Labels** tab.

▶ Click the check boxes next to **Category name** and **Percentages** in the **Label Contains** section.

▶ Uncheck the box next to **Show leader lines**.

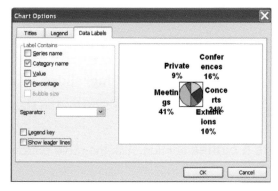

▶ Click **OK**. The chart will reappear.

Now we need to remove the border around the pie chart segments.

- ▶ Right-click in the area between the chart segments and the chart border.

- ▶ Select **Format Plot Area...** from the menu that appears. The **Format Plot Area** dialogue box will be displayed.

- ▶ Click the radio button next to **None** in the **Border** section.

- ▶ Click **OK**.

Finally we need to change the font style and size of the chart text.

- ▶ Use the **Font** box to select the Sans Serif font **Verdana**.

- ▶ Use the **Font Size** to select size **16**.

- ▶ Click on any part of the slide outside the chart area to view the finished pie chart. **Slide 6** of your presentation should now look like the example below.

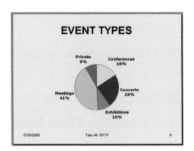

> **TIP**
> Double-click the centre of the chart if you need to return to chart view to make any changes.

 Spelling and Grammar button

- ▶ Now click the **Spelling and Grammar** button on the menu bar.

- ▶ Work through the spellcheck and correct any mistakes.

> **TIP**
> Remember that the spelling and grammar checking facility is not foolproof – sometimes you will need to click the **Ignore** button when a suggested change is *not* required.

Printing individual slides

Now we need to print just slides **2**, **4** and **6** as **individual slides** in **Landscape** orientation.

- ▶ Click **File** on the menu bar, and then click **Page Setup**. The **Page Setup** dialogue box will appear.

- ▶ In the **Notes, handouts & outline** section click the radio button for **Landscape** if it is not already selected.

- ▶ Click **OK**.

- ▶ Click **File** on the menu bar, and then click **Print**. The **Print** dialogue box will appear.

- ▶ Click the radio button next to **Slides** in the **Print range** section and type **2,4,6** in the box.

⊙ Click the down arrow next to the **Print what** box, and then click **Slides** in the drop-down list if it is not already selected.

The options selected in your **Print** dialogue should now be the same as those shown in the example below.

⊙ Click **OK**.

⊙ Click the **Save** button on the Standard toolbar to save the presentation with the new filename **wlcinfo2**.

⊙ Close the presentation and shut **PowerPoint** down.

Task 4 Amending a presentation

This task takes you through the steps needed to edit, hyperlink, hide and delete slides.

⊙ Load **PowerPoint**.

⊙ Open your copy of the presentation called **wlcinfo2**.

Deleting a bullet

First we need to delete the last bullet on **Slide 1**.

⊙ Click **Slide 1** in the Outline pane.

⊙ Click the last bullet **Beautiful location** <u>three</u> times to highlight it. Don't worry if the image seems to disappear – it is still there!

> • Superb facilities
> • Beautiful location

⊙ Press **Delete** to remove the text and the bullet character.

⊙ Click on any blank area of the slide outside the Object Area. **Slide 1** of your presentation should now look like the example below.

Adding bullets

Now we need to add two new bullets to **Slide 1**.

▶ Click at the end of the last bullet **Superb facilities** and press **Enter** to create a new bullet.

▶ Type **Close to the city** and press **Enter**.

▶ Type **Hotels nearby**

▶ Click on any blank area of the slide outside the Object Area. **Slide 1** of your presentation should now look like the example below.

Hiding slides

Slide 6 contains information that could be useful to competitors. This slide needs to be hidden so that it will not automatically appear when the presentation is running.

▶ Click **Slide 6** in the Outline pane.

▶ Click **Slide Show** on the menu bar, and then click **Hide Slide**. A box with a diagonal line through it will appear over the slide number indicating the slide will be hidden when the presentation is viewed.

Creating a hyperlink action button

Next we need to create a hyperlink action button on **Slide 3** that will jump to and display the hidden slide when it is clicked.

Click **Slide 3** in the Outline pane.

Click **Slide Show** on the menu bar, and then click **Action Buttons**. A pop up menu showing available action buttons will appear.

Click the first icon for **Custom** action button. The pointer will change to a thin cross shape.

Position the pointer in the bottom right area of the slide approximately level with the last bullet.

Click and hold the left mouse button.

Drag down and across towards the bottom left corner of the slide. As you drag a dotted line will show you how big the action button will be when you let go of the mouse button. When the action button is roughly the same size as the one shown in the example below, let go of the mouse button.

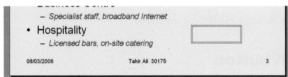

The **Action Settings** dialogue window will appear.

Click the radio button next to **Hyperlink to:** The slide we want this button to link to is not the next slide so we need to change the default option of **Next Slide**.

Click the small down arrow on the right of the box underneath **Hyperlink to:**

Scroll down the list and click **Slide...** The **Hyperlink to Slide** dialogue box will appear.

Click **(6) EVENT TYPES**, then click **OK**.

Taking a screen print

At this point you need to take a screen print as evidence that the action button on **Slide 3** has been linked to **Slide 6**.

Press **PrtSc** to take a screen print of the Action Settings for the button.

▶ Load **Word** and create a new blank document.

▶ Click the **Paste** button on the **Standard** toolbar. The screen print will appear – it should look like the example below.

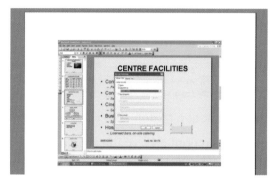

▶ Press **Ctrl**, **Shift** and **Enter** to create a second page in the document – this will be used for another screen print later on.

▶ Save the document in your **Unit 5 PT** folder with the filename **screenprints**.

▶ Click the **PowerPoint** icon at the bottom of the screen. 🔲 Microsoft Power...

▶ Click **OK** to close the Action Settings window.

Labelling an action button

Next we need to label the action button with some text to indicate what information will be displayed when it is clicked.

▶ Right click the action button and select **Add Text** from the pop up menu.

▶ Type **Event Bookings**, and then click away from the action button which should now look like the example below.

> **TIP**
>
> Use the side sizing handles to resize an action button if a label text doesn't fit. Use the **Previous** or **Next** action button types to link to adjacent slides – these don't need labelling.

Testing a hyperlink button

Now we need to test the hyperlink action button to make sure that **Slide 6** is displayed only when the button is clicked.

▶ Click **Slide 3** in the Outline pane.

Slide Show button

▶ Click the **Slide Show** button in the bottom left corner of the screen. The presentation will start at **Slide 3**.

▶ Click or press the **Space bar** to move to the next slide.

▷ Work your way through the presentation – don't click the hyperlink action button on **Slide 3** – the presentation should end at **Slide 5** titled **LOCATION**.

▷ Click to exit the presentation.

▷ Run the presentation from **Slide 3** again – this time click the hyperlink action button on **Slide 3** – the presentation should jump to the hidden **Slide 6** and then end.

Deleting a slide

Next we need to delete **Slide 5** titled **LOCATION** because most of this information has now been added to **Slide 1**.

▷ Right click **Slide 5** in the Outline pane.

▷ Select **Delete Slide** from the pop up menu. The slide will disappear.

Moving a slide

Next we need to move **Slide 2** so that it becomes **Slide 3**.

▷ Click the **Slide Sorter View** icon on the bottom left of the screen. All the slides will be shown in number order as a series of thumbnail images.

Slide Sorter View button

▷ Click on **Slide 2** and hold down the left mouse button.

▷ Drag to the right so that a vertical grey line appears after **Slide 3**. The slides in your presentation should now be in the same order as the example below.

Adding animation effects

PowerPoint allows you to add animation effects to objects such as images, charts and bulleted lists. The most straightforward way to do this is by using the **Slide Design pane** in **Slide Sorter View**. We're going to set some animation effects on **Slide 1** and **Slide 2**.

▷ Click **View, Task pane** on the menu bar if the Task pane isn't already visible.

▷ Click the small down arrow at the top of the Task pane, and then select **Slide Design – Animation Schemes** from the list of options.

▷ Click **Slide 1**.

▷ Click to select an animation effect from the **Slide Design pane**.

> **TIP**
>
> You can use any animation effect you like on a slide unless a specific effect is specified in an assignment. If you don't like an effect, just click another one. Click **No Animation** in the **Slide Design pane** to remove all animation effects from a slide.

▷ Click **Slide 2** and add an animation effect to this slide.

> **TIP**
>
> A symbol with a star will appear under a slide once an animation effect has been set. Clicking this symbol will preview the animation.

Taking another screen print

At this point you need to take another screen print as evidence that a slide has been hidden, animations set and the order of the slides changed.

▷ Press **PrtSc** to take a screen print of **Slide Sorter view**.

▷ Click the **Word** icon at the bottom of the screen. 　📄 screenprints - Mi...

▷ Click the **Paste** button on the **Standard** toolbar. The screen print will appear.

TIP

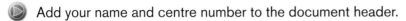 Add your name and centre number to the document header.

 Press **Ctrl**, **Shift** and **Enter** to create another page in the document – this will be used for another screen print in the next task.

The steps to add a document header are described in **Chapter 1** on page **27**.

 Save the document keeping the filename **screenprints**.

Adding speaker's notes

Speaker's notes containing additional information about slides can be added to a presentation to prompt the presenter. These notes are visible only to the presenter, not the audience, either on screen or printed out. We're going to copy and paste some speaker's notes from a text file into **Slide 1** of this presentation.

 Open the text file called **location** which should be in your **My Documents** folder.

Click **Ctrl** and **A** to select all the text.

Click the **Copy** button on the **Standard** toolbar.

Close **Word**.

Click the **PowerPoint** icon at the bottom of the screen if your presentation does not reappear.

Click **Slide 1**.

Click **View** on the menu bar, and then click **Notes Page**.

Click in the notes area underneath the slide labelled **Click to add text**.

Click the **Paste** button on the **Standard** toolbar. The text will appear in the notes area.

TIP

To view speaker's notes on screen, right-click the mouse when you're in Slide Show mode and select **Screen** and then **Speaker Notes**.

Now we need to change the font style and size of the notes text.

Click **Ctrl** and **A** to select all the text in the notes area.

Use the **Font** box to select the Sans Serif font **Verdana**.

Use the **Font Size** to select size **16**.

Printing notes pages

Next we need to print just this slide with the speaker's notes visible in **Portrait** orientation.

Click **File** on the menu bar, and then click **Page Setup**.

In the **Notes, handouts & outline** section click the radio button for **Portrait** if it is not already selected.

Click **OK**.

Click **File** on the menu bar, and then click **Print**. The **Print** dialogue box will appear.

Click the radio button next to **Slides** in the **Print range** section and type **1** in the box.

Click the down arrow next to the **Print what** box, and then click **Notes pages** in the drop-down list.

Click **OK**.

Save the presentation with the new filename **wlcinfo3**

Close the presentation and shut **PowerPoint** down.

Task 5   Creating a timed presentation

This task describes how to create a timed presentation for the White Lake Conference Centre.

Load **PowerPoint**.

Create a **Blank presentation** with a **Title Slide** layout in **Landscape** orientation.

Create two more slides with a **Title Slide** layout.

Using a background graphic

This presentation needs to have a graphic image as the background on all the slides. The image you need to use is called **meeting** – it should be in your **My Documents** folder.

Click **View, Master, Slide Master** on the menu bar to open the master slide.

Click **Format** and **Background...** on the menu bar. The **Background** dialogue box will appear.

Click the small down arrow underneath **Background fill**.

Select **Fill Effects...** from the list of options.

🔘 Click the **Picture** tab.

🔘 Click the **Select Picture...** button. The **Select Picture** dialogue window will appear.

🔘 Click **My Documents**.

🔘 Click the file called **meeting**, and then click **Insert**. A preview of the picture will appear.

🔘 Click **OK**. The **Background** dialogue box will reappear.

🔘 Click the **Apply to All** button.

🔘 Close **Master View**. The three slides of the presentation should now have the same background image like the example below.

Adding text to slides

Now we need to add some text to the slides.

🔘 Click **Slide 1** in the outline pane.

🔘 Click on the text **Click to add title** in the **Title Area**.

Type **White Lake Conference Centre**

Click on the text **Click to add subtitle** in the **Object Area**.

Type **Conferences, Concerts, Exhibitions**

Add the text shown below to the remaining slides.

Slide	Title	Subtitle
2	White Lake Conference Centre	Contact *(insert your name)*
3	White Lake Conference Centre	08900 809800

Spelling and Grammar button

Click the **Spelling and Grammar** button on the menu bar.

Work through the spellcheck and correct any mistakes. Your presentation should look like the example below.

1   2   3

Setting transitions and timings

Transitions change the way a slide opens. You can make the next slide open like a blind or a curtain, for example. Slide timings specify how long a slide will be displayed before the next slide appears. All the commands you need to create transitions and timings are in the **Slide Transition** Task pane.

Click the **Slide Show, Slide Transition** on the menu bar. If the Task pane is already visible you can bring up the **Slide Transition** options by clicking the small down arrow at the top of the Task pane, then clicking **Slide Transition** from the menu that appears.

Click **Slide 1** in the Outline pane.

Click to select a transition effect from the **Slide Transition** pane.

Click the check box next to **On mouse click** in the Task pane to deselect this option.

Click the check box next to **Automatically after** and then click the small up arrow until **00:05** is displayed in the box.

Click the **Apply to All Slides** button.

TIP

You can use any transition effect you like on a slide unless a specific effect is specified in an assignment. You can also apply a different transition to each slide – if you do this take care to make sure the specified slide timings are also set on each slide.

Taking a screen print

Next you need to take another screen print as evidence that the specified transitions and timings have been set on all the slides. We'll put this screen print in the **screenprints** document that you created earlier.

- Switch to **Slide Sorter View** and then press **PrtSc** to take a screen print.
- Load **Word** and open your copy of the document called **screenprints**.
- Press **Ctrl** and **End** to move to the end of the document.
- Click the **Paste** button on the **Standard** toolbar. The screen print will appear – it should look like the example below.

Slide Sorter View

- Press **Ctrl**, **Shift** and **Enter** to create another page in the document – this will be used for another screen later.
- Save the document keeping the filename **screenprints**.

Saving as an automatic slideshow

Next you need to save the presentation in a format that will allow it to be viewed as a self-contained automatic slideshow on computers where **PowerPoint** hasn't been installed. Presentations saved in this way can be either written directly onto a CD or saved to a subfolder on your computer. In this example we'll save the presentation in a subfolder.

- Click the **File, Package for CD** on the menu bar. The **Package for CD** dialogue window will appear.
- Click the **Copy to Folder...** button.
- Type **confcontact** in the box labelled **Folder name:**
- Click the **Browse** button and double-click the **Unit 5 PT** folder in your **My Documents** folder.

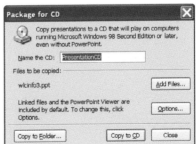

209

▶ Click the **Select** button.

▶ Click **OK**. The presentation will be packaged into a new subfolder called **confcontact**.

▶ Click **Close**.

Next you need to take another screen print as evidence that the presentation has been packaged.

▶ Click **Start, My Documents** and then double-click the **Unit 5 PT** folder.

▶ Double-click the **confcontact** folder.

▶ Take a screen print of the folder's contents and paste it into your **screenprints** document.

▶ Print a copy of the **screenprints** document and close **Word**.

▶ Print the complete presentation as **handouts** in **Portrait** orientation with **3** slides to a page.

▶ Save the presentation with the filename **info** and close **PowerPoint**.

That's the end of the practice tasks. Now try the full New CLAiT Plus assignment that follows.

Practice assignment

Scenario

You are an office assistant at Crossways High School. You have been asked to produce two presentations that will be used to promote the school.

To produce the presentations you will need the following files:

FILENAME	FILETYPE
school	image file
artbg	image file
schinfo	text file
intro	text file
results	datafile

Assessment Objectives

TASK 1

In this task you will prepare a master slide for a presentation that will be used to show to parents looking for a school for their children.

1a
4d

1 a) Select a slide layout that will enable you to enter a title and two levels of bulleted text on each slide.

   b) Set the slide orientation for the master slide to be **portrait**.

1b
1d

2 Set up the master slide as follows:

Background	White
Text for all slides	sans serif (e.g. Arial, Gill Sans, Tahoma)

Item	Font Size	Detail
Header	small	your name and centre number
Footer	small	automatic date – any English format (day, month, year) Slide number to be displayed on all slides

Item	Font Size	Enhancement
Slide headings	large	bold
First level bullet	medium	bold and italic to include a bullet character
Second level bullet	smaller than first level bullets (legible)	to include a bullet character

4a

3 Save the presentation as **crossmast**

Assessment Objectives	**TASK 2**
	Before you begin this task ensure that you have the following files:
	crossmast (that you created in Task 1) **schinfo** **school**
2a 2k	1 a) Using the file **crossmast** check that the layout for the first slide will enable you to enter a title and bulleted list.
	b) Open the text file called **schinfo**.
	Note: In the text file the words, **Slide 1**, **2** etc, **Heading** and **Bullets** are included to show the position of the text on each slide and should **NOT** be included in the presentation.
	c) Copy the prepared text on to the correct slides as indicated in the text file.
	d) Ensure that the formatting of the master slide is applied to all slides.
2d 2e 2f	2 On **Slide 1** titled **CROSSWAYS HIGH SCHOOL**:
	a) insert the image **school**
	b) position the image below the final bullet **Close to the M73**
	c) resize the image maintaining the original proportions. Ensure the image does not touch or overlap any text.
1b	3 On **Slide 2** titled **College Facilities** demote the following bullets to second level:
	Wireless network access **Data Projectors and Interactive Whiteboards** **Swimming Pool** **Multi-gym**
1b 2b	4 On **Slide 2** titled **College Facilities** below the bullet text **Multi-gym** add the following as a second level bullet:
	Sauna
2j	5 Replace the **two** instances of the word **College** with **School**. Maintain the use of case.
4f	6 Print the slides as handouts, 3 to a page.
4a	7 Save the presentation using the filename **crossinf1**

Assessment Objectives	**TASK 3**
	Before you begin this task ensure you have the following files:
	crossinf1 (that you saved in Task 2) **results**
	Some slides need to be added to the presentation. When keying in data ensure that you use upper and lower case as shown.

1a	1	a)	Insert a new slide as **Slide 3**.
1b		b)	Use a slide layout for Slide 3 that will enable you to import data from a
2b			spreadsheet and display it as a table.
2i		c)	Insert the slide heading **GCSE Results**.
2k		d)	Open the datafile **results**.
4a		e)	Insert the information from this file into Slide 3 as a 4 column, 6 row table.
		f)	Display the table showing all borders.
		g)	Format the entire table to be in a sans serif font (e.g. Arial, Gill Sans).
		h)	Format the column headings **Grade**, **%Boys**, **%Girls**, **Combined** to be italic.
		i)	Format all of the columns to be centre-aligned.
		j)	Use any legible font size.
		k)	Ensure all data is displayed in full and that words are not split.
		l)	Save the presentation using the filename **crossinf2**
1b	2	a)	Insert a new slide as **Slide 2**.
2b		b)	Use a slide layout for Slide 2 that will enable you to create an organisation chart
2h			on the slide.
2k		c)	Insert the slide heading **Leadership Team**
		d)	Add the following organisation chart:

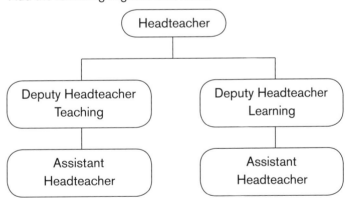

		e)	Format the entire organisation chart to be in a sans serif font (e.g. Arial, Gill Sans).
		f)	Use any legible font size.
		g)	Ensure the text inside the boxes is displayed in full and that words are not split.
1b	3	a)	Insert a new slide as **Slide 5**.
2b		b)	Use a slide layout for Slide 5 that will enable you to create a chart on the slide.
2g		c)	Insert the slide heading **Parental Survey Results**
2k		d)	Use the following data to create a pie chart on Slide 5:

Excellent   61
Good   19
Average   12
Dissatisfied   8

	e)	Display data labels and percentages next to the sectors.
	f)	Do not display a legend.
	g)	Format the entire chart to be in a sans serif font.
	h)	Use any legible font size.
	i)	Ensure the labels and percentages are fully displayed and that words are not split.
2b	4 a)	Spell check your presentation and review your work to ensure all amendments have been made.
4a		
4e	b)	Save your presentation keeping the filename **crossinf2**.
	c)	Print a copy of the following slides as individual slides:

Slide 1 titled **CROSSWAYS HIGH SCHOOL**
Slide 3 titled **School Facilities**
Slide 6 titled **Location**

Assessment Objectives

TASK 4

Before you begin this task ensure you have the following file:

crossinf2 (that you saved in Task 3).

Some amendments need to be made to the presentation to make it suitable for viewing by a variety of audiences.

2l	1	On **Slide 1** titled **CROSSWAYS HIGH SCHOOL**:
	a)	Delete the entire fourth bullet point **Close to the M73**.
	b)	Ensure the bullet character and the line space is also deleted.
3e	2	Hide **Slide 5** titled **Parental Survey Results**.
3f	3	You are going to create a hyperlink to link Slide 4 to Slide 5 and will need to produce a screen print as evidence that this has been done.
		On **Slide 4** titled **GCSE Results**:
	a)	create a hyperlink action button to link **Slide 4** to **Slide 5** titled **Parental Survey Results**
	b)	take a screen print as evidence that the action button on Slide 4 has been linked to Slide 5 Parental Survey Results. Save this screen print for printing later
	c)	ensure the button does not overlap any text or lines
	d)	test the hyperlink to ensure that slide 5 is displayed only when the hyperlink button on Slide 4 is selected.
2k	4	Delete **Slide 6** titled **Location**.
3d	5	Move **Slide 2** titled **Leadership Team** so that it becomes **Slide 3**.
3a	6 a)	Set an animation on Slides 1 and 2.
4h	b)	Take a single screen print to show evidence of the:

hidden slide
hyperlink action button
animations set on Slides 1 and 2
order of slides.

	c)	Ensure the screen print clearly displays all the above.
	d)	You may paste the screen print on the same page as your previous screen print.
	e)	Ensure your name and centre number are displayed on the screen print document(s).
	f)	Print this screen print and the screen print saved at Step 3b.

2b

4g

7　Add speaker's notes to **Slide 1** titled **CROSSWAYS HIGH SCHOOL**.

    a)　Open the text file **intro**.

    b)　Copy the entire text file into the notes page of **Slide 1**.

    c)　Format the text to be in a sans serif font (e.g. Arial, Gill Sans).

    d)　Format the text size to be medium.

    e)　Print **Slide 1** titled **CROSSWAYS HIGH SCHOOL** with speaker's notes.

4a

4c

8　a)　Save your presentation using the filename **crossinf3**

    b)　Close the presentation.

Assessment Objectives

TASK 5

Before you begin this task ensure you have the image **artbg**.

In this task you will create a 3-slide presentation that will be displayed on computer screens.

1a

4d

1　a)　Open your presentation software.

    b)　Create a new presentation.

    c)　Select a Title Slide layout. This layout must be used for all three slides.

    d)　Set the slide orientation to be landscape.

1c

2d

2e

2f

2b

2c

2k

You may use any legible font type and size for all the slides in this presentation.

2　a)　On the master slide, insert the graphic **artbg** as a background for all slides.

    b)　Size this graphic to fill the background.

3　a)　Enter the test on the three title slides as shown below. The heading should be entered on Slide 1 and copied onto Slides 2 and 3.

Slide	Title	Sub-title
1	**Crossways High School**	**Specialist Technology School**
2	**Crossways High School**	**Contact** (insert your name)
3	**Crossways High School**	**01392 231922**

    b)　Spellcheck the presentation.

    c)　Ensure that you have used a consistent layout for all three slides.

3b

3c

4   a)   Set the timings and transitions as follows:

Timings	6 seconds on all slides
Transitions	1 transition on each slide

b)   Take a screen print as evidence that the transitions and timings have been set on all slides.

c)   Ensure the timings and transitions can be clearly seen on the screen print.

d)   Save the screen print for printing later.

4f

5   Print the presentation as handouts, 3 to a page. Ensure the background for each slide is visible on this printout.

6   a)   Save the presentation in a format that will allow it to be viewed as an automatic slideshow, using the filename **crosspres**

b)   Take a screen print as evidence that the file has been saved in this format.

c)   You may paste the screen print on the same page as your previous screen print.

d)   Ensure your name and centre number are displayed on the screen print document(s).

e)   Print this screen print and the screen print saved at step 4d.

4c

7   Close the presentation.

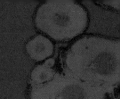

To pass this unit you must be able to:

- ✓ create artwork incorporating text and images in layers

- ✓ edit and retouch scanned images

- ✓ use a variety of graphic effects

- ✓ create a variety of graphic effects

- ✓ prepare artwork for print/electronic publishing.

Before you start this chapter, you or your tutor should download a zipped file called **Resources for Chapter 6** from **www.payne-gallway.co.uk/claitplus**. It will automatically unzip. Specify that the contents are to be saved in your **My Documents** folder.

The practice tasks that follow cover all the techniques you need to learn in order to pass a New CLAiT Plus Unit 6 E-IMAGE MANIPULATION assignment.

Practice tasks

Task 1   Editing an image

Scenario

You're working in the Design Department of a travel company specialising in wilderness adventure holidays. You've been asked to produce some artwork for a poster and an animation for the company's website that will be used to promote a new canyon trekking holiday.

TIP

The steps you need to follow to create a subfolder are described in **Chapter 1** on page **5**.

- ▶ Create a subfolder called **Unit 6 PT** in your **My Documents** folder or network home directory folder where files created as you work through these practice tasks can be stored.

This task describes how to edit an image that will be used to create the poster.

To get started you need to load **Adobe Photoshop**. This can be done in one of two ways:

- ▶ *either* double-click the **Adobe Photoshop** icon on the main screen in Windows,

- ▶ *or* click the **Start** button at the bottom left of the screen, then click **All Programs**, **Adobe Photoshop**.

Adobe Photoshop has been used in this chapter because the photo editing tools supplied with Microsoft Office don't offer all the functions needed to meet the requirements of CLAiT Plus Unit 6. Version CS2 of Photoshop has been used throughout the chapter. Your tutor will need to let you know about any differences in the techniques described here if you're using a different version of Photoshop.

The main **Photoshop** window will be displayed – it should look something like the example below with the **toolbox** on the left of the screen.

If the toolbox isn't visible click **Window** and **Tools** on the menu bar.

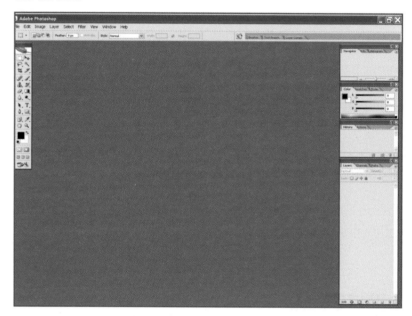

Opening an image

The image you need to edit is called **canyon**. This file should be in your **My Documents** folder.

- Click **File** on the menu bar, and then click **Open**.
- Click the down arrow next to the **All Formats box** if it is not already selected.
- Click on the file called **canyon**, and then click **Open**. The image will be opened and it should look like the example below.

Adjusting colours, contrast and brightness

Next we need to adjust the colours, contrast and brightness in the image.

⊙ Click **Image, Adjustments** on the menu bar, and then click **Auto Levels**. Your image should look now look like the example below.

Removing scratches

Next we need to remove the scratches in the top left-hand corner of the image.

⊙ Click the **Zoom** tool on the toolbox. The pointer will change shape into a magnifying glass when you hold it over the image.

Zoom tool

219

▷ Position the pointer in the top left corner of the image just above the scratches.

▷ Click and hold the left mouse button and drag down and across to the right.

▷ Let go of the mouse button when the scratched area of the image is completely surrounded by a dashed outline.

Now that the scratched area of the image can be seen in more detail we can select the area that needs to be treated.

Lasso tool

▷ Click the **Lasso** tool on the toolbox. The pointer will change shape into a lasso when you hold it over the image.

▷ Position the pointer in the top left corner of the image just above the scratches.

▷ Click and hold the left mouse button and drag to the right. A thin line will appear as you drag – work your way around the scratched area back to the point where you started.

▷ Let go of the mouse button. The line around the scratched area will change into a flashing dashed line.

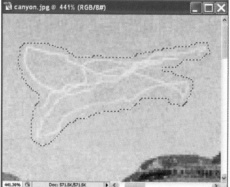

▷ Click **Filter, Noise** on the menu bar, and then click **Dust & Scratches...** The **Dust & Scratches** dialogue box will appear.

▷ Click in the **Radius:** box, type **10** and then click **OK**. The scratches will disappear – this area of your image should now look like the example below.

TIP

Try changing the value in the **Radius:** box if all of the dust and scratches in a selected area are not completely removed.

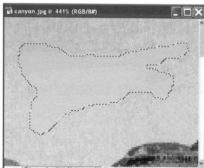

- Right click anywhere inside the selected area, and then click **Deselect** on the pop up menu to remove the selection.

- Click **View** on the menu bar, and then click **Actual Pixels** to return to a full view of the image.

Removing an unwanted object

Next we need to remove the hiker from the bottom left corner of the image. We'll start by selecting the area that needs to be replaced.

- Use the **Zoom** tool to view the area of the image containing the hiker in more detail.

- Use the **Lasso** tool to outline the hiker.

- Press the **Del** or **Backspace** key to remove the selection containing the hiker. The hiker will disappear – this area of your image should now look like the example below.

- Right click anywhere inside the selected area, and then click **Deselect** on the pop up menu to remove the selection.

Replacing the background

Now we need to replace the blank area of the image with a background to match the surrounding area.

▶ Use the **Zoom** tool to view the top of the empty section in more detail.

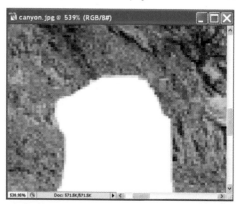

▶ Use the **Lasso** tool to outline a section of the image just to the top left of the empty section.

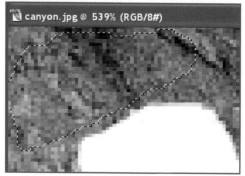

▶ Position the pointer anywhere inside the selected area.

▶ Press and hold the **Ctrl** and **Alt** keys and then click and hold the left mouse button. Drag to the right. A copy of the selected area will move with the pointer.

▶ Position the copied selection over the top portion of the empty section.

▶ Use the scroll bar on the right of the image window to move down and view more of the empty section.

▶ Select another section of the image next to the empty section and use the same technique to replace another blank area. Carry on like this until all of the blank area has been replaced.

▶ Click **View** on the menu bar, and then click **Actual Pixels** to return to a full view of the image. Your image should now look something like the example below.

Printing and saving

Finally we need to print the edited image in colour before saving it and closing **Photoshop**.

 Click **File** on the menu bar, and then click **Print**. The **Print** dialogue box will appear.

 Click the small down arrow next to **Name** in the **Printer** section.

A list of available printers will appear. At this stage you need to select a suitable colour printer from the list of available printers. Your tutor will tell you which printer to choose.

 Click on the name of the printer you want to use.

 Click **OK.**

> **TIP**
>
> When you're asked to print in colour make sure that a suitable colour printer is available. It is not acceptable to print in black and white unless you are specifically instructed to do so.

Finally we'll save the image keeping the name **canyon**.

 Click **File** on the menu bar, and then click **Save**.

 Click **File** on the menu bar, and then click **Exit**, or click **(x)** in the top-right hand corner of the screen to close **Photoshop**.

Task 2   Combining text and images

This task will take you through the steps needed to begin creating a poster to match the Layout Sketch shown below.

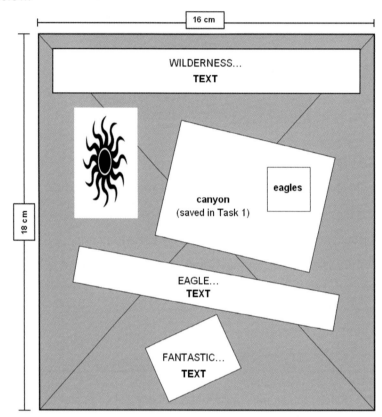

Setting canvas size and resolution

To get started we need to create a new **Photoshop** file and set the canvas size and resolution as specified in the Layout Sketch. The **resolution** determines the number of pixels or coloured dots that make up an image. High resolution images give much better print quality than low resolution images but they take up much more disk storage space. Typical resolution for printed artwork starts around 150 ppi (pixels per inch) going up to 300 ppi or higher where very high quality photographs need to be reproduced.

- ▶ Load **Photoshop**.

- ▶ Click **File** on the menu bar, and then click **New**. The **New** dialogue box will appear.

- ▶ A default file name, something like **Untitled-1,** will be highlighted in the box labelled **Name:** Type the new name **canpost**

- ▶ Click the small down arrow on the second box next to **Width:** and select **cm** from the drop-down list.

- ▶ Double-click in the first box next to **Width:** and type **16**.

▶ Double-click in the first box next to **Height:** and type **18**

▶ Double-click in the first box next to **Resolution:** and type **200**

▶ Click the small down arrow on the box next to **Background Contents:** and select **Transparent** from the drop-down list.

TIP

If you're asked to use an edited image as the background for a new piece of artwork, open the image and click **Image, Image Size…** to open the **Image Size** dialogue box. If the **width** and **height** settings don't match those specified, click the check box next to **Constrain Proportions** and enter the new values. Set the resolution, and then click **OK**.

Taking a screen print

At this point you need to take a screen print as evidence that the canvas size and resolution have been set as specified in the Layout Sketch.

▶ Load **Word** and create a new blank document.

Next you need to insert a **header** that contains your name and centre number.

▶ Click **View** on the menu bar, and then click **Header and Footer**.

▶ Type **your name (first name and last name)** and **centre number** in the header section. You'll need to ask your tutor for the correct centre number.

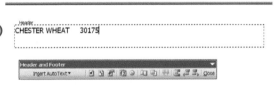

▶ Click the **Close** button on the **Header and Footer** toolbox.

▶ Press **PrtSc** to take a screen print of the **New** dialogue box.

▶ Click the **Paste** button on the **Standard** toolbox. The screen print will appear – it should look like the example below.

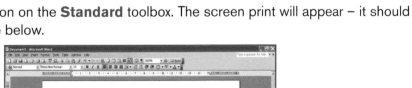

Close

Close button

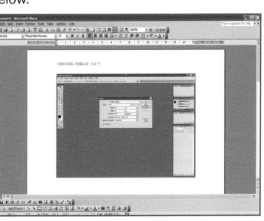

- Click anywhere on empty space to the right of the image.

- Press **Ctrl**, **Shift** and **Enter** to create a second page in the document – this will be used for another screen print later on.

- Save the document in your **Unit 6 PT** folder with the filename **screenprints**

- Click the **Photoshop** icon at the bottom of the screen. 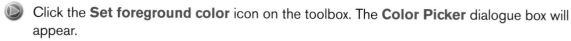 Adobe Photoshop

- Click **OK** to close the **New** dialogue box.

Filling the background

Next we need to fill the background of the artwork with colour. The fill colour needs to be a gradient changing from red in the top left corner of the page to yellow in the bottom right corner of the page.

Maximize icon

- Click the **Maximize** icon to view the artwork as a full page.

Now we need to choose a foreground colour. This will be the starting colour for the fill.

Set foreground
color icon

- Click the **Set foreground color** icon on the toolbox. The **Color Picker** dialogue box will appear.

- Click in the box next to the radio button labelled **R:** if the value **0** is not already highlighted, and then type **255**. This will highlight plain red in the box labelled **Select foreground color**.

- Click **OK**.

Next we need to choose a background colour. This will be the end colour for the fill.

Set background
color icon

- Click the **Set background color** icon on the toolbox. The **Color Picker** dialogue box will reappear.

- Click a shade of yellow in the box labelled **Select background color**.

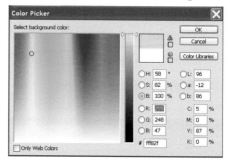

- Click **OK**.

Now we can apply the gradient fill to the background.

Paint Bucket
Tool icon

- Click and hold the **Paint Bucket Tool** icon on the toolbox, and then click **Gradient Tool** in the pop up list.

If you can't see the **Paint Bucket Tool**, the **Gradient Tool** will be displayed on the toolbar – this toolbar button 'toggles' between the **Paint Bucket** and **Gradient** tools when you click and hold it.

Linear Gradient
button

▶ Click the **Linear Gradient** button on the toolbox at the top of the screen if it is not already selected.

▶ Position the pointer – this will be a thin cross – in the top left corner of the page, and then hold down the left mouse button.

▶ Drag down and across to the bottom right corner of the page. A line will appear as you drag, and then let go of the mouse button. The gradient fill will be applied to the background. Your artwork should now look something like the example below.

To use a solid background colour choose a colour using the **Set foreground color** icon then select the **Paint Bucket Tool** and click anywhere on the page.

Importing an image

Artwork created in Photoshop consists of **layers**. Each layer can contain different images, text or effects. Layers are stacked on top of one another to build up a complete piece of artwork. The main advantage of using layers is that the individual components can be edited without affecting the others. So far our artwork has just one *background* layer containing the gradient fill. Next we need to import the **canyon** image on a new layer.

▶ Click **File** on the menu bar, and then click **Place…** The **Place** dialogue box will appear.

The **canyon** image was saved in the **Unit 6 PT** subfolder inside your **My Documents** folder.

▶ Double-click the **Unit 6 PT** folder if its contents are not already visible.

▶ Click the file called **canyon**, and then click **Place**. The image will appear in the centre of the artwork. A new layer called *canyon* will also appear in the **Layers panel** on the right of the **Photoshop** window.

Photoshop automatically creates new layers when images or text are added to artwork. When you're asked to create a new layer during a Unit 6 assignment just carry on and insert the required text or image.

Positioning and resizing an image

Next we need to position the **canyon** image as shown on the Layout Sketch.

▶ Position the pointer over the image and then click and hold the left mouse button.

▶ Drag towards the top right corner of the artwork – let go of the mouse button when the image is in approximately the same position as the example below.

227

▶ Click the right mouse button and select **Place** from the pop up menu or press **Enter**.

Move tool

▶ Click the **Move Tool** on the toolbox. Square sizing handles will appear around the edges of the image.

Next we need to resize the image so that it is approximately the same size as shown on the Layout Sketch.

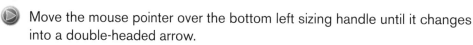

▶ Move the mouse pointer over the bottom left sizing handle until it changes into a double-headed arrow.

▶ Click and hold the left mouse button.

▶ Drag down towards the bottom left corner of the artwork. The image will increase in size as you drag. Let go of the mouse button when the image is approximately the same size as the example below.

Move tool

TIP

To reposition an object after placing, click the layer containing the object on the layer panel, and then select the **Move Tool** on the toolbox. Click anywhere on the object, hold the left mouse button, drag the object into position and then let go of the mouse button.

Rotating an image

Next we need to rotate the image to approximately the same angle as shown on the Layout Sketch.

Move tool

▶ Click the **Move Tool** icon on the toolbox if it is not already selected.

▶ Position the pointer just above the sizing handle on the top right corner of the image.

Angle

▶ Click and hold the left mouse button when the pointer changes into a curved arrow with two heads.

▶ Drag towards the bottom of the artwork. Let go of the mouse button when the image is at approximately the same angle as the example below.

> **TIP**
>
> The angle of rotation will be displayed in the **Rotate** box on the toolbox at the top of the screen when an object is rotated by hand. To rotate an object by an exact angle just click inside this box and type the angle you need.

▶ Click the right mouse button and select **Place** from the pop up menu or press **Enter** to place the image again.

Setting layer opacity

The **opacity** of a layer determines how much of the layer underneath will be seen. As the opacity of a layer is increased it becomes more transparent revealing more of the layer underneath. Next we need to insert the **eagles** image and then reduce the layer opacity so that the rocks in the **canyon** image underneath can be seen.

▶ Click **File** on the menu bar, and then click **Place...** The **Place** dialogue box will appear.

The **eagles** image should already be in your **My Documents** folder.

▶ Click the **My Documents** icon on the left of the dialogue box.

▶ Click the file called **eagles**, and then click **Place**. The image will appear in the centre of the artwork.

▶ Position and resize the image over the **canyon** image to match the example below.

229

Now we're ready to set the **opacity** of the new *eagles* layer to **60%**.

▶ Click the **eagles** layer in the **Layers Panel** if it is not already highlighted blue.

▶ Double click in the box labelled **Opacity:** in the **Layers Panel** and type **60**. The layer opacity will be reduced revealing more of the rocks in the **canyon** image underneath.

> **TIP**
>
> If you need to make a layer completely transparent set the **layer opacity** to **100%**

▶ Press **PrtSc** to take a screen print of the opacity setting for this layer.

▶ Click the **Word** icon at the bottom of the screen.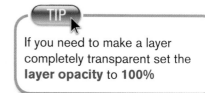

▶ Click the **Paste** button on the **Standard** toolbox. The screen print will appear.

▶ Press **Ctrl**, **Shift** and **Enter** to create another page in the document – this will be used for another screen print in the next task.

▶ Save the document keeping the filename **screenprints**.

▶ Close **Word**.

Adding and formatting text

Next we need to add the text shown at the bottom of the Layout Sketch in the box labelled **FANTASTIC...**

Text tool

▶ Click the **Text Tool** icon on the toolbox.

▶ Click anywhere in the lower half of the artwork underneath the **canyon** image – a new text layer will be created automatically.

▶ Enter the following text:

FANTASTIC TWO WEEK TOUR
Horse Riding
White Water Rafting
Flying

▶ Press **Ctrl** and **A** to highlight all the text.

Now we can format the text using the formatting tools at the top of the screen.

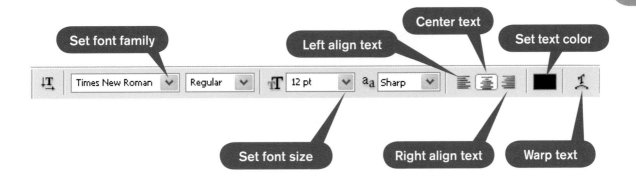

Set font family

Left align text

Center text

Set text color

Times New Roman | Regular | 12 pt | Sharp

Set font size

Right align text

Warp text

Click the down arrow next to the **Set the font family** box, and select **Impact** from the drop-down list.

Click the down arrow next to the **Set the font size** box, and select **18 pt** from the drop-down list.

Click the **Center text** button.

Click the **Set the text color** box. The **Color Picker** dialogue box will appear.

Position the pointer over the **Color slider** in the centre of the dialogue box, hold down the left mouse button. Drag up until a dark shade of red appears in the **Adjusted color** box, and then let go of the mouse button.

Click **OK**.

Color slider

Adjusted color

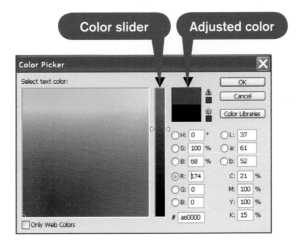

Repositioning and rotating text

Next we need to reposition and rotate the text to match the Layout Sketch.

Position the pointer just outside the highlighted text – it will change shape into an arrow head with a cross – and hold down the left mouse button. Drag the text into approximately the same position as the example below.

Now we can rotate the text.

- Press and hold the **Ctrl** key. The text will be surrounded by an outline with square marquees on the sides and corners.

- Position the pointer just above the top right corner of the outline around the text.

- Click and hold the left mouse button when the pointer changes into a curved arrow with two heads.

Drag up and let go of the mouse button when the text is at approximately the same angle as the example below.

Saving artwork

Finally we'll save the artwork with the name **wilderness**.

- Click **File** on the menu bar, and then click **Save**.

- Double click the **Unit 6 PT** folder if it is not already selected.

- Click in the **File name** box and type **wilderness**

- Click **Save**.

- Close **Photoshop**.

Task 3 Layer styles, shapes and filters

This task takes you through the steps needed to add standard shapes and apply special effects to artwork.

▶ Load **Photoshop**.

To work through this task you need to load your copy of the artwork called **wilderness**.

▶ Click **File** on the menu bar, and then click **Open**.

▶ Double-click the **Unit 6 PT** folder.

▶ Click on **wilderness** and **Open**.

Applying a dropped shadow to a layer

Next we need to add the text shown at the top of the Layout Sketch in the box labelled **WILDERNESS...**

▶ Click the **Text Tool** icon on the toolbox.

▶ Click anywhere in the top left corner of the artwork.

▶ Enter the following text:

Wilderness Travel

Text tool

Next we need to format this text.

▶ Press **Ctrl** and **A** to highlight all the text.

▶ Select the font type **Impact** in the **Set the font family** box.

▶ Select the font size **48 pt** in the **Set the font size** box.

▶ Click the **Set the text color** box and choose a shade of yellow.

Now we need to add a **dropped shadow** to this layer.

▶ Click **Layer**, **Layer Style** on the menu bar, and then click **Drop Shadow...** The **Layer Style** dialogue box will appear.

▶ Double-click in the box labelled **Distance:** and type **30** – this will offset the shadow further from the text making it stand out more.

▶ Click **OK** – the dropped shadow effect will be applied to the layer.

▶ Reposition the text to match the example below.

If you need to make a drop shadow stand out more try adjusting other options such as distance, spread and size with the sliders in the **Layer Style** dialogue box.

Warping text

Next we need to add the text shown at the top of the Layout Sketch in the box labelled **EAGLE PEAK...**

▶ Add the text **Eagle Peak Canyon** underneath the **canyon** image.

▶ Format this text as follows:

Font type: **Impact**
Font size: **48 pt**
Font colour: **Black**

A warped effect also needs applying to this text.

With the text highlighted click the **Warp Text** button on the toolbox at the top of the screen. The **Warp Text** dialogue box will appear.

Warp Text button

▶ Click the down arrow next to the **Style:** box, and select **Flag** from the drop-down list.

▶ Click the radio button next to **Horizontal** if this option is not already selected.

▶ Click **OK**. The warped effect will be applied to the text.

▶ Reposition and rotate the text to match the example below.

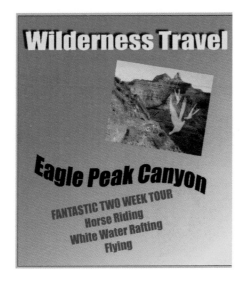

Drawing standard shapes

Next we need to add the sun image shown on the Layout Sketch using the **Custom Shapes** tool.

⊙ Click the **Rectangle Tool** button on the toolbox and hold the left mouse button. Let go of the mouse button when a pop up menu of other shape tools appears.

Rectangle Tool
button

⊙ Click the **Custom Shape Tool** option.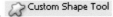

A box labelled **Shape:** will appear on the toolbox at the top of the screen.

⊙ Click the small down arrow next to this box to view the current shape collection.

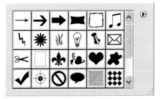

⊙ Click the circular arrow button on the top right corner of the current shape collection box. A pop up menu listing all the available shape collections will appear.

⊙ Select **Nature** from the list, and then click **OK** to replace the current shapes.

⊙ Select the first sun shape in the collection, then click anywhere in the grey area around the artwork.

Sun

⊙ Click the **Color:** box on the toolbox at the top of the screen and use the **Color Picker** dialogue box to choose a shade of yellow.

Color box

⊙ Click underneath the **Wilderness Travel** text on the left of the artwork, hold the left mouse button and drag down and across to the right. Let go of the mouse button when the sun shape is approximately the same size as the example below.

TIP

Click the **Shape Layers** button on the toolbar at the top of the screen if the color box isn't visible when you're using the **Custom Shape** tool.

Shape Layers
button

Move tool

TIP

To repostion a shape click on the layer for the shape in the **Layers Panel**, and then click the **Move Tool** on the toolbox. Click and hold the left mouse button, drag the shape into position and let go of the mouse button.

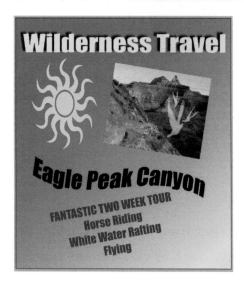

TIP

To resize a shape click the **Show Transform Controls** check box on the toolbar at the top of the screen and then click on the layer for the shape in the **Layers Panel**. Square marquees will appear around the shape. Position the pointer over a marquee until it changes into a double-headed arrow, click and hold the left mouse button and drag to resize the shape.

Applying a filter to a layer

Next we need to apply a special effect filter to change the appearance of the **canyon** image.

▶ Click the *canyon* layer in the **Layers Panel**.

▶ Click **Filter**, **Distort** on the menu bar, and then click **Diffuse Glow**.

▶ Click **OK** when the message below appears.

▶ The **Filter** dialogue window will appear with a preview of the filter effect.

▶ Click **OK**. The artwork will be displayed with the filter effect applied to the **canyon** image. It should look something like the example below.

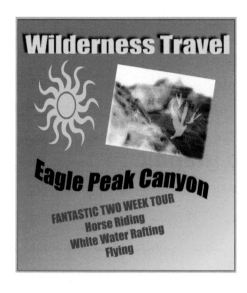

TIP

You can choose any filter effect in an assignment unless a specific type is specified but take care to make sure that the original image does not become unrecognisable. To change the filter click the small down arrow next to the box containing the filter name on the right of the window, and then select another filter type from the drop-down list. You can also use the sliders underneath the filter name box to adjust the effect.

Printing with crop marks

Next we need to print a copy of the artwork showing the **crop marks**. Crop marks are used as guides to trim artwork to size when it is smaller or larger than the paper it has been printed on.

▶ Click **File** on the menu bar, and then click **Print with Preview...** The **Print** dialogue window will appear.

▶ Click the box underneath the preview of the printed artwork in the top left corner of the window and select **Output**.

▶ Click the check box next to **Corner Crop Marks**.

▶ Click the check box next to **Center Crop Marks**.

▶ Click the **Print** button in the top right corner of the window – select a colour printer.

Click **OK** to print the artwork.

Save the artwork keeping the filename **wilderness**.

Close **Photoshop**.

Task 4   Creating an animated graphic

This task will take you through the steps needed to create an animated graphic to match the Design Sketch show below.

Frame 1

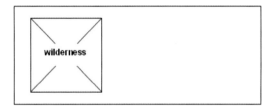

width = 450 pixels   height = 100 pixels
Background gradient fill orange on the left to yellow on the right
Image **wilderness** on the left
This will form the background for all frames.

Frame 2

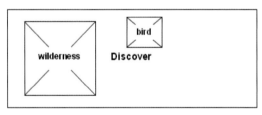

Discover text in black with warped effect to the right of image **wilderness**
bird image above **Discover** text

Frame 3

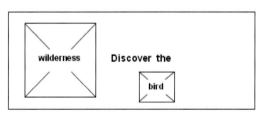

the text in black to the right of image **Discover** text
bird image below **Discover the** text

Frame 4

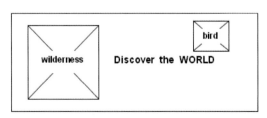

WORLD text in black with warped effect to the right of image **Discover the** text
bird image above **WORLD** text

Creating a new piece of artwork

To get started we need to create a new piece of artwork and set the width and height to match the measurements given for the animation on the Design Sketch.

- ▶ Load **Photoshop**.

- ▶ Click **File**, **New** on the menu bar to open the **New** dialogue box.

- ▶ Double-click in the **Name:** box and type **discover**

- ▶ Click the small down arrow on the **Width:** box and select **pixels** from the drop-down list if it is not already selected.

- ▶ Double-click in the **Width:** box and type **450**

- ▶ Click the small down arrow on the **Height:** box and select **pixels** from the drop-down list if it is not already selected.

- ▶ Double-click in the **Height:** box and type **100**

At this point you need to take a screen print as evidence that the width and height measurements for this animation have been set correctly.

- ▶ Take a screen print of the **New** dialogue box.

- ▶ Load **Word** and open your **screenprints** document.

- ▶ Press **Ctrl** and **End** to move to the last page of the document.

- ▶ Paste the screen print into the document.

- ▶ Click anywhere on empty space to the right of the image.

- ▶ Press **Ctrl**, **Shift** and **Enter** to create a blank page for another screen print.

- ▶ Save the document keeping the filename **screenprints**.

- ▶ Click the **Photoshop** icon at the bottom of the screen. ⬛ Adobe Photoshop

- ▶ Click **OK** to close the **New** dialogue box.

Creating layers

Next we're going to add the image and text layers needed for this animation.

- ▶ Double-click the name **Layer 1** in the layers panel and type the new name **background** for this layer.

- ▶ Fill the background of this layer with a gradient fill changing from orange on the left to yellow on the right.

Your artwork should now look something like the example below.

> **TIP**
>
> The technique for creating a gradient fill on a background layer is described on page **226**.

Next we need to place and position the **wilderness** image shown on **Frame 1** of the Design Sketch on a new layer. This image should already be in your **My Documents** folder.

▶ Place and position the **wilderness** image on the artwork to match the example below.

Next we need to add the text shown on **Frame 2** of the Design Sketch.

▶ Add the text **Discover** to the artwork.

▶ Format this text as follows:

Font type: **Arial**
Font size: **36 pt**
Font colour: **Black**

▶ Add a warped flag effect to the text and position it to match the example below.

Now we need to place and position the **bird** image shown on **Frame 2** of the Design Sketch on a new layer. This image should already be in your **My Documents** folder.

▶ Place and position the **bird** image on the artwork to match the example below.

▶ Change the name of this layer to **bird frame 2**

Now we need to add the text shown on **Frame 3** of the Design Sketch.

▶ Add the text **the** to the artwork.

▶ Format this text as follows:

Font type: **Arial**
Font size: **36 pt**
Font colour: **Black**

▶ Position the text to match the example below.

Next we need to place and position the **bird** image shown on **Frame 3** of the Design Sketch on a new layer.

▶ Place and position the **bird** image on the artwork to match the example below.

▶ Change the name of this layer to **bird frame 3**

Next we need to add the text shown on **Frame 4** of the Design Sketch.

▶ Add the text **WORLD** to the artwork.

▶ Format this text as follows:

Font type: **Arial**
Font size: **36 pt**
Font colour: **Black**

▶ Add a warped flag effect to the text and position it to match the example below.

Now we need to place and position the **bird** image shown on **Frame 4** of the Design Sketch on a new layer. This image should already be in your **My Documents** folder.

▶ Place and position the **bird** image on the artwork to match the example below.

▶ Change the name of this layer to **bird frame 4**

Creating animation frames

Now we're ready to use the various objects in the layers of this artwork to create the frames that make up the animation.

▶ Click **Window, Animation** on the menu bar to open the **Animation Panel** at the bottom of the screen.

To create the first frame of the animation we need to hide the layers containing objects that will appear later in the animation.

▶ Click the eye symbol next to every layer except the *wilderness* and *background* layers. When you've finished your **Layers Panel** should look like the example below.

Eye symbol

To create the second frame of the animation we'll duplicate the first frame and reveal the layers containing objects that must appear at this point in the animation.

Duplicate

Layer Visibility box

▶ Click the **Duplicate** symbol at the bottom of the **Animation Panel**.

▶ Click the **Layer Visibility** box next to the *bird frame 2* and *Discover* layers to show the layer contents. When you've finished your **Layers Panel** should look like the example.

▶ Duplicate the second frame.

To create the third frame of the animation we'll duplicate the second frame and hide the layers containing objects that must not appear in this frame.

▶ Click the eye symbol next to the *bird frame 2* layer to hide the contents of this layer.

Now we need to reveal the layers containing objects that must appear in this frame.

▶ Reveal the *bird frame 3* and *the* layers. When you've finished your **Layers Panel** should look like the example on the next page.

Finally we'll duplicate the third frame and reveal and hide layers to create the fourth frame.

▶ Duplicate the **third frame**.

 Hide the *bird frame 3* layer.

 Reveal the *bird frame 4* and *WORLD* layers. When you've finished your **Layers Panel** should look like the example below.

Setting frame duration

Next we need to specify how long each frame of the animation must be displayed.

Click the small down arrow at the bottom of the first frame in the **Animation Panel** and select **0.5** from the pop up menu.

Use the same technique to set a delay of **1.0** second for the other frames. When you've finished your **Animation panel** should look like the example below.

At this point you need to take another screen print as evidence that the frame delay times for this animation have been set correctly.

▶ Press **PrtSc** to take a screen print that includes the animation window.

▶ Click the **Word** icon at the bottom of the screen. screenprints - Mi...

▶ Paste the screen print at the end of the document.

▶ Print the document.

▶ Save the document keeping the filename **screenprints**.

▶ Close **Word**.

Now we're ready to preview the animation.

Play button

▶ Click the **Play** button at the bottom of the animation window.

Stop button

▶ Click the **Stop** button once you've watched the animation through a few times and made sure that the contents of each frame match the Design Sketch.

> **TIP**
>
> If a frame doesn't have the right contents click on the frame in the **Animation Window** and use the **Layers** panel to reveal or hide layers.

Saving an animation

Finally we need to save the animation using a **GIF file format** so that it can be used on the company's website.

▶ Click **File** on the menu bar, and then click **Save for Web…**

▶ Click the down arrow next to the file type box and choose **GIF** if this is not already selected.

▶ Click **Save** and then close **Photoshop**.

> **TIP**
>
> **GIF** (Graphics Interchange Format) is a type of graphics file commonly used to create small animated graphics for use on web pages.

That's the end of the practice tasks. Now try the full New CLAiT Plus assignment that follows.

Practice assignment

Scenario

You are working as a Graphic Designer for a record company. You have been asked to produce a CD cover design for a popular group's new album.

Assessment Objectives	TASK 1
	Before you begin this task make sure that you have the file **tower**.
	In this task you will edit an image that you will use to create the CD cover.
1a	1 a) Load software that will enable you to edit an image.
	b) Open the file **tower**.
2c	2 Use the colour correction tools of your software to adjust the contrast and brightness of the image so that it does not appear under exposed.
2a	3 Remove the scratches from the top right corner of the image.
2b	4 Use the image editing features of your software to:
2c	a) remove the tree on the right-hand side of the image
	b) replace the area, where the tree has been removed, with a background to match the surrounding area.
5a	5 Save your amended image as **cdtower** in a **.jpg** or **.jpeg** format (in any file size).
5c	6 a) Print your edited image in colour.
	b) Ensure your name and centre number are displayed on this print. This may be handwritten.

Assessment Objectives	TASK 2
	Before you begin this task ensure you have the file **cdtower** that you saved in **Task 1**. In this task you will create a piece of artwork that will combine text and images to create the CD cover.
1a	1 Use the file **cdtower** that you created in **Task 1** as a background for a new piece of artwork.
1b	2 a) Amend your artwork canvas to be:
5d	Width: **12 cm**
	Height: **12 cm**
	Resolution: **180 pixels/inch (ppi) or 80 pixels/centimetre**
	b) Make sure the picture content remains unchanged.
	c) Take a screen print to show these settings.
	d) Ensure your name and centre number are displayed on this print. Print the screen print in colour or black and white.

| 3   a)   Refer to the Layout Sketch for the CD shown below.

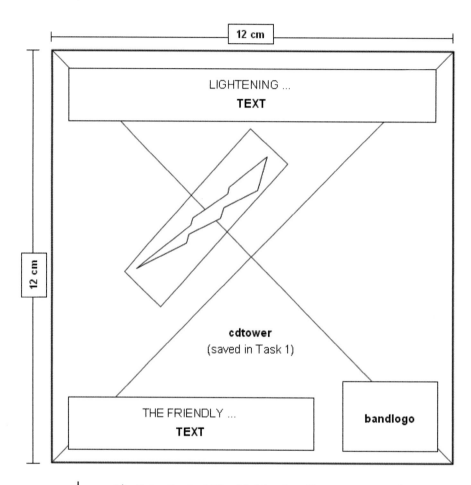

b)   Enter the text **The Lightening Tower** as a new layer.

c)   Position this text as shown in the Layout Sketch.

d)   Ensure your text fills most of the width of your artwork.

e)   Colour the text **white**.

f)   Ensure that the background of this layer is transparent.

g)   Format the shape of this text to give a visible arch effect.

4   Save your artwork using the filename **cdcover**

Assessment **TASK 3**
Objectives

Before you begin this task ensure you have the following files:

bandlogo

cdcover (that you saved in **Task 2**).

In this task you will use the editing and drawing features of your software to amend the CD cover that you created in **Task 2**.

1c	1	Using the file **cdcover** that you saved in **Task 2**:
1d		a) insert the file **bandlogo** as a new layer
		b) position this as shown in the Layout Sketch on page 246
		c) ensure that the background of this layer is transparent
		d) set the opacity for this layer to be **70%**
		e) take a screen print to show this has been done.
1c	2	Create a new layer that will allow you to draw graphic shapes.
1d		a) Draw a lightening bolt shape in the position shown in the Layout Sketch on
3a		page 246.
3b		b) Fill this shape with **white**.
1e	3	a) Enter the text **The Friendly Natives** as a new layer, as shown on the
3d		Layout Sketch on page 246.
3e		b) Colour the text **white**.
3f		c) Ensure that the background of this layer is transparent.
5d		d) Create a dropped shadow effect for this text.
5a	4	Save your artwork keeping the filename **cdcover**.
5b	5	a) Print the CD cover in colour showing crop marks.
5c		b) Ensure your name and centre number are displayed on this print. This may be
		handwritten.
3c	6	You have been asked to use a special effect to create an alternative CD cover. The
5a		alternative artwork must be noticeably different from the original cover but must still
5c		display at least an outline of the tower.
		a) On the background layer use a special effect to create an alternative CD cover.
		b) Save your amended CD cover using the filename **cdeffect**
		c) Print your amended CD cover in colour.
		d) Ensure your name and centre number are displayed on this print. This may be
		handwritten.
		e) Close any open files.

Assessment Objectives	TASK 4
	Before you begin this task ensure you have the file **bandlogo**.
	In this task you will create a 3-frame animation which will be displayed on the company website. You will need to refer to the Design Sketch below to complete this task.
1a	1 a) Create a new animation.
4a	b) Set the size of the animation to be:
4b	Width: **460 pixels** Height: **110 pixels**
	c) Take a screen print to show that this has been done.
	d) Ensure your name and centre number are displayed on this print. Print this screen print in colour or black and white.
3b	2 Create each frame of the animation according to the Design Sketch for the animation
4c	shown below.

Design Sketch for Animation

Frame 1

Width = 460 pixels   Height = 110 pixels
Background gradient fill dark blue in the top left corner to red in the bottom right corner.
Image **bandlogo** on the left. **This will form the background for all frames.**
Text **The** in white to the right of image **bandlogo**.

Frame 2

Text **LIGHTENING** with arch effect in white to the right of text **The**.

Frame 3

Text **TOWER** with arch effect in white underneath and to the right of text **LIGHTENING**.

4d 3 Set the duration of each frame as follows:

Frame 1	1 second
Frame 2	1 second
Frame 3	3 seconds

5a 4 a) Check your work carefully to ensure you have not made any errors.

5c b) Save your work in a format appropriate for running an animation.

5d c) Print the three frames of the animation in colour showing the timings and the file name (this may be a screen print).

d) Ensure that the text and graphics are clearly visible on each of the frames.

e) Ensure your name and centre number are displayed on this print. This may be handwritten.

f) Close all open software.

To pass this unit you must be able to:

- ✓ identify and use web publishing software correctly
- ✓ create web pages from unformatted source material
- ✓ use and format images, text and tables
- ✓ create and format an interactive form
- ✓ create links/hyperlinks
- ✓ save and upload the website.

You don't need to have any resources in your **My Documents** folder before starting work on this chapter – resources must be downloaded and saved during an assignment in order to meet the assessment criteria for Unit 7.

The practice tasks that follow cover all the techniques you need to learn in order to pass a New CLAiT Plus Unit 7 WEBSITE CREATION assignment.

Practice tasks

This chapter describes how to set up a simple website by creating and linking together some web pages. Web pages are created using **Hypertext Mark-up Language**, or **HTML**, which is a fairly simple computer programming language. Computer users who have no knowledge of HTML can use **Web design packages** to produce web pages in a **WYSIWYG** environment very similar to that offered by word processing or DTP software to produce printed publications. **WYSIWYG** stands for **'What you see is what you get'**. This means that the way web pages look in the web design package will be almost the same as they'll actually appear when they're viewed on the Internet with a web browser like **Internet Explorer**. The web design package we're going to use in this chapter is **Microsoft FrontPage 2003**.

Task 1   Creating a new website

Scenario

You are working as a Web Developer for **XS Marketing**. The owner of a florist called **Floral Seasons** has asked you to develop a website to promote their business.

Creating a website folder

To get started you need to create a subfolder for the new website in your **My Documents** folder or network home directory.

TIP

The steps you need to follow to create a subfolder are described in **Chapter 1** on page **5**.

- Create a subfolder called **floral (your initials)** in your **My Documents** folder or network home directory folder. For example: **floral bm**

- Create another subfolder inside the new subfolder called **images**.

Downloading and storing files

Next we need to download and store all the files needed for the website from the Internet. To access the Internet and download the files we need to load **Internet Explorer**:

- *either* double-click the **Internet Explorer** icon on the main screen in Windows,

- *or* click the **Start** button at the bottom left of the screen, then click 🔵 **Internet** Internet Explorer ·

Internet
Explorer

The default web page that Internet Explorer is set up to open when it is loaded will appear.

- Click in the address box and type:

  www.payne-gallway.co.uk/xs-marketing

- Press **Enter**, then click on the **Downloads** button. It should look like the example below.

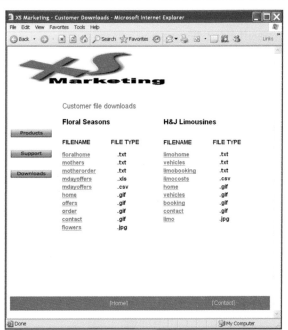

We'll start by downloading all the text-based files for the website and saving them in the **floral (your initials)** website folder.

- Position the pointer over the **floralhome** hyperlink in list of files for **Floral Seasons**.

- Click the right mouse button when the pointer changes to a hand shape.

- Select **Save Target As...** from the pop up menu. The **Save As** dialogue box will appear.

- Click the **My Documents** icon on the left of the dialogue box if the contents of your **My Documents** folder aren't already visible.

- Double-click the **floral (your initials)** website folder, and then click the **Save** button to start the download.

- Click the **Close** button when the **Download complete** dialogue box appears.

- Download and save the remaining text-based files – **mothers.txt, motherorder.txt, mdayoffers.xls, mdayoffers.csv** – to the **floral (your initials)** website folder in exactly the same way.

Next we need to download all the image files for the website and save them in the **images** subfolder of the **floral (your initials)** website folder.

- Position the pointer over the <u>home</u> hyperlink in the list of files for **Floral Seasons**.

- Click the right mouse button and select **Save Target As...** from the pop up menu.

- Double-click the **images** subfolder, and then click the **Save** button to start the download.

- Download and save the remaining image files – **home.gif, offers.gif, order.gif, contact. gif, flowers.jpg** – to the **images** subfolder in exactly the same way.

Creating a new website

Next you need to load **Microsoft FrontPage** and set up a new website.

You can load FrontPage in one of two ways:

Microsoft Office
FrontPage
2003

- *either* double-click the **Microsoft FrontPage** icon on the main screen in Windows

- *or* click the **Start** button at the bottom left of the screen, then click **Programs, Microsoft Office** and .

  The main FrontPage window will be displayed.

- Click **Create a new page or site...** at the bottom of the **Task pane**.

- Click **One page Website...**

  The **Website Templates** dialogue window will appear.

- Click once on **One Page Website** if it isn't already selected.

TIP

If you can't see the **Task pane**, click **View** and **Task pane** on the menu bar.

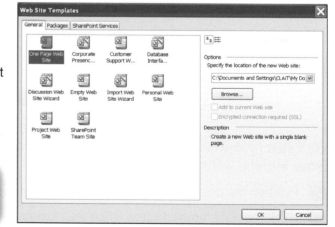

- Click the **Browse** button.
- Click the small down arrow next to the **Look in:** box and click on your **My Documents** or network home directory folder if it is not already selected.
- Click <u>once</u> on the folder called **floral (your initials)**.
- Click **Open**.
- Click **OK**. The website will be created and a list of available files will be displayed.

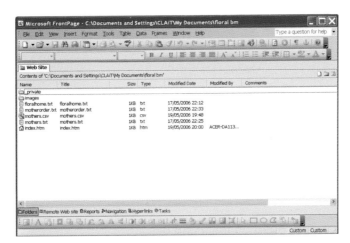

Closing FrontPage

Finally you need to close the website and shut **FrontPage** down.

- Click **File** on the menu bar, and then click **Close Site.**
- Click **File** on the menu bar, and then click **Exit**, or click **(x)** in the top right-hand corner of the screen.

Task 2   Creating a master page

This task describes how to create a **master page** for a website. Master pages are used to specify the same general layout and colour scheme for every page in a website. Once a master page has been created it can be used to create all the pages for a site. This maintains a consistent design throughout a site making it look much more professional.

Creating a blank web page

To get started we need to create and save a new blank web page.

- Load **FrontPage**.
- Click **File** on the menu bar, and then click **Open Site**. The **Open Site** dialogue window will appear.

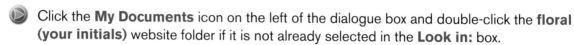

New button

Save button

▶ Click the **My Documents** icon on the left of the dialogue box and double-click the **floral (your initials)** website folder if it is not already selected in the **Look in:** box.

▶ Click **Open**. The contents of the website subfolder will be displayed.

▶ Click the **Create a new normal page** button on the **Standard** toolbar. Your screen should now look something like the one below.

Now we can save the page:

▶ *either* click **File** and then **Save** on the menu bar,

▶ *or* click the **Save** button on the **Standard** toolbar. The **Save As** dialogue window will appear.

▶ Double-click in the **File name:** box if the default filename is not already highlighted, and then type **masterfloral**

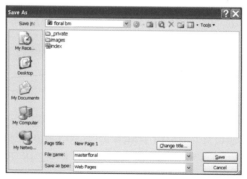

▶ Click **Save**. The name **masterfloral.htm** will be displayed on the page tab at the top of the screen.

Setting page properties

Next we need to set the page properties specified in the table below.

background colour	#FFFF66
text colour	#660033
hyperlink colour	#006600
visited hyperlink colour	#99FF66

 Click **File** on the menu bar, and then click **Properties...** The **Page Properties** dialogue window will appear.

 Click the **Formatting** tab.

 Click the small down arrow next to **Background:** in the **Colors** section.

 Click **More Colors...**

 Double-click inside the box labelled **Value:** and type **FFFF66**

> **TIP**
>
> You will be expected to specify the colours for a master page by using the **Hex Code** for the colour. Hex Codes always start with a **#** symbol followed by a combination of letters and numbers. You don't need to use capital letters when entering a Hex Code in FrontPage.

 Click **OK**.

 Set the text colour, link colour and visited link colour in exactly the same way. When you've finished your **Page Properties** dialogue window should look like the example below.

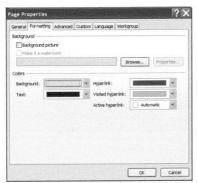

 Click **OK** to close the **Page Properties** dialogue window.

Creating META tags

META tags provide search engines with information about the contents of a website. Search engines use these tags to generate a list of relevant links when you type in keywords. We need to create the META tags specified in the table below for the Floral Seasons website.

keywords	florist, flowers, deliver
author	your name and centre number
description	*contents to be entered on each page*

▶ Click the **Code** tab at the bottom of the page. The HTML code for the page will be displayed – it should look like the example below.

```
1  <html>
2
3  <head>
4  <meta http-equiv="Content-Language" content="en-gb">
5  <meta name="GENERATOR" content="Microsoft FrontPage 6.0">
6  <meta name="ProgId" content="FrontPage.Editor.Document">
7  <meta http-equiv="Content-Type" content="text/html; charset=windows-1252">
8  <title>New Page 1</title>
9  </head>
10
11 <body text="#660033" bgcolor="#FFFF66" link="#006600" vlink="#99FF66">
12 </body>
13
14 </html>
15
```

▶ Click after the head tag **<head>** and press **Enter** to create a new line.

▶ Create another new line and type **<meta name="keywords" content="florist, flowers, deliver">**

▶ Create another new line and type **<meta name="author" content="**

▶ Type **your name and centre number** followed by **">**

▶ Press **Enter**.

▶ Type **<meta name="description" content="enter contents here">** The HTML code for your page should look something like the example below.

TIP

A keywords META tag can also be created by clicking the **General** tab in the **Page Properties** dialogue window and typing the keywords in the **Keywords:** box.

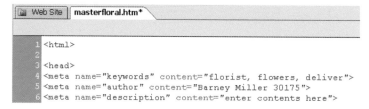

```
1  <html>
2
3  <head>
4  <meta name="keywords" content="florist, flowers, deliver">
5  <meta name="author" content="Barney Miller 30175">
6  <meta name="description" content="enter contents here">
```

▶ Click the **Design** tab at the bottom of the page.

Creating a table

Ordinary HTML code can only be used to place objects on the left, right or centre of a page. Most web designers get around this problem by basing their page layout designs around tables. This allows objects to be positioned by placing them inside individual cells in the table. We're going to create an ordinary table and modify it to match the layout guide shown below.

Heading area	Blank
Navigation Table	Body text area
Blank	Copyright text

The first thing we need to do is create an ordinary table. We can work out what size our table needs to be by counting the maximum number of rows and columns shown in the layout guide. If you do this you'll see there are **two columns across** and **six rows down**. So the table we need to start off with must be this size.

▶ Click and hold the **Insert Table** button on the **Standard** toolbar at the top of the screen.

Insert Table button

▶ Drag down and to the right until a **6 by 2 Table** is selected, then let go of the mouse button. The table will appear on the page.

6 by 2 Table

Setting table properties

Next we need to set the table properties specified in the table below.

width	**740 pixels**
table alignment	**left**
border	3
cell padding	2
cell spacing	3

> **TIP**
>
> The boxes in a table are called **cells**. The space between cells can be changed by adjusting the **cell padding** and **cell spacing**. The thickness of the border around cells can be changed by adjusting the value for the border – a value of 0 gives an invisible border and larger values a thicker border.

▶ Click **Table, Table Properties** on the menu bar, and then click **Table**. The **Table Properties** dialogue window will appear.

▶ Click the small down arrow next to the **Alignment:** box in the **Layout** section and choose **Left** if it is not already selected.

▶ Click the check box next to the **Specify width:** if it is not already selected.

▶ Click the radio button box next to **In pixels**.

⊙ Double-click in the box underneath **Specify width:** and type **720**.

⊙ Click the small up arrow next to the **Cell padding:** <u>once</u> to change the value to **2**.

⊙ Click the small up arrow next to the **Cell spacing:** <u>once</u> to change the value to **3**.

⊙ Click the small up arrow next to the **Size:** box in the **Borders** section <u>twice</u> to change the value to **3**.

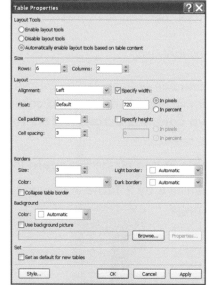

⊙ Click **OK**. Your table should now look like the example below.

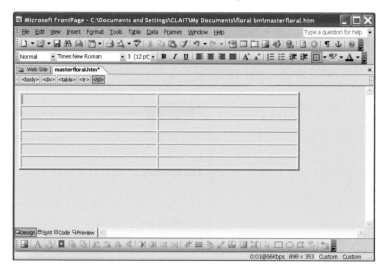

Setting cell properties

Now we need to set the cell properties specified in the table below.

Column	Width	Horizontal alignment	Vertical alignment
1ˢᵗ column	**115 pixels**	**centre**	**middle**
2ⁿᵈ column	**600 pixels**	**left**	**top**

Click anywhere in the first column.

Click **Table, Select** on the menu bar, and then click **Column**. The cells in the first column will be highlighted.

Click **Table, Table Properties** on the menu bar, and then click **Cell**.

The **Cell Properties** dialogue window will appear.

Click the check box next to **Specify width:**.

Double-click in the box underneath **Specify width:** and type **115**

Click the small down arrow next to the **Horizontal alignment:** box in the **Layout** section and select **Center**.

Click the small down arrow next to the **Vertical alignment:** box in the **Layout** section and select **Middle**.

Click **OK**.

Highlight the second column and set the cell properties for this column in the same way. The **Cell Properties** dialogue window should look like the example below when you've finished.

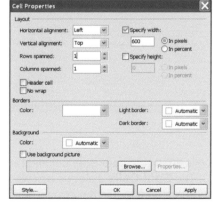

Click **OK**. Your table should now look like the example below.

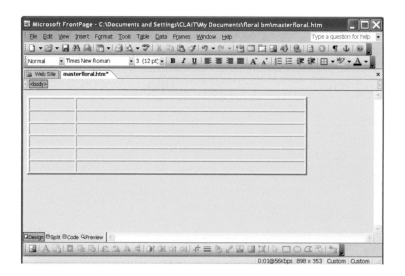

TIP

You could be asked to set the cell properties for **rows** during a Unit 7 assignment. The technique for this is virtually the same – click anywhere in the row, then click **Table, Select** and **Row**. Click **Table, Table Properties** and **Cell** to open the **Cell Properties** dialogue window.

Merging cells

Now the standard table has been created and formatted we need to merge some of the cells in the second column to form the **Body area** shown on the layout guide.

▶ Click in the second cell of the second column and hold down the left mouse button.

▶ Drag down until the middle four cells are highlighted, and then let go of the mouse button.

▶ Click **Table** on the menu bar, and then click **Merge Cells**. The highlighted cells will be merged to form a single cell.

▶ Click anywhere outside the table to remove the highlighting. Your table should now look like the example below.

TIP

You could also be asked to split cells apart to create extra columns in a table. To do this click in the cell and click **Table, Split Cells...** The **Split Cells** dialogue box will appear. Click the radio button next to **Columns** if it is not already selected and use the arrows next to the **Number of columns:** box to select the required number of columns.

Creating a navigation table

Next we need to build the navigation table shown on the layout guide.

Position in Column 1	Image	Alt text	Link to
Row 2	**home.gif**	**home**	**index.htm**
Row 3	**offers.gif**	**special offers**	**offers.htm**
Row 4	**order.gif**	**place order**	**order.htm**
Row 5	**contact.gif**	**contact us**	**floral-seasons@payne-gallway.co.uk**

▶ Click inside **Row 2** in **Column 1**.

▶ Click **Insert** on the menu bar, and then click **Picture, From File**.

▶ *Or* click the **Insert Picture From File** button on the **Standard** toolbar.

Picture button

The **Picture** dialogue box will appear. The first image file we need is called **home.gif** and should be in the **images** subfolder of the **floral (your initials)** website folder.

▶ Click the **My Documents** icon on the left of the dialogue box.

▶ Double-click the **floral (your initials)** website folder.

▶ Double-click the **images** subfolder.

▶ Click on **home** and **Insert**.

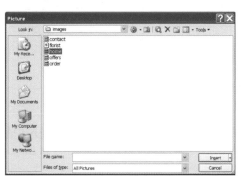

▶ Insert the remaining navigation images in **Column 1** in exactly the same way. Your navigation table should look like the example below when you've finished.

261

Seven   Website Creation

Chapter 7

Now that all the images have been inserted we can add the hyperlinks to them.

▶ Double-click the **Home** image. The **Picture Properties** dialogue box will appear.

▶ Click the **General** tab.

▶ Click the check box next to **Text:** in the **Alternative representations** section.

▶ Click in the box next to **Text:** and type **home**

▶ Click in the box next to **Location:** in the **Default hyperlink** section, type **index.htm** and click **OK**.

TIP

You'll be asked to create three types of hyperlink during a Unit 7 assignment – **internal**, **external** and **email**. Internal hyperlinks load other pages within the same website, external hyperlinks load pages from other websites and email hyperlinks open an email editor window with a blank message window ready to send an email to a specified address.

▶ Create the **Offers** and **Order** image hyperlinks specified in the table on page **261** in exactly the same way.

TIP

During a Unit 7 assignment you'll be asked to create **relative hyperlinks**. The hyperlinks we're creating here are all relative because they give just the filename of the page such as **index.htm**. Relative hyperlinks don't specify the exact location of a page on the computer's hard disk drive such as **C:\Documents and Settings\CLAIT\floral bm\index.htm** – a hyperlink with this type of exact physical location is referred to as an **absolute hyperlink**.

The last hyperlink is slightly different because it must allow website users to contact the company by email. When this link is clicked an email editor like MS Outlook will be loaded with a blank message window.

▶ Click <u>once</u> on the **Contact** image.

▶ Click **Insert** on the menu bar, and then click **Hyperlink**.

Hyperlink button

▷ *Or* click the **Insert Hyperlink** button on the **Standard** toolbar. The **Insert Hyperlink** dialogue box will appear.

▷ Click the **E-mail Address** button in the **Link to:** column.

▷ Type **floral-seasons@payne-gallway.co.uk** in the **E-mail address:** box

The text **mailto:** will appear in front of the email address as you type – don't worry about this – just carry on typing.

▷ Click **OK** – you will test this link later along with the others.

Next we need to add the alternative text for this image given in the table on page **261**.

▷ Double-click the **Contact** image to open the **Picture Properties** dialogue box.

▷ Click the **General** tab if it is not already selected.

▷ Click the check box next to **Text:** in the **Alternative representations** section.

▷ Click in the box next to **Text:** type **contact us** and then click **OK**.

Creating a style sheet

A **style sheet** is a set of instructions that defines how a web page should look. Style sheet instructions are stored in a separate file from the HTML code for a page. Style sheets are linked to web pages using a special HTML command. Using style sheets offers the advantage of being able to change the appearance of a complete website or group of pages by editing just one set of instructions.

Next we need to create a style sheet for our website and define the styles specified in the table below.

Name	Font face	Size	Emphasis	Alignment
heading	**sans serif** (e.g. Arial, Helvetica)	**HTML 5 (18 pt)**	**strong (bold)**	**left**
body	**sans serif**	**HTML 3 (12 pt)**	**none**	**left**

New Page button

Style Sheets tab

▶ Click the small down arrow next to the **Create a new normal page** button on the **Standard** toolbar.

▶ Click **Page...** to open the **Page Templates** dialogue window.

▶ Click the **Style Sheets** tab.

▶ Click the **Normal Style Sheet** icon if it is not already selected, and then click **OK**. The new style sheet will appear along with the **Style** toolbar. We'll create the **heading** style first.

▶ Click the **Style...** button on the **Style** toolbar. The **Style** dialogue window will appear.

▶ Click the **New...** button. The **New Style** dialogue window will appear.

▶ The cursor will be flashing inside the **Name (selector):** box – type **Heading**.

▶ Click the **Format** button and select **Font...** from the drop-down list. The **Font** dialogue window will appear.

▶ Scroll through the list of fonts underneath the **Font:** box and select **Arial**.

▶ Click **Bold** in the list of font styles underneath the **Font style:** box.

▶ Scroll through the list of font sizes underneath the **Size:** box and select **18pt**.

▶ Click **OK** to return to the **New Style** dialogue window.

▶ Click the **Format** button and select **Paragraph...** from the drop-down list. The **Paragraph** dialogue window will appear.

▶ Click the small down arrow next to the **Alignment:** box and select **Left**.

▶ Click **OK** to return to the **New Style** dialogue window.

▶ Click **OK** to close the **New Style** dialogue window.

▶ Click **OK** to close the **Style** dialogue window and define the new style. Your style sheet page should now look like the example below.

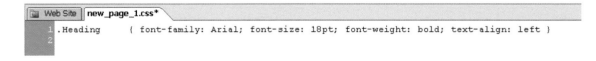

Click the **Style...** button on the **Style** toolbar and define the **Body** style in the same way. Your style sheet page should look like the example below when you've finished.

```
  Web Site  new_page_1.css*
 1 .Heading    { font-family: Arial; font-size: 18pt; font-weight: bold; text-align: left }
 2 .Body       { font-family: Arial; font-size: 12pt; text-align: left }
```

Now we can save the new style sheet:

Save button

 either click **File** and then **Save** on the menu bar,

 or click the **Save** button on the **Standard** toolbar. The **Save As** dialogue window will appear.

 Double-click in the **File name:** box if the default filename is not already highlighted, and then type **styles**

 Click **Save**. The name **styles.css** will be displayed on the page tab at the top of the screen.

 Click **File** and **Close**.

Creating an external hyperlink

Next we need to add the **Copyright text** shown in the layout guide on page **257** and create an external hyperlink to the **xs-marketing** website.

 Click inside **Row 3** in **Column 2** and type **Copyright**

 Press the **Spacebar**, and then click **Insert**, **Symbol...** on the menu bar. The **Symbol** dialogue box will appear – we need to use this to insert a copyright symbol © in the text.

 Click the small down arrow next to the **Font:** box, scroll through the list and select **Arial** – this will make the symbol match the font selected for the Body and Heading text on the style sheet.

 Scroll down though the symbols, double-click the copyright symbol ©, and then click **Close**.

 Press the **Spacebar**, and then type **XS Marketing Group**

 Highlight the text by clicking it <u>three</u> times.

▶ Open the **Insert Hyperlink** dialogue box and click **Existing File or Web Page** under **Link to:** if it is not already selected.

▶ Type the website address **www.payne-gallway.co.uk/xs-marketing** in the **Address:** box. The text **http://** will appear in front of the website address as you type – don't worry about this – just carry on typing.

▶ Click **OK** – we'll test this link later.

Attaching a style sheet and applying a style

Next we need to format the copyright text by applying the **Body** style to it. To get started we need to attach the style sheet created earlier to the page.

▶ Click **Format** on the menu bar, and then click **Style Sheet Links...** to open the **Link Style Sheet** dialogue window.

▶ Click the **Add...** button. The **Link Style Sheet** dialogue window will list the style sheets available in the current website folder.

▶ Click **styles.ccs**, and then click **OK**.

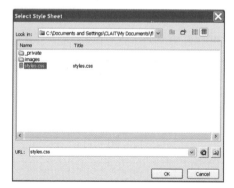

▶ Click **OK** to close the **Link Style Sheet** dialogue window.

▶ Save the master page keeping the filename **masterfloral**.

Now we're ready to apply the **Body** style to the copyright notice text.

▶ The text **Copyright © XS Marketing 2006** should still be highlighted – if it isn't, click it <u>three</u> times.

▶ Click the small down arrow next to the **Style** box on the **Formatting** toolbar and select **Body** from the list. The style will be applied to the text. It should look like the example below.

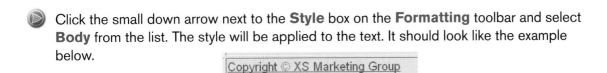

▶ Save the web page keeping the name **masterfloral**.

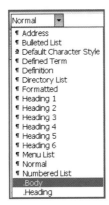

That's the master page completed. Now we can save the website and shut **FrontPage** down. In the next task we'll use a copy of the master page to create a home page for the Floral Seasons website.

▶ Click **File** and **Close Site** to close the website.

▶ Shut **FrontPage** down.

Task 3   Creating a home page

This task describes how to create a home page for Floral Seasons website by inserting and formatting text on a copy of the master page.

Creating a new page from a master page

To get started we need to load the master page called **masterfloral.htm** created and saved in the last task.

▶ Load **FrontPage**.

▶ Click **File** on the menu bar, and then click **Open Site**. The **Open Site** dialogue window will appear.

▶ Click the **My Documents** icon on the left of the dialogue box and double-click the **floral (your initials)** website folder if it is not already selected in the **Look in:** box.

▶ Click **Open**. The contents of the website subfolder will be displayed.

▶ Double-click **masterfloral** in the list of files to open the master page.

Next we need to save a copy of the master page with the name **index.htm**.

 Click **File** and then **Save As...** on the menu bar.

 Click the **Change title...** button – the **Set Page Title** dialogue window will appear – type **Floral Seasons Florist** and click **OK**.

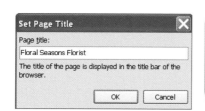

> ### TIP
> The **title** tag tells web browsers what to display at the top of the browser window. **Untitled Document** is displayed when a title is not specified. Specifying a title looks more professional and is used by web search engines to compile and list search results.

 Type **index.htm** in the **Filename:** box, and then click **Save**.

 Click **Yes** when you see the warning message below.

> ### TIP
> If you don't give a home page the name **index** users will get a blank page instead of the home page when they enter the website. FrontPage automatically creates an index page when a new site is set up – we're replacing this page with one based on the master page for the website.

 The name **index.htm** will be displayed on the page tab at the top of the screen.

Next we need to add a heading to the page.

 Click in the page heading area and type **Welcome to Floral Seasons**

Entering a description META tag

Next we need to complete the description META tag for the page.

⊡Code
Code tab

 Click the **Code** tab at the bottom of the page to view the HTML code for the page.

 Replace the text **enter contents here** in the **<meta name="description"** tag with **About Floral Seasons Florist**

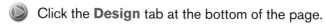

⟐Design
Design tab

 Click the **Design** tab at the bottom of the page.

Inserting a text file

Next we need to insert the **body text** for this page to match the outline below.

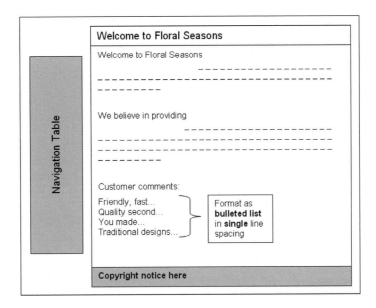

The body text is in the pre-prepared text file called **floralhome** that you downloaded and saved in the **floral (your initials)** website folder.

▶ Click in the **Body text area** of the page.

▶ Click **Insert** on the menu bar, and then click **File...** The **Select File** dialogue window will appear.

▶ Click the **My Documents** icon on the left of the dialogue box and double-click the **floral (your initials)** website folder if it is not already selected in the **Look in:** box.

▶ Click the small down arrow next to the **Files of type:** box, and then click **Text Files (*.txt)** in the drop-down list of file types.

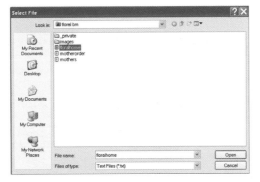

▶ Click on the file **floralhome**, and then click **Open**.

▶ Click the radio button next to **Normal paragraphs** when the **Convert Text** dialogue box appears.

Click **OK**. The text in the file will be inserted on the web page – it should look like the example below.

Adding line spaces

Next we need to make sure that each paragraph or block of text has at least one blank line before the next one. This was done automatically for most of the text when the text file was inserted. The page outline shows that the last block of text also needs separating into single lines of text.

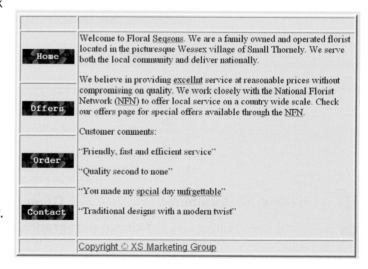

Click before the text starting **"Friendly...** and press **Enter**.

Click before the text starting **"Quality...** and press **Enter**.

Click before the text starting **"You...** and press **Enter**.

Click before the text starting **"Traditional...** and press **Enter**.

Your web page should now look like the example opposite.

Line spacing and bullets

Next we need to format the last five lines of text on the page to be a **bulleted list** with **single line spacing**. We'll set the line spacing first and then add the bullets.

▶ Highlight the last five lines of text.

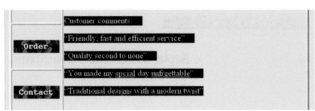

▶ Click **Format** and **Paragraph...** on the menu bar to open the **Paragraph** dialogue window.

▶ Click the small down arrow next to the box under **Line spacing:** and choose **Single** if it is not already selected.

▶ Click the small down arrow next to the **Before:** box to set a value of **0**.

▶ Click the small down arrow next to the **After:** box to set a value of **0**.

▶ Click **OK**. The spacing between the lines will disappear.

Now we can apply the bullets.

▶ Click away from the highlighted text to deselect it.

▶ Highlight the <u>last four lines</u> of text – don't include the section heading **Customer comments:** in the selection.

▶ Click the **Bullets** button on the **Formatting** toolbar. Click away from the text – the bottom of your page should now look like the example below.

Applying styles

Next we need to apply the Heading and Body styles to the page.

▶ Highlight the text **Welcome to Floral Seasons** in the page heading area.

Welcome to Floral Seasons

▶ Click the small down arrow next to the **Style** box on the **Formatting** toolbar and select **Heading** from the list. The style will be applied to the text.

▶ Highlight all the text in the body text area.

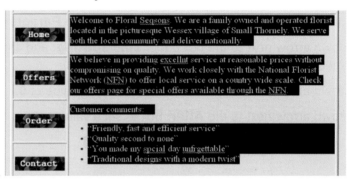

▶ Click the small down arrow next to the **Style** box on the **Formatting** toolbar and select **Body** from the list. The style will be applied to the text.

▶ Click away from the text to remove the highlighting. Your page should look like the example below.

Spelling and
Grammar button

▶ Now click the **Spelling and Grammar** button on the menu bar.

▶ Work through the spellcheck and correct any mistakes.

Remember that the spelling and grammar checking facility is not foolproof – sometimes you'll need to click the **Ignore** button when a suggested change is not required.

That's the home page completed. In the next task we'll create another web page for the Floral Seasons website.

- Click the **Save** button on the **Standard** toolbar.
- Close the website and shut **FrontPage** down.

Save button

Task 4   Combining text and images

So far we've created a text-based home page. Now we're going to create a web page that contains text and an image.

Creating a new web page

- Load **FrontPage** and open the **floral (your initials)** website.
- Open the master page **masterfloral.htm**.
- Save a copy of the master page with the title **This month's offers** and the filename **offers. htm**
- Click in the page heading area and type **Mother's Day Offers**
- Click the **Code** tab and enter the text **Offers this month** in the description META tag.
- Click the **Design** tab.

Inserting and formatting body text

Next we need to insert the **body text** for this page to match the outline below.

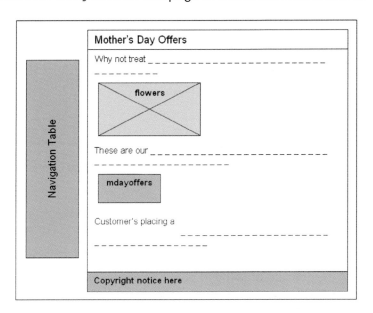

The body text is in the pre-prepared text file called **mothers** that you downloaded and saved in the **floral (your initials)** website folder.

Insert the **mothers** text file in the body text area of the page – it should look like the example below.

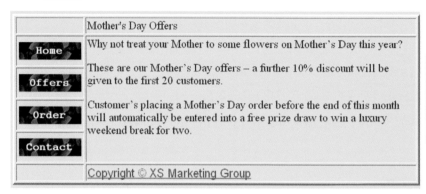

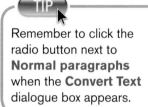

TIP

Remember to click the radio button next to **Normal paragraphs** when the **Convert Text** dialogue box appears.

Applying Heading and Body styles

Next we need to apply the **Heading** and **Body** styles to the page.

Highlight the text **Mother's Day Offers** in the page heading area and apply the **Heading** style.

Highlight all the text in the body area and apply the **Body** style.

Click away from the text to remove the highlighting. Your page should look like the example below.

Spelling and
Grammar button

Now click the **Spelling and Grammar** button on the menu bar, work through the spellcheck and correct any mistakes.

Inserting an image

Next we need to insert the image **flowers** under the first line of text ending **...this year?**

Click at the end of the first line of text and press **Enter**.

Click **Insert** on the menu bar, and then click **Picture, From File**.

Or click the **Insert Picture From File** button on the **Standard** toolbar.

The **Picture** dialogue box will appear.

Picture
button

Click the **My Documents** icon on the left of the dialogue box and double-click the **floral (your initials)** website folder if it is not already selected in the **Look in:** box.

Double-click the images **subfolder**.

Click on **flowers** and **Insert**. The image will be inserted on the page – it should look like the example below.

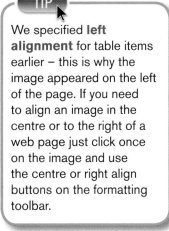

TIP

We specified **left alignment** for table items earlier – this is why the image appeared on the left of the page. If you need to align an image in the centre or to the right of a web page just click once on the image and use the centre or right align buttons on the formatting toolbar.

Formatting an image

Next we need to format the image by flipping it horizontally, reducing the resolution and reducing its size. We'll start by flipping the image horizontally.

Click once on the image to select it.

Click the **Flip Horizontal** button on the **Pictures** toolbar at the bottom of the screen.

Flip Horizontal button

Flip Vertical button

TIP

If the **Pictures** toolbar isn't visible click **View**, **Toolbars** and **Pictures**.

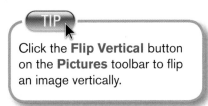

TIP

Click the **Flip Vertical** button on the **Pictures** toolbar to flip an image vertically.

Next we're going to reduce the resolution of the image. This will lower the overall quality of the image but will reduce the time it will take for the web page to download over the Internet.

Right-click the image and select **Change Picture File Type...** from the pop up menu. The **Picture File Type** dialogue window will appear.

Click the check box next to **Settings:** to remove the tick and access the options in this section.

Click the small down arrow next to the box labelled **Quality:** until the value is **65**.

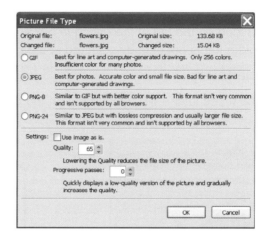

⏵ Click **OK**.

Reducing the quality value of an image compresses it, reducing the resolution. You can experiment with the quality value at this stage. Click the **Undo** button on the **Standard** toolbar if you use a quality value that noticeably reduces the quality of the image because it is too low.

Next we're going to reduce the image size.

⏵ Right-click the image and select **Picture Properties** from the pop up menu. The **Picture Properties** dialogue window will appear.

⏵ Click the **Appearance** tab if it is not already selected.

⏵ Click the check box next to **Keep aspect ratio** to remove the tick. This will allow us to set a specific width and height for the image.

⏵ Double-click in the box labelled **Width:** and type **350**

⏵ Double-click in the box labelled **Height:** and type **230**

The **aspect ratio** of an image refers to the relation of the width of the image to the height. Resizing an image with the **Keep aspect ratio** option checked avoids distorting the image. If you are asked to use specific values for the heights and width of an image always make sure you deselect the **Keep aspect ratio** option first.

Now we need to specify some alternative text for this image.

▶ Click the **General** tab.

▶ Click the check box next to **Text:** in the **Alternative representations** section.

▶ Click in the box next to **Text:** and type **flowers**

▶ Click **OK**. Your web page should now look like the example below.

Inserting a data file and creating a table

Next we need to insert the text file called **mdayoffers** underneath the flowers image as shown on the page outline. The data from this file needs to be displayed as a two column table.

▶ Insert a line space after the text ending **...first 20 customers**.

▶ Click **Insert** on the menu bar, and then click **File...**

▶ Click the **My Documents** icon on the left of the **Select File** dialogue box and double-click the **floral (your initials)** website folder if it is not already selected in the **Look in:** box.

▶ Click the small down arrow next to the **Files of type:** box, and then click **All Files (*.*)** in the drop-down list of file types.

mdayoffers

> **TIP**
>
> You downloaded two different versions of the **mdayoffers** file in Task 1 – an **EXCEL Workbook** and a **CSV** file. We're going to use the CSV file in this example. These files have very similar icons but you can identify the CSV file by looking for a letter **a** in the bottom right corner of the icon or by holding the pointer over the icon and checking the pop up description which reads **Microsoft Office Excel Comma Separated Values File**.

▷ Click on the **CSV** version of the **mdayoffers** file, and then click **Open**.

▷ Click the radio button next to **Normal paragraphs with line breaks** when the **Convert Text** dialogue box appears.

▷ Click **OK**. The file will be inserted on the page – it should look like the example below.

▷ Highlight the three new lines of text.

▷ Click **Table**, **Convert** on the menu bar, and then click **Text to Table...** The **Convert Text To Table** dialogue box will appear.

▷ Click the radio button next to **Commas**, and then click **OK**. The text will appear in a table.

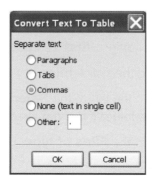

Now we need to format the table by changing the width of the columns to exactly fit the text inside them.

▶ Position the pointer over the line separating the two columns and wait for the pointer to change into a double-headed arrow.

▶ Click and hold the left mouse button, and then drag to left of the page. The width of the first column will reduce as you drag – let go of the mouse button when the column looks like the example below.

These are our Mother's Day offers – a further 10% discount will
be given to the first 20 customers.

Hand-Tied Bouquet   £14.95
Mixed Country Basket £12.95
Seasonal Bouquet   £10.50

Customer's placing a Mother's Day order before the end of this

▶ Adjust the width of the second column in exactly the same way – let go of the mouse button when the column looks like the example below.

These are our Mother's Day offers – a further 10% discount will
be given to the first 20 customers.

Hand-Tied Bouquet   £14.95
Mixed Country Basket £12.95
Seasonal Bouquet   £10.50

Customer's placing a Mother's Day order before the end of this

That's the offers page completed. In the next task we'll create a web page containing an interactive form.

▶ Save the web page keeping the name **offers**.

▶ Click **Yes** if you're prompted to save embedded files.

▶ Close the website and shut **FrontPage** down.

Task 5   Creating an interactive form

This task describes how to create a web page containing an interactive form. To get started we need to save another copy of the master page.

Creating a new web page

▶ Load **FrontPage** and open the **floral (your initials)** website.

▶ Open the master page **masterfloral.htm**.

▶ Save a copy of the master page with the title **Mother's Day Order** and the filename **order.htm**

- Click in the page heading area and type **Mother's Day Order Form**
- Click the **Code** tab and enter the text **Order flowers** in the description META tag.
- Click the **Design** tab.

Creating a form and inserting body text

Next we need to create a blank form and insert the **body text** for this page.

- Click in the **Body text area** of the page.
- Click **Insert, Form** on the menu bar, and then select **Form**. A blank form containing a **Submit** button and **Reset** button will be inserted in the **Body text area** of the page.
- Press **Enter** to create a blank line space above the form buttons.

The body text for this page is in a pre-prepared text file called **motherorder** that you downloaded and saved in the **floral (your initials)** website folder.

- Click in the blank linespace above the buttons and insert the **motherorder** text file.
- Apply the **Heading** and **Body** styles to the page. Your page should look like the example below.

> **TIP**
>
> Remember to click the radio button next to **Normal paragraphs** when the **Convert Text** dialogue box appears.

Setting form properties

Next we need to set the properties for the form to specify what needs to happen when a user completes and submits the form online.

- Click **Insert, Form** on the menu bar, and then select **Form Properties...** The **Form Properties** dialogue window will appear.
- Click the radio button next to **Send to other**.
- Click in the **Form name:** box and type **order**

 Click the **Options** button. A second dialogue box headed **Options for Custom Form Handler** will appear.

 Type **http://www.payne-gallway.co.uk/xs-marketing/cgi-bin/webmail.cgi** in the box labelled **Action:**

> **TIP**
>
> When an interactive form is submitted, the values in each form field – the **form results** – are sent to a program called a **form handler** on the web server hosting the site. The form handler processes the form results. FrontPage also supports several form handlers including **CGI** (Common Gateway Interface) which is the one you'll be expected to use during a Unit 7 assignment. Before you create an interactive form, ask your Internet Service Provider (ISP) which technology their web servers support.

 Click the small down arrow next to the box labelled **Method:** and select **POST** if this option is not already displayed.

 Click **OK**.

 Click **OK** again to close the **Form Properties** dialogue window.

Inserting and positioning form fields

Next we need to insert and position the form fields shown on the outline below.

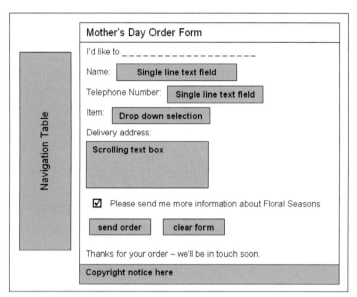

Mother's Day Order Form

I'd like to _

Name: Single line text field

Telephone Number: Single line text field

Item: Drop down selection

Delivery address:

Scrolling text box

☑ Please send me more information about Floral Seasons

send order   clear form

Thanks for your order – we'll be in touch soon.

Copyright notice here

Navigation Table

▶ Click after the text **Name:** and press the **Spacebar**.

▶ Click **Insert, Form** on the menu bar, and then select **Textbox**. A single line text box will appear.

▶ Click after the text **Telephone Number:** press the **Spacebar**, and then add another single line text box.

▶ Click after the text **Item:** and press the **Spacebar**.

▶ Click **Insert, Form** on the menu bar, and then select **Drop-Down Box**. A small box with a drop-down arrow on the right will appear.

▶ Click after the text **Delivery Address:** and press **Enter** to create a blank line space.

▶ Click **Insert, Form** on the menu bar, and then select **Text Area**. A box with a scroll bar on the right will appear.

▶ Click at the start of the line beginning **Please send me...** so that the cursor is flashing before the first word.

▶ Click **Insert, Form** on the menu bar, and then select **Checkbox**. A check box will appear at the start of the line.

Next we need to move the text starting **Thanks for your order...** so that it appears after the **Submit** and **Reset** buttons.

▶ Highlight all of the line beginning **Thanks for your order...**

✂ **Cut button**

▶ Click the **Cut** button on the **Standard** toolbar.

▶ Click after the **Reset** button and press **Enter**.

📋 **Paste button**

▶ Click the **Paste** button on the **Standard** toolbar.

▶ Click above the **Submit** and **Reset** buttons and press the **Backspace** key to remove the blank line space.

Now we need to separate the **Submit** and **Reset** buttons.

▶ Click in-between the **Submit** and **Reset** buttons so that the flashing cursor appears – this can be quite tricky and you might need a few attempts before you see the flashing cursor.

▶ Press the **Spacebar** <u>three</u> times to move the buttons apart.

That's all of the form items inserted and positioned. Your interactive form should now look like the example below.

Adding a hidden field

Next we need to add a hidden field to the form. Hidden fields are used by form handlers on web servers; they are not visible to website users. We're going to add a hidden field to specify an email address that information from completed forms should be sent to.

▶ Click **Insert, Form** on the menu bar, and then select **Form Properties...** to open the **Form Properties** dialogue window.

▶ Click the **Advanced...** button. The **Advanced Form Properties** dialogue window will appear.

▶ Click **Add...** Another dialogue window headed **Name/Value Pair** will appear.

▶ Type **recipient** in the **Name:** box.

▶ Type **floral-seasons@payne-gallway.co.uk** in the **Value:** box, and then click **OK**.

▶ Click **OK** to close the **Advanced Form Properties** dialogue window.

▶ Click **OK** to close the **Form Properties** dialogue window. The hidden field information will be added to the **HTML** code for the page but there will be no obvious change to the page in **Design View**.

Changing field settings

Next we need to change the settings of the form fields to specify both how they should appear and behave.

▶ Double-click the **Textbox** field next to **Name:** The **Text Box Properties** dialogue window for this field will appear.

▶ Type **name** in the box labelled **Name:**.

▶ Click <u>three</u> times inside the box labelled **Width in characters:** and type **40**

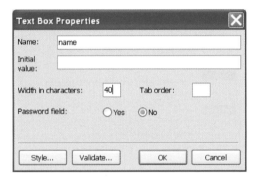

▶ Click **OK** to close the properties box for this form field.

▶ Double-click the **Textbox** field next to **Telephone Number:** Enter the name **telephone** for this field and set the width to **20**.

▶ Double-click the **Drop-Down Box** next to **Item:** The **Drop-Down Box Properties** dialogue window for this field will appear.

▶ Enter the name **items** for this field.

▶ Click the **Add...** button. Another dialogue window headed **Add Choice** will appear.

▶ Type **Hand-Tied Bouquet** in the **Choice** box, and then click **OK**. The choice will appear in the centre panel of the dialogue window.

▶ Add the choices: **Mixed Country Basket** and **Seasonal Bouquet** in exactly the same way. The **Drop-Down Box Properties** dialogue window should look like the example below when you've finished.

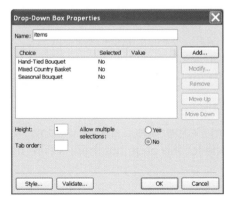

- Click **OK** to close the **Drop-Down Box Properties** dialogue window.

- Double-click the **Text Area** field under **Delivery address:** The **TextArea Box Properties** dialogue window for this field will appear.

- Enter the name **address** for this field and set the width to **45**

- Click <u>three</u> times inside the box labelled **Number of lines:** and type **5**

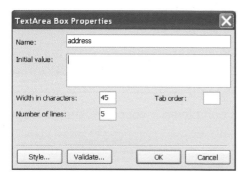

- Click **OK** to close the properties box for this form field.

- Double-click the **Checkbox** field next to the text beginning **Please send...** The **Check Box Properties** dialogue window for this field will appear.

- Enter the name **moreinfo** for this field.

- Click inside the box labelled **Value:** and add the text **or OFF**

- Click **OK** to close the **Check Box Properties** dialogue window.

- Double-click the **Submit** button. The **Push Button Properties** dialogue window will appear.

- Type the name **submit** in the **Name:** box.

- Click <u>three</u> times inside the box labelled **Value/label:** and type **send order**

▶ Click **OK** to close the **Push Button Properties** dialogue window.

▶ Double-click the **Reset** button. Enter the name **reset** for this button, type **clear form** in the box labelled **Value/label:** and then click **OK**.

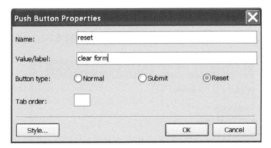

That's all the form field settings completed – your form should look like the example below now.

That's the order page completed.

▶ Save the web page keeping the name **order**.

▶ Close the website and shut **FrontPage** down.

Testing the form

Next we need to test the form. To do this we need to view the page in **Internet Explorer**. You can load Internet Explorer in one of two ways:

▶ *either* load **Internet Explorer**,

▶ *or* click **File** on the menu bar, and then click **Open**. The **Open** dialogue box will appear.

▶ Click the **Browse** button. The **Microsoft Internet Explorer** dialogue box will appear.

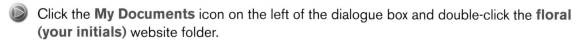 Click the **My Documents** icon on the left of the dialogue box and double-click the **floral (your initials)** website folder.

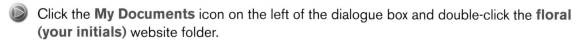 Click on **order** and **Open**.

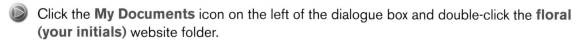 Click **OK** to close the **Microsoft Internet Explorer** dialogue box and open the web page.

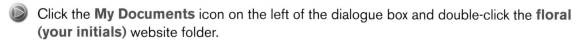 Enter a name in the text box next to **Name:** and then click the **clear form** button. The text you entered should disappear.

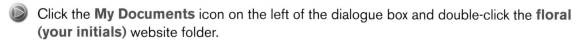 Complete the form in full using the example data below or your own data if you prefer.

 Click the **send order** button.

TIP

If you don't see a message saying that the form information has been sent, load **FrontPage** and open the **form** page. Click **Insert, Form** on the menu bar, and then select **Form Properties...** Check that the settings in the **Form Properties** dialogue window match those given in the assignment. If the form settings are correct there is either a problem with your Internet connection or the website the form information is being sent to – you'll need to check this with your tutor.

Testing the website

The order page was the last of the three web pages specified on the Site Map so the website is now complete and ready to be tested. To get started we need to open the home page of the Floral Seasons website in **Explorer**.

▷ Open the **index.htm** page – it should look like the example below.

Offers button

▷ Click the **offers** navigation button.

The **offers** page should be loaded and displayed – it should look like the example below.

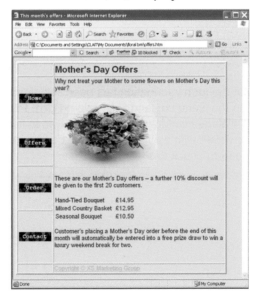

Home button

▷ Click the **home** navigation button – the Floral Seasons home page should reappear.

TIP

If the correct page is not displayed from a navigation button, open the page in **FrontPage**. Right-click the navigation button and select **Hyperlink Properties...** and check that the correct page is displayed in the **Address:** box.

▶ Click the **order** navigation button.

Order button

▶ The **order** page should be loaded and displayed – it should look like the example below.

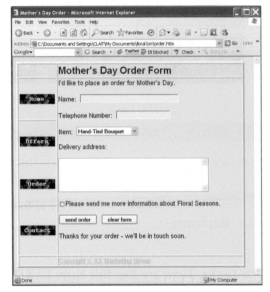

▶ Click the **home** navigation button – the Floral Seasons home page should reappear.

▶ Click the **contact** navigation button. The default email editor for your computer should be loaded with a new blank message window. In the example below the email editor is **Microsoft Outlook** – your tutor will let you know if this is different on the computer you're using.

Contact button

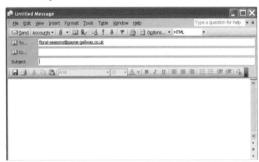

▶ Click **File** on the menu bar, and then click **Exit**, or click **(x)** in the top right-hand corner of the email editor window to close the program. Click **No** if you're prompted to save any changes to the message.

▶ Click the **home** navigation button – the Floral Seasons home page should reappear.

▶ Click the copyright hyperlink at the bottom of the page. The home page of the XS Marketing website should be loaded from the Internet and displayed.

Welcome to XS Marketing - the first choice for web design solutions

Products

Support

Downloads

[Home]   [Contact]

 Back

Back button

⊙ Click the back button on the toolbar at the top of the screen. The Floral Seasons home page should reappear.

⊙ Click **File** on the menu bar, and then click **Exit**, or click **(x)** in the top right-hand corner of the browser window to close **Explorer**.

That's the end of the practice tasks. Now try the full New CLAiT Plus assignment that follows.

Practice assignment

Scenario

You are working for **H&J Limousines**, a company offering classic chauffeur driven American limousines for hire. You have been asked to create a website which will be hosted by XS Marketing.

All of the text and graphics for each of the pages have been prepared in advance by a designer. You must download these from the **downloads** page at: **www.payne-gallway.co.uk/xs-marketing**.

NOTE: You will need to download 3 text files (.txt), 5 images files (.gif/.jpg) and one datafile (.csv).

You are not required to provide any printouts for this assignment.

H&J LIMOS SITE MAP

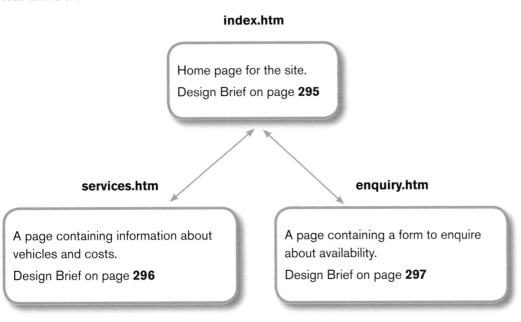

index.htm

Home page for the site.

Design Brief on page **295**

services.htm

A page containing information about vehicles and costs.

Design Brief on page **296**

enquiry.htm

A page containing a form to enquire about availability.

Design Brief on page **297**

Assessment Objectives	TASK 1
	In this task you will download and store all the files for your website.
1c	1 a) In your working area create a folder for your website called **HandJ** (your initials) e.g. **HandJbm**.
	b) Within this folder create a subfolder called **images**.
	c) **All image files for your website must be contained within the images subfolder. All other files must be contained within the website folder HandJ(your initials).**
1b	2 a) Locate the web page:
1h	**http://www.payne-gallway.co.uk/xs-marketing**
	b) Press **Enter**, then click on the **Downloads** button.

c) Download the following four files and place them in your website folder **HandJ(your initials).**

FILENAME	FILE TYPE
limohome	.txt
vehicles	.txt
limobooking	.txt
limocosts	.csv

d) Download the following five files and place them in the **images** subfolder that you created in Step 1b.

FILENAME	FILE TYPE
home	.gif
vehicles	.gif
booking	.gif
contact	.gif
limo	.jpg

Assessment Objectives

TASK 2

In this task you will create a master page/template that you will use to create all your web pages to ensure they have a consistent style.

All links to files and images on the website must be **relative**, not absolute.

1a

1d

1f

1g

1h

1 a) Load software that will allow you to create web pages.

b) Create a new web page.

c) Save this web page in your website folder **HandJ(your initials)** using the filename **HandJmast**.

d) Set the page properties as follows:

title	(as specified for each page)
background colour	**#FFFFCC**
text colour	**#CC3399**
hyperlink colour	**#660066**
visited hyperlink colour	**#FF9999**

1e

1g

2 Create the following META tags and insert the information shown:

keywords	limousine, rental, hire
author	your name and centre number
description	(as specified for each page)

1g

2j

2l

2m

3 You will now create a table to align the contents of your page. A guide is shown below:

Heading area		Blank	
Body text area			
Link button	Link button	Link button	Link button
Copyright text		Blank	

a) Create a table of **two** columns and **four** rows.

b) Set the table properties as follows:

width	600 pixels
table alignment	left
border	0
cell padding	3
cell spacing	3

c) In the **second row** only merge the cells to create **one column**.

d) In the **third row** only split the cells to create **four columns**.

e) Set the cell properties as follows:

Row	Width	Horizontal alignment	Vertical alignment
2nd row	600 pixels	left	top
3rd row	150 pixels	centre	middle

4a

4c

4d

4e

4 Create a navigation table in the **third** row of your table. The images must be formatted as below:

Position in Row 3	Image	Alt text	Link to
Column 1	home.gif	home page	index.htm
Column 2	vehicles.gif	vehicle information	vehicles.htm
Column 3	booking.gif	booking enquiry	enquiry.htm
Column 4	contact.gif	contact us	h&j@payne-gallway.co.uk

a) All images in the third row have a height of **30** pixels and a width of **110** pixels which should be retained.

2g

      b)   Check to ensure all links are relative.

5   You will now create a style sheet that must be applied to the appropriate areas of each web page (see guide shown in Step 3 on page **293**).

    a)   Create a style sheet as follows:

Name	Font face	Size	Emphasis	Alignment
heading	**sans serif** (e.g. Arial, Helvetica)	**HTML 6 (24 pt)**	**strong (bold)**	**centre**
body	**sans serif**	**HTML 4 (14 pt)**	**none**	**left**

    b)   Save your style sheet as appropriate to your software.

1f   6   The copyright notice needs to be displayed at the bottom of each page.

2a   a)   In the first cell of the last (bottom) row of the table, key in the following text:

4b   **Copyright © XS Marketing**

        b)   Link this text to **www.payne-gallway.co.uk/xs-marketing**.

        c)   Format in the body text style.

1h   7   Save your master page/template in your website folder **HandJ(your initials)** retaining the filename **HandJmast**.

Assessment Objectives | **TASK 3**

1e   1   a)   Open a copy of the master page/template **HandJmast**.

1h   b)   Save this in your website folder **HandJ(your initials)** using the filename **index. htm**.

        c)   Title the page: **H&J Limousine Rental**

        d)   In the description META tag enter the following description:

            Chauffeur driven American stretch limousines

2a   2   In the heading area key in the text:

        H&J Limousines

2a   3   a)   Insert the text file **limohome** in the body text area, following the outline

2h   shown below.

2i

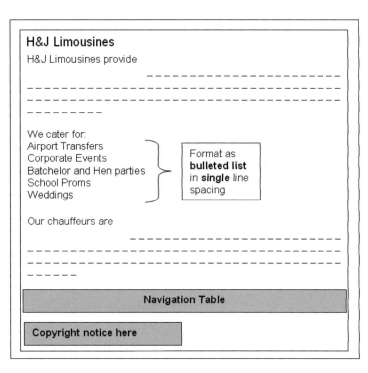

H&J Limousines

H&J Limousines provide

– –
– –
– –
– – – – – – – –

We cater for:
Airport Transfers
Corporate Events
Batchelor and Hen parties
School Proms
Weddings

Format as **bulleted list** in **single** line spacing

Our chauffeurs are

– –
– –
– –
– – – – – –

Navigation Table

Copyright notice here

b) Ensure each paragraph is separated by at least one clear line space.

c) Format the five lines after the text **We cater for:** as a bulleted list in single line spacing.

d) Ensure that the style sheet has been applied to the appropriate parts of the text.

2b   4   Spellcheck and proofread your web page and correct any errors.

1h   5   Save your web page in your website folder **HandJ(your initials)** retaining the filename **index.htm**.

Assessment Objectives	TASK 4
	In this task you will need to insert several files.
1e	1 a) Open a copy of the master page/template **HandJmast**.
1h	b) Save this in your website folder **HandJ(your initials)** using the filename **vehicles. htm**.
	c) Title the page: **Our vehicles**
	d) In the description META tag enter the following description:
	Vehicles available to rent
2a	2 In the heading area key in the text:
	About our vehicles
2a	3 a) Insert the text file **vehicles**, the image file **limo** and the table from the file
2g	**limocosts**, following the outline shown below:

2k

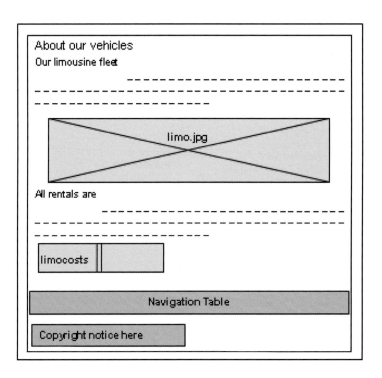

b) Make sure the file **limocosts** is displayed in two columns.

c) Ensure that the style sheet has been applied to the appropriate parts of the text. The body text style should also be applied to the **limocosts** table.

2c

4 Apply the following formatting to the image **limo**.

2d

a) Flip the image horizontally.

2e

b) Reduce the resolution.

2f

c) Reduce the size of the image

d) Set the image attributes as follows:

width	**500 pixels**
height	**190 pixels**
alt text	**limousine**

5 Save your web page in your website folder **HandJ(your initials)** retaining the filename **vehicles.htm**.

Assessment Objectives | TASK 5

1e

1 a) Open a copy of the master page/template **HandJmast**.

1h

b) Save this in your website folder **HandJ(your initials)** using the filename **enquiry.htm**

c) Title the page: **Booking enquiry**

d) In the description META tag enter the following description:

Enquire about booking

2a | 2 | In the heading area key in the text:

Booking enquiry

3 You are going to create an interactive form. An outline of the form is shown below:

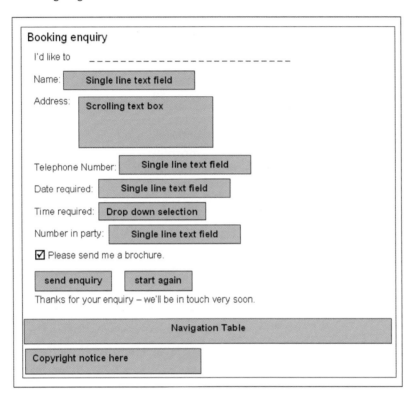

a) Insert the text file **limobooking** in the body text area, following the outline shown above.

b) Ensure that the style sheet has been applied to the appropriate parts of the text.

3a | 4 | Create an interactive form as follows:

start of form	after the text: **below**
end of form	before the text: **Thank you for your enquiry**
form method	**POST**
form action	**http://www.payne-gallway.co.uk/xs-marketing/cgi-bin/webmail.cgi**

3b
3c | 5 | Add form items according to the following table, placing them where shown in the outline above.

Type	Name	Field settings
hidden field	**recipient**	h&j@payne-gallway.co.uk
single line text field	**name**	width **40**
scrolling text box	**address**	width **6** lines of **40** characters
single line text field	**telephone**	width **20**
single line text field	**date**	width **10**
drop-down selection	**time**	options: **morning afternoon evening**
single line text field	**number**	width **2**
check box	**brochure**	on or off
submit button	**submit**	value = send enquiry
reset button	**reset**	value = start again

1h   **6**   Save your web page in your website folder **HandJ(your initials)** retaining the filename **enquiry.htm**.

3d   **7**   Test the interactive form to ensure that it correctly sends the information to the recipient.

5c
5d   **8**   Save and close your website and exit the software securely.

9   You will now load and test your website to make sure that all pages work correctly.

4f   Load your website in a browser and check that all:

5a   a)   pages load correctly

5b   b)   links function properly

c)   page content and image(s) are displayed

d)   links to other pages and images in the website are relative NOT absolute

e)   pages have been formatted accurately

f)   pages are free from spelling errors.

Save or copy all files to the disk, drive or network location specified by your tutor.

No printouts should be submitted for this assignment.

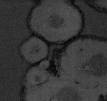

To pass this unit you must be able to:

☑ use advanced email features to co-ordinate information

☑ set up distribution lists and use address book

☑ manage mailbox and folders.

The practice tasks that follow cover all the techniques you need to learn in order to pass a **New CLAiT Plus Unit 8 ELECTRONIC COMMUNICATION** assignment.

Practice tasks

This chapter describes how to work with **email** and organise a diary using **Personal Information Manager (PIM)** software. The software we're going to use in this chapter is **Microsoft Outlook**.

Task 1   Contacts and distribution lists

Scenario

You are working as an Office Assistant for the Vocational team at Payne Gallway publishers. You use Personal Information Manager (PIM) software to help you organise your appointments and keep details of co-workers and business contacts. You use email software to send and receive email communications.

 Create a subfolder called **Unit 8 PT** in your **My Documents** folder or network home directory folder where files can be saved as you work through these practice tasks.

This task describes how to add the details of new contacts to your address book and create email distribution lists.

To get started we need to load **Outlook** – you can do this one of two ways:

The steps you need to follow to create a subfolder are described in **Chapter 1** on **page 5**.

 either double-click the **Outlook** icon on the main screen in Windows,

 or click the **Start** button at the bottom left of the screen, then click **Programs, Microsoft Office** and E-mail
Microsoft Office Outlook   .

Microsoft
Outlook

The main **Outlook** window will be displayed. You should see a window something like the one below.

Adding new contacts

You need to add the new contact details shown below to your address book.

Full name	Sue Marshall
Job title	Commissioning Editor
Work telephone	01649 721396
Email	sue.marshall@payne-gallway.co.uk

Full name	Barbara Wheat
Job title	Copy Editor
Work telephone	01649 721394
Email	barbara.wheat@payne-gallway.co.uk

New button

▶ Click the small down arrow next to the **New** button on the **Standard** toolbar, and select **Contact** from the drop-down menu. A new window headed **Untitled – Contact** will appear.

▶ Click in the box next to **Full Name...** and type **Sue Marshall**

▶ Click in the box next to **Job title...** and type **Commissioning Editor**

▶ Click in the box next to **Business...** in the **Phone numbers** section and type **01649 721396**

▶ Click in the box next to **E-mail...** and type **sue.marshall@payne-gallway.co.uk**

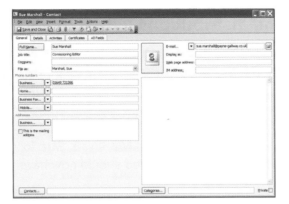

▶ Click **Save and Close** on the toolbar.

▶ Add the details for **Barbara Wheat** in exactly the same way.

Creating a distribution list

Next we need to create a **distribution list**. Distribution lists are used to send the same email message to a group of recipients. Every recipient of a distribution list message sees their own name and the names of all the other recipients in the **To:** line of the message window.

▶ Click the small down arrow next to **New** on the **Standard** toolbar, and then click **Distribution List** from the drop-down menu. A new window headed **Untitled – Distribution List** will appear.

New button

▶ Type **Team** in the **Name:** box.

▶ Click the **Select Members...** button. The **Select Members** dialogue box will appear.

▶ Click **Barbara Wheat** in the list of members if this contact is not already highlighted, and then click **OK**.

▶ Add the details for **Sue Marshall** in exactly the same way – your distribution list window should now look like the example below.

▶ Close the **Distribution List** window by clicking **(x)** in the top right-hand corner.

▶ Click **Yes** when you are prompted to save changes.

Printing contacts and distributions lists

Now we need to print a copy of the new contacts and new distribution list.

▶ Click **Contacts** at the bottom of the **Folder** bar on the left of the screen. All your contacts will be listed in alphabetical order.

Next we need to select the contacts that need to be printed.

▶ Hold **Ctrl** and then click the grey bar labelled **Marshall, Sue** followed by the grey bars labelled **Team** and **Wheat, Barbara**. You should now have three contact details highlighted.

▶ Click the **File** button on the **Standard** toolbar, and then click **Print...** to open the **Print** dialogue box.

▶ Select the printer you want to use in the **Name:** box.

▶ Click **Memo Style** in the **Print style** section.

▶ Click the check box **Start each item on a new page** in the **Print options** section to remove the tick if it is already selected.

▶ Click **Page Setup...** and click the **Header/Footer** tab.

▶ Click in the first box in the **Header** section and type your name.

▶ Click in the second box **Header** section and type your centre number.

▶ Click the **Preview** button. A preview of the printout will appear – it should look something like the example below.

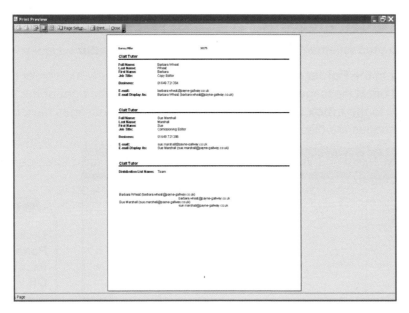

Click **Print...** followed by **OK** to print the page.

Now we can shut **Outlook** down.

Click **File** on the menu bar, and then click **Exit**, or click **(x)** in the top right-hand corner of the window.

Task 2   Saving and extracting attachments

This task describes how to open email messages and work with attached files.

Creating an archive folder

To get started we're going to create a folder to store messages from your Team Leader.

Load **Outlook**.

Click the small down arrow next to the **New** button on the **Standard** toolbar, and select **Folder...** from the drop-down menu. A new window headed **Create New Folder** will appear.

New button

Type **team leader** in the **Name:** box, and then click **OK**.

Reading an email message

Next you need to read an email message sent by your **Team Leader** welcoming you to the team.

Inbox

 Click **Inbox** in the **Folder** bar on the left of the screen to view the contents of your **Inbox**. All received email messages in your Inbox will be listed on the right of the screen. The number next to the **Inbox** folder tells you how many new messages have been received. Unread messages are displayed in bold text in the list.

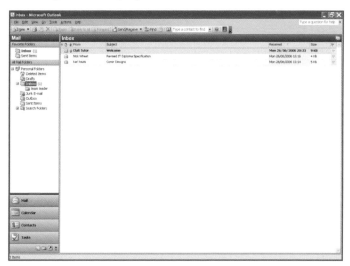

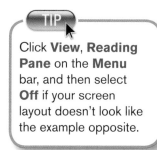

TIP

Click **View**, **Reading Pane** on the **Menu** bar, and then select **Off** if your screen layout doesn't look like the example opposite.

The message you need to read will have the subject heading **Welcome** – it should already have been sent to you by your tutor.

 Double-click this message to view it in a new window.

Maximize button

 Click the **Maximize** button in the top right corner of the message window. Your message window should look like the example below.

Saving an attached file

Before opening or saving an email attachment you should use antivirus software to scan it for viruses. Most antivirus software can be configured to scan email attachments automatically.

Once you're sure that antivirus software will scan email attachments automatically you can carry on and save the attachment in the email sent by your tutor.

TIP

If the contents of your **My Documents** folder aren't listed click the **My Documents** button on the left of the **Save As...** window.

▶ Click **File** on the menu bar, and then click **Save Attachments...**

▶ The **Save Attachment** dialogue window will appear with the contents of your **My Documents** listed.

▶ Double-click the **Unit 8 PT** folder.

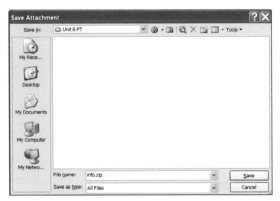

TIP

Attachments can also be saved by right-clicking them and selecting **Save As...** from the pop up menu.

▶ Click the **Save** button.

Adding an address

Next you need to add the email address of the person who sent this message to your address book.

▶ Right-click the email address in the **From:** box.

▶ Click the **Add to Outlook Contacts...** in the drop-down list of options. A window showing details for the new contact will appear.

▶ Click in the **Job title:** box and type **Team Leader**

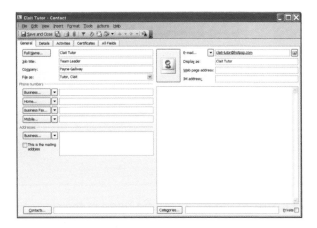

- Click in the **Company:** box and type **Payne-Gallway**
- Click in the **Save and Close** button on the **Standard** toolbar at the top of the window.

  💾 Save and Close

Moving a message

Next you need to move a message to the **team leader** folder.

- Click the **Move to Folder** button on the **Standard** toolbar at the top of the message window.
- Click the **team leader** in the drop-down list of folders.
- Close the message window by clicking **(x)** in the top right-hand corner.

Taking a screen print

At this point you need to take a screen print of the **team leader** folder as evidence that it has been created and the message from your Team Leader has been moved into it.

- Click **team leader** in the **Folder** bar on the left of the screen to view the contents of the folder. 📁 team leader
- Take a screen print of the current window by holding down the **Alt** key and then pressing the **Print Scr** key.
- Load **Word** and create a new blank document.
- Add your **Name** and **Centre Number** to the document header.
- Click the **Paste** button on the **Standard** toolbar. The screen print will appear – it should look something like the example below.

> **TIP**
>
> The steps to add a document header are described in **Chapter 1** on page **27**.

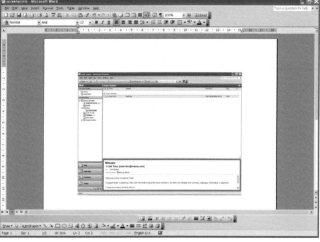

- Press **Ctrl**, **Shift** and **Enter** to create a second page in the document – this will be used for another screen print later on.

Save the document in your **Unit 8 PT** folder with the filename **screenprints**

Close **Word**.

Close **Outlook**.

Extracting zipped files

Next you need to extract the three files contained in the zipped folder that you saved earlier.

Click **Start** on the **Taskbar** at the bottom of the screen.

Click the **My Documents** icon to view the contents of your **My Documents** folder.

Double-click the **Unit 8 PT** folder.

Click <u>once</u> on the **info** zipped folder.

Click **File** and **Extract All...** on the menu bar to start the **Extraction Wizard**, and then click **Next**.

Click **Next** again, and then click **Finish** to extract the files into a new subfolder called **info**.

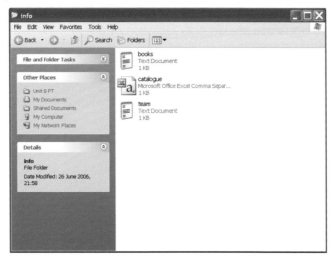

Close the folder window by clicking **(x)** in the top right-hand corner.

Task 3   Sending messages

This task describes how to create and send a new email message with attachments to the recipients in a distribution list.

Creating an email signature

An **email signature** is a block of formatted text that appears at the end of a message identifying the sender and giving their contact details. You can tell **Outlook** to automatically add the same signature at the end of every new message or create a number of different signatures and select them from a list.

⊙ Load **Outlook**.

⊙ Click **Tools** on the menu bar, and then click **Options**. The **Options** dialogue box will appear.

⊙ Click the **Mail Format** tab, and then click the **Signatures...** button.

⊙ Click **New** when the **Create Signature** dialogue box appears.

⊙ Type **work signature** in the box labelled **Enter a new name for your signature:** and then click **Next**. The **Edit Signature** dialogue box will appear.

⊙ Type the following:

> **Your name and centre number**
> **Office Assistant**
> **Vocational Team**
> **Payne-Gallway Publishers**

> **TIP**
>
> You can format signature text by highlighting it and clicking the Font button, alternatively enter and format your text in Word and then copy and paste it into the **Signature** area of the **Edit Signature** dialogue box.

Your **Edit Signature** dialogue box should now look something like the example below.

Taking a screen print

At this point you need to take a screen print of the **Edit Signature** dialogue box as evidence that the signature has been created.

⊙ Take a screen print of the current window by holding down the **Alt** key and then pressing the **Print Scr** key.

⊙ Load **Word** and open the **screenprints** document.

⊙ Press **Ctrl** and **End** to move to the blank page at the end of the document.

⊙ Click the **Paste** button on the **Standard** toolbar. The screen print will appear.

⊙ Create a new page at the end of the document. This will be used for another screen print later on.

⊳ Save the document keeping the filename **screenprints**.

⊳ Click the **Outlook** icon at the bottom of the screen. Inbox - Microsof...

⊳ Click **Finish** and **OK** to return to the **Options** dialogue box.

⊳ Click the small down arrow next to **Signature for new messages:** and select **work signature** if this is not already displayed. Your **Options** dialogue box should now look like the example below.

⊳ Click **OK**.

Creating a new message

Now we're ready to create a new message.

⊳ Click the **New** button on the **Standard** toolbar. A window headed **Untitled Message** will appear with your **work signature** already inserted.

New button

This message needs to be sent to the recipients in the **team** distribution list created in **Task 1**.

⊳ Click the **To:** button at the top of the message window to open the **Select Names** dialogue box.

To button

⊳ Click **Team** in the list of names, and then click **OK**.

Using the copy facility

You need to send a copy of this message to a colleague.

 Click in the **Cc:** box and type the email address:

jane.kauffman@payne-gallway.co.uk

 Click in the **Subject:** box and type **ICT Diploma**

 Click in the message text box above the signature text and type:

A meeting to review first proofs of the new ICT Diploma book will take place on 3 August at 10.30 am.

Please let me know if you can't attend.

Now we need to check the message for spelling errors.

 Click the **Tools** on the menu bar, and then click **Spelling and Grammar...** Work through the spellcheck correcting any errors, and then click **OK** when the spellcheck is complete.

Using the confidential facility

Next we need to make sure that another copy of this message will be sent to the **Senior Commissioning Editor**. The **Senior Commissioning Editor's** email address must not be visible to the other recipients of the message. To do this we need to use the **Bcc (blind carbon copy)** facility.

To button

 Click the **To:** button at the top of the message window to open the **Select Names** dialogue box.

 Click in the **Bcc:** box and type the email address:

yasemin.kazan@payne-gallway.co.uk

 Click **OK**.

Attaching files to a message

Now we need to attach the files extracted from the zipped folder to the message.

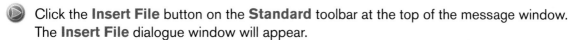 Click the **Insert File** button on the **Standard** toolbar at the top of the message window. The **Insert File** dialogue window will appear.

Insert File button

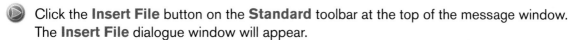 Click the **My Documents** icon if the contents of your **My Documents** folder aren't already visible.

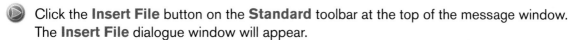 Double-click the **Unit 8 PT** folder.

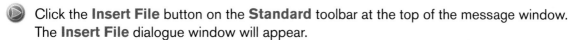 Double-click the **info** folder. Take care at this point <u>not</u> to double-click the zipped info folder.

 Click <u>once</u> on the books **file** and hold the **Shift** key, then click <u>once</u> on the **catalogue** file and <u>once</u> on the **team** file. Let go of the **Shift** key – all three files should be highlighted like the example below.

 Click the **Insert** button.

 The **Attach:** box will appear with the three files **books**, **catalogue** and **team** listed.

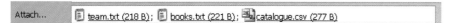

Marking a message high priority

Now we need to mark the message as high priority so that a red exclamation mark symbol appears next to the message in every recipient's Inbox.

 Click the **Importance: High** button on the **Standard** toolbar at the top of the message window. The button will change colour to show that the message priority has been set.

Priority button

You can also click the **Importance: Low** button on the **Standard** toolbar at the top of the message window if the contents of a message aren't urgent. High or Low importance can be turned off by clicking the toolbar button again to deselect the option.

 The message is ready to send now. Check that your message window looks like the example below before you carry on.

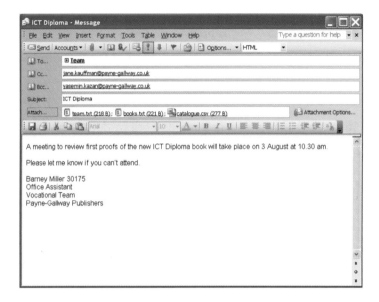

Taking another screen print

Next you need to take a screen print of the message window to show that the correct recipients have been selected and the specified files have been attached.

▶ Take a screen print of the message window by holding down the **Alt** key and then pressing the **Print Scr** key.

▶ Click the **Word** icon at the bottom of the screen. 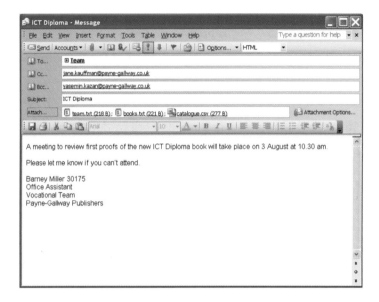 screenprints - Mi...

▶ Press **Ctrl** and **End** to move to the blank page at the end of the document.

▶ Click the **Paste** button on the **Standard** toolbar. The screen print will appear.

▶ Create a blank page at the end of the document – this will be used for another screen print in the next task.

▶ Save the document keeping the filename **screenprints**.

▶ Close **Word**.

Saving Sent Items

Before you send any messages you need to check that copies will be saved in the **Sent Items** folder. **Outlook** should do this automatically but it is still worth knowing how to check this.

▶ Click the **Outlook** icon at the bottom of the screen. Inbox - Microsof...

▶ Click **Tools** on the menu bar and then click **Options...** The **Options** dialogue box will appear.

▶ Click the **Preferences** tab if it is not already selected and then click the **E-mail Options...** button. The **E-mail Options** dialogue box will appear.

Click the check box next to **Save copies of messages in Sent Items folder** if it is not already checked.

 Click **OK**.

Sending and printing messages

Now we're ready to send the message.

 Click the **ICT Diploma** message icon at the bottom of the screen.

 Click the **Send** button on the toolbar at the top of the screen. The message will be sent to your tutor and the new message window will be closed.

Send button

Next we need to print a copy of the sent message.

 Click **Sent Items** in the **Folder** bar on the left of the screen. All the email messages you've sent will be listed.

Sent Items button

 Click on the message with the subject heading **ICT Diploma**.

 Click **File** on the menu bar, and then click **Print** to open the **Print** dialogue box.

 Select the printer you want to use, and then click **OK**.

 Close **Outlook**.

Task 4   Using the calendar

This task describes how to use the Calendar facility in **Outlook** to organise your diary. You need to schedule the following meetings and appointments for next week:

Day	Start Time	Duration	Memo/Description and location	Repeating/ Recurring	Alarm
Monday	**0900**	**30 mins**	**Team Briefing Meeting Room 1**	**Recurring every week**	**No**
Monday	**1330**	**2 hours**	**Induction Training Team Leader's Office**	**Not recurring**	**Yes**
Thursday	**1100**	**1 hour**	**Copy Editor's Meeting Meeting Room 2**	**Recurring every week**	**No**
Friday	**1230**	**1 hour**	**Team Lunch Meeting Room 1**	**Not recurring**	**Yes**

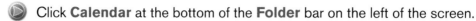

New button

Recurrence button

(▷) Load **Outlook**.

(▷) Click **Calendar** at the bottom of the **Folder** bar on the left of the screen.

Adding a recurring event

We'll start by adding the first event for **Monday**. This event is specified as **Recurring every week** so it needs to be set up to automatically reappear in the diary from week to week.

(▷) Click the **New** button on the **Standard** toolbar. A new window headed **Untitled – Appointment** will appear.

(▷) Click in the **Subject:** box and type **Team Briefing**

(▷) Click in the **Location:** box and type **Meeting Room 1**

(▷) Click the **Recurrence...** button on the **Standard** toolbar at the top of the appointment window. The **Appointment Recurrence** dialogue box will appear.

(▷) Click the down arrow on the box next to **Start:** in the **Appointment time** section and select **09:00** from the drop-down list.

This event is set to last for **30 minutes**.

(▷) Click the down arrow on the box next to **Duration:** Scroll through the drop-down list and select **09:30**. The **End:** time will be automatically updated.

(▷) Click the radio button next to **weekly** in the **Recurrence pattern** section if it is not already selected.

> **TIP**
>
> Click in the **Start:** or **End:** box and type the time you need if it doesn't appear in the list.

(▷) Click the check box next to **Monday** in the **Recurrence pattern** section if it is not already selected.

(▷) Click the down arrow on the box next to **Start:** in the **Range of recurrence** section. A drop-down panel showing the current month will appear with a box around the current date. Click on the date for next Monday.

Your **Appointment Recurrence** dialogue box should now look something like the example below.

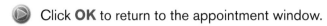 Click **OK** to return to the appointment window.

This event <u>does not</u> need a reminder alarm.

 Click the check box next to **Reminder** to remove the tick if it is already selected.

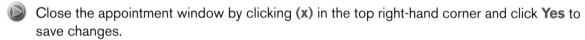 Close the appointment window by clicking **(x)** in the top right-hand corner and click **Yes** to save changes.

Adding a non-recurring event

Next we'll add the second event for **Monday**. This event is specified as **Not recurring** so it does not need to be set up to automatically reappear in the diary.

 Create a new appointment.

 Click in the **Subject:** box and type **Induction Training**

 Click in the **Location:** box and type **Team Leader's Office**

 Click the down arrow on the first box next to **Start time:** and click on the date for next Monday.

 Click the down arrow on the second box next to **Start time:** and select **13:30**.

> **TIP**
>
> If you've already entered the same location for another event just click the down arrow next to **Location:** and select the location from the drop-down list to save time.

This event is set to last for **2 hours** so it will end at **15:30**.

 Click the down arrow on the second box next to **End time:** and select **15:30**.

This event <u>does</u> need a reminder alarm.

 Click the check box next to **Reminder** if it is not already selected.

Your appointment window should now look something like the example below.

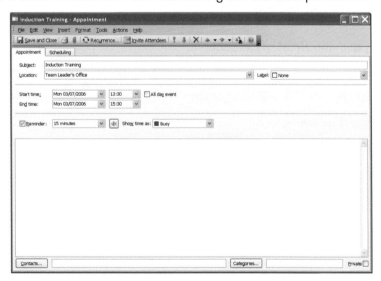

▷ Add the remaining events shown in the table above.

Now you need to check that all the specified events have been correctly placed in your diary.

▷ Click the **Work Week** button on the **Standard** toolbar if it is not already selected.

▷ Click the date on the calendar that you set for your first event. Events for the week will be displayed – your screen should look like the example below.

08⁰⁰					
09⁰⁰	Team Briefing (Meeting Room				
10⁰⁰					
11⁰⁰			Copy Editor's Meeting (Meeting Room 2)		
12⁰⁰					Team Lunch (Meeting Room 1)
13⁰⁰	Induction Training (Team Leader's Office)				
14⁰⁰					
15⁰⁰					
16⁰⁰					

TIP

Double-click an event on the calendar to open the Appointment window and edit the details. Right-click an appointment and select **Delete** to completely remove an appointment.

Printing diary pages

Next we need to print the diary pages for Monday, Thursday and Friday.

▷ Click the **File** button on the **Standard** toolbar, and then click **Print...** to open the **Print** dialogue box.

▷ Select the printer you want to use in the **Name:** box.

▷ Click **Daily Style** in the **Print style** section.

▷ Click **Page Setup...** and click the **Format** tab if it is not already selected.

▷ Deselect any checked boxes next to **Include:** in the **Options** section.

▷ Click the **Header/Footer** tab.

▷ Click in the first box in the **Header** section and type your name.

▷ Click in the second box in the **Header** section and type your centre number.

- Click **OK** to return to the **Print** dialogue box.

- Click the down arrow next to the **End:** box in the **Print range** section and select the date for Monday that's displayed in the **Start:** box above. Your **Print** dialogue box should now look something like the example opposite.

- Click the **Preview** button. A preview of the diary page for Monday will appear – it should look something like the example below.

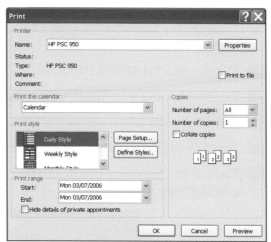

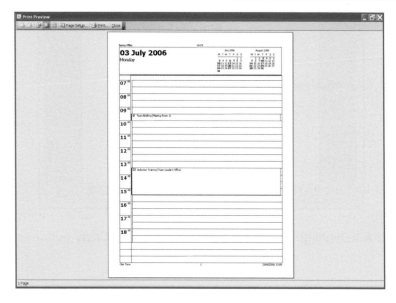

- Click **Print...** followed by **OK** to print the diary page.

Print the diary pages for **Thursday** and **Friday** in exactly the same way taking care to change the **Start:** and **End:** dates in the **Print range** section of the **Print** dialogue box each time.

Creating a notes page

Now you need to use the text file **team** that you extracted and saved in **Task 2** to create a **notes page** in the diary. The notes page will store information about the Vocational Team members. To get started you need to open the text file **team** in **Word** and copy all of the text to the clipboard.

Load **Word**.

Click **File** on the menu bar, and then click **Open**.

Open button

Or click the **Open button** on the **Standard** toolbar.

Click the **My Documents** icon if the contents of your **My Documents** folder aren't already visible.

Double-click the **Unit 8 PT** folder.

Double-click the **info** folder. Take care at this point <u>not</u> to double-click the zipped info folder.

Click the down arrow next to the **Files of type:** box.

Scroll through the drop-down list of options and click **Text Files**.

Click on the file called **team**, and then click **Open**. The text file will be opened – it should look like the example below.

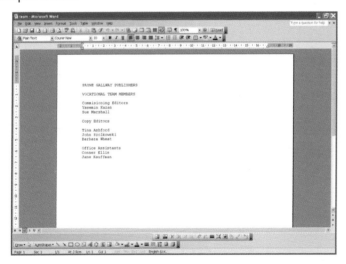

Press **Ctrl** and **A** to highlight all the text, and then click the **Copy** button on the **Standard** toolbar.

Close **Word**.

Click the **Notes** icon at the bottom of the **Calendar** panel on the left of the screen.

Notes button

New Note

Click the small down arrow next to the **New** button on the **Standard** toolbar, and select **Note** from the drop-down menu. A new **notes page** will appear.

Right-click anywhere in the notes page, and select **Paste** from the pop up menu. The text from the clipboard will be pasted into the note which should now look like the example below.

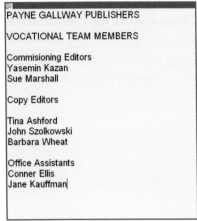

Next we need to print the **notes page**.

Click the menu icon in the top left corner of the **notes page**, and select **Print...** from the drop-down menu to open the **Print** dialogue box.

Select the printer you want to use in the **Name:** box.

Click **Page Setup...** and click the **Header/Footer** tab.

Click in the first box in the **Header** section and type your name.

Click in the second box **Header** section and type your centre number.

Click the **OK** button to return to the **Print** dialogue box.

Click the **Preview** button. A preview of the **notes page** will appear – it should look something like the example below.

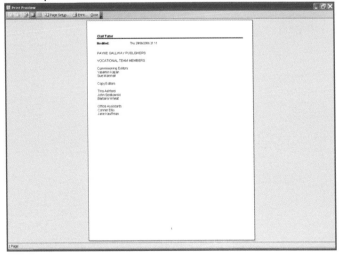

Click **Print...** followed by **OK** to print the **notes page**.

▷ Close the **notes page** by clicking **(x)** in the top right-hand corner.

▷ Close **Outlook**.

That's the end of the practice tasks. Now try the full New CLAiT Plus assignment that follows.

Practice assignment

Scenario

You work as an Office Assistant for Seaforth Animal Rescue, a local charitable organisation. You use Personal Information Manager (PIM) software to organise your diary and to keep details of contacts. You use email software to send and receive email communications.

During this assignment you may need to take a number of screen prints. All screen prints may be contained in one document and printed at the end of the assignment.

You must ensure that all printouts of calendar, notes pages and to-do task lists include your personal details, i.e. name and centre number. These details may be handwritten.

Assessment Objectives	TASK 1
2a	1 Two new staff have been appointed. Enter only the following details in your address book:

Full name	Andy Yarker
Job title	Veterinary Surgeon
Work telephone	01294 656821
Email	sar.ayarker@hotmail.co.uk

Full name	Justine Rowley
Job title	Veterinary Nurse
Work telephone	01294 656823
Email	sar.jrowley@hotmail.co.uk

2b

2 a) Create an email distribution list.

    b) Name the distribution list **vetstaff**

    c) Add the two contacts entered at Step 1 to the distribution list.

    d) Save and close the distribution list.

2d

3 a) You need to print a copy of these contacts and the distribution list.

    b) These may be printed on the same sheet.

    c) Print a copy of the contacts showing the **Full name, Job title, Work telephone** and **Email address** of each contact.

    d) Print a copy of the distribution list **vetstaff** showing the name of the distribution list, the **Full name** and **Email address** of each of the contacts.

    e) Ensure that your name and centre number are displayed on the printouts.

Assessment Objectives			TASK 2
3a	1	a)	You need to create an archive folder to store messages from the **Business Manager**.
		b)	Within your email system, create a new folder.
		c)	Name this folder **busmgr**
2a	2	a)	The **Business Manager** has sent you an email message concerning a **Fundraising Meeting**.
3b			
3c		b)	Read the message entitled **Fundraising Meeting**.
		c)	Store the attached zipped/compressed file **fundsmtg** outside the mailbox folder in your working area.
		d)	Add the **Business Manager's** email address and **Job Title** to the applications address storage facility.
		e)	Move the message entitled **Welcome Conference** to the folder **division**.
1f	3	a)	Locate the zipped/compressed file **fundsmtg** that you stored at Step 2.
3c		b)	Extract the files contained in the compressed file **fundsmtg** and store them in your working area.
		c)	Check that you have extracted three files **volunteers**, **events** and **raised**.

Assessment Objectives			TASK 3
			You need to send an email message.
1a	1	a)	In your email software create an email signature as follows:
			Your name and centre number
			Office Assistant
			Seaforth Animal Rescue
		b)	Produce evidence, in the form of a screen print, to show that this has been done.
		c)	Ensure your name and centre number are displayed on the printout.
		d)	You may print this document now or save the document and print all screen prints when you have completed the assignment.
1b	2	a)	Create a new email message.
1c		b)	Address the email to the **vetstaff** group.
1d		c)	You must retrieve this distribution list from your address book.
1e		d)	Enter the details shown below in the appropriate parts of the email:
1g			
2c			

Subject:	**Fundraising**
Message:	**A meeting of the fundraising subcommittee will take place on 10 June at 9.30 am in the Atrium Annexe. Please confirm your attendance.**

e) Add the signature that you created at Step 1 to the end of this message.

f) Attach to the email the three files **volunteers.txt**, **events.txt** and **raised.csv** that you extracted in Task 2. The files must be attached as three **separate** files. Do not attach the compressed file.

g) Use the copy facility to ensure this email will also be sent to

   sar.bm@hotmail.co.uk

h) Use the confidential facility to send the email to the **Business Manager** ensuring confidentiality of the Business Manager's address. You must retrieve this address from your address book.

i) Mark the message **high priority**.

j) Before sending this email take a screen print of the message showing all recipients, priority and evidence of the three attached files.

k) Ensure that all the evidence is clearly shown on the screen print.

l) You may print this document now or save the document and print all screen prints when you have completed the assignment.

m) Ensure that a copy of the sent message will be saved.

n) Send the message.

o) Print a copy of the sent email.

Assessment Objectives

TASK 4

You need to enter some information into your Personal Information Manager software.

2e

1 Schedule the following meetings and appointments for next week:

Day	Start Time	Duration	Memo/Description and location	Repeating/ Recurring	Alarm
Monday	**1000**	**1 hour**	**Re-homing Meeting Atrium Annexe**	**Not recurring**	**Yes**
Thursday	**1330**	**30 mins**	**Planning Meeting Office 1**	**Recurring every week**	**No**
Thursday	**0930**	**3 hours**	**St. Wilfred's School Visit Atrium Annexe**	**Not recurring**	**Yes**

2f

2 You need to print a copy of your diary pages for Monday and Thursday only. Preview your printout(s) to ensure that evidence of the following will be shown:

- the day, date, start and finish time of meetings
- memo/description and location
- the alarm
- the recurring meeting

- text in full

- your name and centre number.

If necessary additional screen prints may be used.

2e

2f

3   You need to keep a note of volunteers working for the charity.

a)   Open the file **volunteers** that you stored in Task 2.

b)   Copy the entire file into a notes page.

c)   Preview a print of your notes page.

d)   Ensure all details have been included in the note.

e)   Ensure that your name and centre number will be shown on this printout.

f)   Print a copy of your notes page.

Assessment Objectives

TASK 5

1h

1   You need to print a copy of the contents of the **busmgr** folder. A screen print may be used to provide this evidence. If a screen print is used it may be copied and pasted into the same document you used for screen prints from other tasks.

a)   Print the contents of the folder **busmgr**.

b)   Ensure the contents of the folder are clearly shown.

c)   Ensure your name and centre number are clearly displayed on the printout.

d)   Ensure you have printed all the screen print(s) taken during the assessment.

e)   Save and close any open documents.

f)   Close any open software and exit the system securely.

Index

absolute cell references 58–9

absolute hyperlinks 262

Access 93–4, 101, 111, 119–20, 126, 130

action buttons 200–3

adding
    addresses 305–6
    bullets 200
    calculated fields to queries 119
    contacts 300–1
    footers 27–8, 39, 69, 73–4, 130, 140–1, 164
    formulae 75–7
    headers 27–8, 39, 61–2, 140–1, 164
    hidden fields 283
    images 161
    line spaces 270
    non-recurring events 315–16
    recurring events 314–15
    text 81–2, 158–60
        to images 230–1
        to slides 183–5, 207–8

addresses 305–6

adjusting
    column widths 33–4, 53–4, 115
    image colour/contrast/ brightness 219
    leading 151–3
    margins 155–6

Adobe Photoshop 217–49

Align Left button 141, 150

Align Right button 140

alignment
    images 275
    text 19, 31

All Files 29

amending
    data 116–17
    existing documents 34
    presentations 199–206

animations 204, 238–44

antivirus software 304–5

applying
    dropped shadows 233–4
    filters 236–7
    special effects to text 165–6
    styles 266–7, 272–4

Appointment window 314–16

archive folders 303

archiving files 39–41

artwork 232, 239
    see also images

Ascending button 103

aspect ratio, images 276

attaching
    datafiles 7
    files to messages 310–11
    style sheets 266–7

attachments 303–7

Auto Fill Options button 56

AutoForm 99

automatic slideshows 209–10

AutoSum 54–5

Avery labels 107

axes scales 79–80

background
    filling 226–7
    placing images 158
    replacing 222–3
    slides 179–80, 206–7

Backup Tapes 39

bar graphs 77–86

bars 84–5

Bcc (blind carbon copy) 310

blank publications 137

blind carbon copy (Bcc) 310

body styles 274

body text
    formatting 273–4
    inserting 268–70, 273–4, 280

borders 31–3, 53, 143, 193–4

Borders button 33

brightness 219

bullets
    adding 200
    deleting 199–200
    demoting 188
    formatting 180–1
    line spacing 271

Bullets button 22

calculated fields 119

Calendar facility 313–20

canvas size, setting 224–5

Cc: box 310

CD-ROMs 39

cells 257
    formatting 31–2, 51–2
    merging 31–2, 51–3, 260
    naming 54–5
    setting properties 258–60
    splitting 260

Center button 31, 52, 105, 140, 159, 193

CGI see Common Gateway Interface

Index

changing
- axes scales   79–80
- y-axis scales   85

Chart Wizard tool   64–6, 78, 83

charts
- creating   196–7
- formatting   197–8
- highlighting   65
- labels   66–7
- legends   66–7
- moving segments   68
- PowerPoint   190–9
- printing   62–4, 69, 85–6
- recolouring   68

clicking and dragging   33

closing
- Access   111, 119, 126, 130
- documents   12
- Excel   192
- FrontPage   253
- PowerPoint   183, 206, 210
- Publisher   154, 165, 168

codes in fields   96–7

colour
- adjusting   219
- background   226–7
- fonts   159
- printing   223
- slides   179–80
- text   32

colour-separated copies   167–8

columnar reports   126–30

columns
- deleting   71

hiding   62–4
setting   139–40
splitting   260
tables   191, 257
width   33–4, 53–4, 115

combining
- files for mail merge   15–28
- text and images   224–32, 240–1, 273–9

Common Gateway Interface (CGI)   281

composite copies   153–4

conditional functions   56–7

confidential facility, email   310

Connect Text Boxes toolbar   145

contacts   299–303

content slides   190–1

contrast   219

converting data   30–1

Copy button   142, 163, 184–5, 192

copy facility, email   310

copying
- objects   163
- text from datafiles   191–2

correcting proof marks   148

Create Text Box Link button   145–6

critical errors   9

cropping images   164–5, 237–8

CSV files   278

currency   60–1, 125

Custom Shapes tool   235

custom sized publications   155

Cut button   35, 124

data
- amending   116–17

conversion to table format   30–1
entry forms   99–101
filtering   69–74
formatting   59–61
highlighting   65
saving   73–4
sorting   69–74

data points   80–1

databases
- creating   93–101, 111–19
- opening   101
- practice assignments   131–5
- tables   94–6

datafiles
- attaching   7
- copying   191–2
- importing/inserting   111–14, 277–9
- mail merge   28–34
- opening   65, 69–70, 74–5, 77
- saving   49–53, 65, 69–70, 74–5, 77–8

decimal places   59–61, 95, 125

deleting
- appointments   316
- bullets   199–200
- columns   71
- rows   70–1
- slides   203
- text   34–5

demoting bullets   188

description META tags   268

Design View, reports   123–6

Index

diary pages   316–18
    see also Calendar facility

distribution lists   299–303

document format   17

document text   9–10

downloading   251–2

draft documents   16

dragging and dropping   33

drawing
    lines   160–1
    shapes   235–6

Drawing toolbar   32, 81

dropped shadows   233–4

duration, frames   243–4

e-image manipulation
    see images

editing images   217–23

email   299–324
    creating   309
    hyperlinks   262–3
    moving   306
    printing   313
    reading   304
    sending   307–13
    signatures   307–8

entering
    records in table
      views   98–9
    search criteria   118, 127–8

Excel   25–7, 49–53, 191, 192

exiting *see* closing

exploded pie charts   64–9

external hyperlinks   262, 265–6

extracting
    attachments   303–7
    zipped files   307

fields
    characteristics   114–15
    codes   96–7
    forms   281–6
    text   97

files
    attachments   304–5, 310–11
    downloading   251–2
    storing   251–2
    types   29, 42
    zipped   307
    see also datafiles; text files

filling background   226–7

filtering data   69–74

filters   233–8

Find and Replace   35–6, 70, 116

first page layout   141–4

flipping images   275

folders
    email   303, 306–7, 312–13
    websites   251

Font Color button   32

fonts
    colour   32, 159
    size   9–10, 21, 31, 52, 159, 181
    types   9–10, 21, 37, 149, 180, 193

footers
    adding 39, 69, 73–4, 164

graphs   82–3
labels   109–11
reports   105–6, 130
    see also headers and footers

form fields   281–6

form handlers   281

form results   281

Format Picture button   24, 26

formatting
    bullets   180–1
    cells   31–3, 51–2
    charts   67, 197–8
    data   59–61, 80–1
    email signatures   308
    formulae   75–6
    headers   180–1
    images   186–8, 275–7
    tables   193–4
    text   9–10, 20–2, 149–50, 158–60, 230–1, 273–4

forms
    interactive   279–90
    properties   280–1
    testing   286–7

formulae   56, 75–7

frames
    animations   241–4
    setting duration   243–4

FrontPage   250–98

GIF (Graphics Interchange Format)   244

Gradient tool   226

grammar checker   37–9, 272

graphics
    animated   238–44

Index

backgrounds 206–7
see also images

Graphics Interchange Format
(GIF) 244

graphs
bar 77–86
inserting footers 82–3
printing 82–3
text boxes 81–2
XY scatter 77–86

greater than symbol 118
gridlines 32–3
grouped reports 120–6
grouping objects 163

handouts 189–90
headers and footers
adding 27–8, 61–2
formatting 180–1
slides 181–2
toolbar 28, 39,
140–1, 164
see also footers

heading styles 274
Hex Codes 255
hidden fields 283
hiding
columns 62–4
slides 200

high priority messages
311–12

highlighting
data 65
text 20

home pages 267–73

HTML (Hypertext Mark-up
Language) 250, 256

hyperlinks
action buttons 200–3
creating 200–1, 262–3,
265–6
testing 202–3

Hypertext Mark-up Language
(HTML) 250, 256

hyphens 151

images 217–49
adding 161
adjustments 219
alignment 275
backgrounds 158
combining with text
224–32, 240–1, 273–9
editing 217–23
formatting 186–8, 275–7
importing 22–3, 156–7,
227
inserting 186–8, 274–5
opening 218–19
positioning 157, 227–8
practice assignments
245–9
printing 223, 237–8
replacing 163–4
resizing 23–5, 157–8,
227–8
rotating 228–9
saving 223

Import Text Wizard 112

Import Wizard 113

Importance button,
email 311–12

importing
datafiles 29–30, 111–14
graphs 25–7

images 22–3, 156–7, 227
text files 146–7
text from files 166–7

index page 268
Insert AutoText button 28
Insert date button 141
Insert Function button 55
Insert Page number
button 140
Insert Picture button 22
inserting
datafiles 277–9
files 268–70
footers 82–3
form fields 281–3
images 186–8, 274–5
merge fields 8–9
organisation charts
194–6
page breaks 27
rows 72
special symbols 36–7
text 268–70,
273–4, 280
see also adding

interactive forms 279–90
internal hyperlinks 262
Internet *see* websites
Internet Explorer 251, 286
italic button 21, 159,
181, 193

Justify button 19, 149

Keep aspect ratio option 276
keyword META tags 255–6

Index

Label Wizard   101, 106–9

labelling

    action buttons   202

    bars   84–5

    charts   66–7

labels   101–11

landscape orientation   101

Lasso tool   220–2

layers   227

    animated graphics 239–41

    dropped shadow   233–4

    filter application   236–7

    opacity   229–30

    styles   233–8

leading adjustments   151–3

legends, charts   66–7

Line button   160

line spacing   20, 270, 271

Line/Border Style
button   143

Linear Gradient button   227

lines, drawing   160–1

linking

    spreadsheets   74–7

    text boxes   145–6

loading

    Access 93–4, 101, 111,
    120, 126

    Excel   50, 191

    FrontPage   252

    Internet Explorer 251, 286

    Outlook   299–300

    Photoshop   217–18

    PowerPoint   178, 190

    Publisher 137, 162, 165

    Word   5–6,
    183, 202

    see also opening

location, non-recurring
events   315

Lookup Wizard   96

mail merge

    archiving files   39–41

    changes   34–9

    combining files   15–28

    creating
    documents   4–12

    datafiles and
    tables   28–34

    practice
    assignments   42–8

    queries   12–15

margins   6, 18, 137–9,
    155–6

marking messages
high priority   311–12

master documents   4

master page

    creating   253–67

    new page from   267–8

master slides   177–83

mathematical functions   55

Maximize button 106, 115,
    118–19, 123

Merge Cells button   31

merge fields   8–9

merging cells   31–2, 51–3,
    260

messages *see* email

META tags   255–6, 268

Microsoft software *see*
    Access; Excel; Frontpage;
    Internet Explorer; Outlook;
    PowerPoint; Publisher; Word

modifying

    field characteristics
    114–15

labels page

    footer   109–11

    reports 104–6, 123–6

    template
    publications   162–5

moving

    email messages   306

    pie chart segments   68

    slides   203–4

    see also positioning

My Documents

    datafiles   7, 29

    saving attachments   305

    subfolder creation   5

    website folders   251

naming cells   54–5

navigation

    buttons   288–9

    tables   261–3

New Slide button   185

non-recurring events 315–16

notes pages   205–6,
    318–20

number formatting   59–61

Objects toolbar 141, 158,
    160, 165

opacity, layers   229–30

Open button   162, 191

opening

    databases   101

    datafiles 65, 69–70,
    74–5, 77

    images   218–19

    password protected
    files   12–13

    pre-prepared text
    files   34

    see also loading

Index

organisation charts 194–6

orientation, page 6, 18, 101, 137–9

orphans *see* widows and orphans

Outlining toolbar 188

Outlook 299–324

    Calendar facility 313–20

    loading 299–300

    practice assignments 321–4

Outside Borders button 53

page

    breaks 27

    layout 141–5

    orientation 6, 18, 101, 137–9

    properties 254–5

    see also web pages

Page Setup 6, 63, 138

Paint Bucket tool 226

Paper size 6, 18, 155

password protected documents 11–12

Personal Information Manager (PIM) 299–324

Photoshop 217–49

Pictures toolbar 275

pie charts 64–9

PIM *see* Personal Information Manager

pixels 224

Portrait orientation 18

positioning

    form fields 281–3

    images 24, 157–8, 227–8

    see also moving; repositioning

PowerPoint

    closing 183, 206, 210

    loading 178, 190

    practice assignments 211–16

    presentations 199–210

    slides 177–90

    tables and charts 190–9

practice assignments

    databases 131–5

    images 245–9

    mail merge 42–8

    Outlook 321–4

    PowerPoint 211–16

    Publisher 169–76

    spreadsheets 87–92

    websites 291–8

pre-prepared text files 34

preparing master slides 177–83

presentations

    amending 199–206

    creating 178–9

    saving 182–3, 190

    timed 206–10

primary keys 96, 113

Print button 126

Print Scrn key 41

    see also screen prints

printing

    charts 62–4, 69, 85–6

    colour-separated copies 167–8

    composite copies 153–4

    contacts 302–3

    crop marks 164–5, 237–8

    diary pages 316–18

    distribution lists 302–3

    emails 313

    graphs 82–3

    images 223, 237–8

    labels report 111

    mail merge 10–11

    notes pages 205–6, 319

    publications 153–4

    reports 106, 130

    slides 198–0

    spreadsheets 74, 76–7

    Word documents 39

    see also screen prints

proof marks 148

publications 136–62, 165–8

Publisher

    closing 154, 165, 168

    columns 139–40

    cropping 164–5

    custom sized publications 155

    headers and footers 140–1, 164

    hyphens 151

    images 156–8, 161, 163–4

    layout 141–5

    leading 151–5

    loading 137, 162, 165

    margins 137–9, 155–6

    practice assignments 169–76

    printing 153–4, 167–8

    proof marks 148

    publications 137, 154–62, 165–8

Index

saving publications 153, 162

text 145–7, 149–50, 158–60, 165–7

widows and orphans 151

quality value, images 276
queries 117–19, 126–7
Query Design toolbar 118
Query Wizard 126

Radius: box 220
recolouring

bars 84–5

pie chart segments 68

records in table view 98–9
recurring events 314–15
relative hyperlinks 262
removing

hyphens 151

objects 221

scratches from images 219–21

widows and orphans 151

replacing

backgrounds 222–3

images 163–4

text 189

replicating formulae 56
Report Wizard 101, 120–1, 128
reports

columnar reports 126–30

footers 105–6, 130

grouped 120–6

labels 111

layout 104–5

modifying 104–5, 123–6

printing 106, 111, 130

repositioning

shapes 236

text 231–2

see also positioning

resizing

images 23–5, 157–8, 227–8

shapes 236

resolution, images 224–5
rotating

images 228–9

text 231–2

rows

cell properties 260

deleting 70–1

inserting 72

tables 191, 257

Run button 118–19, 128

saving 39, 251–2

animations 244

artwork 232

attachments 303–7

data 73–4

datafiles 49–53, 65, 69–70, 74–5, 77–8

emails 312–13

images 223

mail merge 10–11

presentations 182–3, 190

publications 153, 162

slideshows 209–10

spreadsheets 76–7

tables 98

text files 17

scales, y-axis 85
Scaling 63

scratches, images 219–21
screen prints

archived files 41

email

folders 306–7

message windows 312

signatures 308–9

hyperlink action buttons 201–2

image settings 225–6

password protected files 13

slides 204–5, 209

search criteria 118, 127–8
search engines 255
segments of pie charts 68
sending emails 307–13
Sent Items folder 312–13
setting

canvas size 224–5

cell properties 258–60

form properties 280–1

frame duration 243–4

layer opacity 229–30

margins 137–9

page properties 254–5

resolution 224–5

table properties 257–8

text field lengths 97

transitions and timings 208–9

setting up documents 17–20
Shading Color button 32
shapes 233–8
signatures, email 307–8
Simple Query Wizard 117
sizing handles 23–4, 157–8, 186–7

Index

Slide Master View toolbar 182

slides

    backgrounds 179–80

    creating 183–90

    deleting 203

    headers and footers 181–2

    hiding 200

    moving 203–4

    printing 198–9

    text 183–5, 207–8

    timings 208

slideshows 209–10

sorting data 69–74

source datafiles 4

speaker's notes 205–6

special effects 165–6

    see also animations

special symbols 36–7

spell checker 37–9, 198, 272

Spelling and Grammar button 208

splitting cells 260

spreadsheets

    creating 49–64

    linking 74–7

    practice assignments 87–92

    printing 74, 76–7

    saving 76–7

square text wrapping 24

standard functions 54–5

storing files 251–2

    see also saving

structures in tables 98

style sheets

    attaching 266–7

    creating 263–5

styles

    applying 266–7, 272–3, 274

    layers 233–8

subfolders 5, 136, 177, 251

superscript formatting 37

symbols

    currency 60–1

    greater than 118

    inserting 36–7

tables

    columns 115

    creating 94–6, 191, 256–7, 261–3, 277–9

    data conversion 30–1

    databases 94–6

    entering records 98–9

    formatting 32–3, 193–4

    mail merge 28–34

    PowerPoint 190–9

    properties 257–8

    saving 98

Tables and Borders toolbar 31–3

tabular reports 101–11

tags *see* META tags

Task pane 252

template publications

    creating 154–62

    modifying 162–5

testing

    forms 286–7

    hyperlink buttons 202–3

    websites 288–90

text

    adding 158–60, 230–1

    alignment 31

    boxes 81–2, 145–6, 166–7

    colour 32

    combining with images 224–32, 240–1, 273–9

    datafiles 191–2

    deleting 34–5

    field lengths 97

    formatting 9–10, 149–50, 158–60, 230–1

    importing 166–7

    proof marks 148

    replacing 189

    repositioning 231–2

    rotating 231–2

    slides 183–5, 207–8

    special effects 165–6

    tables 193

    warping 234–5

    wrapping 53–4

Text Box button 141, 143, 158, 159

text files

    importing 146–7

    inserting 268–70

    spreadsheets 50

Text Wrapping button 24, 26

timings, slides 208

title tag 268

toolbars

    Connect Text Boxes 145

    Drawing 32, 81

    Header and Footer 28, 39, 140–1, 164

Index

Mail Merge 7–9, 14
Objects 141, 143, 158, 160, 165
Organisation Chart 194–5
Outlining 188
Query Design 118
Slide Master View 182
Tables and Borders 31–3
toolbox 110, 123, 218
top and bottom text wrapping 24
transitions, slides 208
transparency, layers 229–30

Undo button 56
unwanted objects 221

View button 125
viruses 304–5

warping text 234–5
web design packages 250
web pages 253–73, 279–80
websites 250–98
  combining text and images 273–9
  creating 250–3
  folders 251

home page
  creation 267–73
interactive forms 279–90
master page
  creation 253–67
practice
  assignments 291–8
testing 288–90
what you see is what you get (WYSIWYG) 250
widows and orphans 151
width, columns 33–4
Word
  document format 17
  exiting 12
  loading 5–6, 183, 202
  saving 17
WordArt 165–6
workbooks 25–7, 49–53
wrapping text 53–4
WYSIWYG (what you see is what you get) 250

XY scatter graphs 77–86

y-axis scale 85

zipped files 39–40, 307
Zoom tool 221–2